POLITICS
ISLAM AND THE
End Times

Fred DeRuvo

STUDY · GROW · KNOW

Published in Scotts Valley, California, by Study-Grow-Know
www.studygrowknow.com • www.adroitpublications.com

Scripture quotations unless otherwise noted, are from The Holy Bible, King James Version. This version is in the public domain.

Images used in this publication (unless otherwise noted) are from clipartconnection.com and used with permission, ©2007 JUPITERIMAGES, and its licensors. All rights reserved.

Any Woodcuts used herein are in the Public Domain and free of copyright.

All Figure illustrations used in this book were created by the author and protected under copyright laws, © 2010, unless otherwise noted.

Cover Design and Interior Layout: Fred DeRuvo

Edited by: Hannah Richards

Library of Congress Cataloging-in-Publication Data

DeRuvo, Fred, 1957 –

ISBN 098264437X
EAN-13 9780982644379

1. Religion – Demonology & Satanism

CONTENTS

"Nation will rise against nation, and kingdom against kingdom. There will be great earthquakes, famines and pestilences in various places, and fearful events and great signs from heaven." (Luke 21:10-11)

• *FOREWORD* •

This book actually began being written in June of 2009. It has taken that long to write it because in many ways, it is an ongoing book. The chapters that you'll read here were all published on my blog, which you can find at **http://www.studygrowknowblog.com**.

As I look back over some of these, I marvel at how much life has changed in just over one year. I have not published everything I have blogged about, but I have simply taken the ones I liked the best, that I believe have moved us forward in time.

The world is not the same today as it was prior to President Obama becoming our current president. While he ran for the office of president, it seemed like he could do no wrong, and get by with saying nothing specific. In fact, some of the catch phrases connected with his campaign – *"Yes, we can!"* and *"Change is coming!"* have certainly come true. The difficulty is that they are both open-ended statements. *"Yes, we can...**what**?"* *"What change is coming?"*

Since his election, President Obama has not failed to show the people of the United States and the world what *he* meant by the phrases *"Yes, we can!"* and *"Change is coming!"* In both cases, they likely differed in the minds of those who voted for Obama from what has actually been put into effect.

This book of my blogging presents a bit of a chronological thought process related to many of the things that Obama has accomplished and sought to accomplish since being sworn into office. A number of the blogs are out of order, but most are included in the order that they were published on my blog. Some of the titles were changed in order to shorten them for this book. As this book's foreword was written, a number of things were still in the works, like the Cordoba House (the Ground Zero mosque, which only last night Obama finally came out and expressed his support for, but then today tried to backpedal on what he meant), and his plan to grant blanket amnesty to millions of people illegally here from Mexico.

So what can you do? Well, the first thing you can do is become educated. Do not stick your head in the sand because you do not think you can do anything.

If you are one of those individuals who voted for and now continues to support Obama, then this book is definitely not for you. If you have gotten to this point in life and you still believe Obama is the closest thing to the Messiah, you are, unfortunately, deluded. You live in a world that really does not exist, except in *your mind*. You wrongly believe that the world needs only love and everything will be just swell because of it.

Obama wants to take what you have and give it to others. That much he said during his campaign. He actually tipped his hat to his socialistic tendencies then, but the media gave him a pass.

We have a president who is likely the first president with no legal right to be president because he was, in all probability, not born in any portion of the United States (including any U.S. military base away from the United States). He is also the first to *cancel* the National Day of Prayer because he thought it might *offend*, and then head off to pray with 50,000 other Muslims not far from the White House. He has a very strange definition of "offend."

Obama is the first president to sue one of the states in the United States for attempting to put into practice what was already Federal Law. Obama is doing his level best to shipwreck this country, and so far he has done a very good job. I would like to thank all those who voted for him. It is because of their blindness that he is in office.

People like me are seen as part of the lunatic fringe, with no real footing in reality. Of course, I disagree and see those who pander after

Obama (including the media) as the ones who have lost connection with reality.

It is certainly not too late to do anything about the current administration. ***We can all call for his resignation***. Short of that, ***we can all pray that God will bring about Obama's resignation***. He is a cancer on this great country of ours, and he needs to step down. God may, in fact, have Obama as president as part of the judgment of this nation. If so, so be it.

The United States as a country was never meant to be a socialist or communist state. However, that is what is becoming, and it is moving rapidly to that point under Obama's rule. I know that God is fully in control. I have never doubted that. What I have doubted is whether there is something else I should be doing other than simply *thinking* about it.

I have opted to do two things: 1) write about it, and 2) pray for Obama's resignation. If God wants to keep Obama in office, then I thank Him for His will. I want His will, not mine. In the meantime, barring any type of new understanding from God about this situation, I am going to spend time asking God to force Obama's resignation. Will you join me in that prayer?

Fred DeRuvo, September 2010

1

Middle East Madness

(Blogged: 06/18/2009)

Not long into his presidency, President Obama gave a speech in Cairo, in which he seemed to ignore the *character* of specific nations and how they view Israel. What President Obama attempted to hide during his election campaign has now become plainly (and painfully) obvious. It is apparent that Obama is a *Muslim* and prefers to cater to the Muslim world, even if it means tossing Israel (and the United States) under the bus, so to speak. (The fact that he changed his name from Barry Soetero to Barack H. Obama reveals that fact alone.)

For many decades, Israel has only had the United States to rely on for support in her war against terrorists. This will obviously be changing now that President Obama has taken the reigns of this country. It was not too many years ago that it seemed a bit rare to hear much about the trouble in the Middle East. Within the last few years, things seem to have taken a turn in which the situation has ramped up. The rhetoric continues to fly from both sides, and in spite of the concessions made by Israel, it appears that the Arab world will have none of it.

To the Arab world, the fact that Israel is a presence in the Middle East at all is something neither appreciated nor wanted. In fact, it is obvious that if Israel could be eliminated from of the Middle East altogether, most, if not all in the Arab world would be ecstatic about it. With President Obama's vision for the Middle East and his insistence that a two-state solution is the only solution, with Jerusalem split into two parts as well, the Arab world may get its wish.

Of course, this begs the question of what God wants and will achieve. Many Christians today are under the unfortunate delusion that God finished with Israel years ago, in A.D. 70 to be exact. This was the time when Rome stormed Jerusalem and destroyed it, taking with it the Temple that Herod designed. True to Christ's prophetic words, not one stone was left standing on itself (cf. Matthew 24). The Romans removed each stone to get at the gold.

That event was part of the fulfillment of what Christ indicated would occur in the Olivet Discourse. Many believe that event signaled God permanently parting ways with Israel. These folks state unequivocally that Israel is done, over as a nation. God has no plan or purpose for Israel any longer and has now switched His attention to the Church. Of course, this assumes a couple of things:

First, that God will *break* His promises (cf. Abrahamic, Land and Davidic Covenants of the Old Testament), thereby making Him a liar.

Second, God had no previous knowledge that Israel would get to the point where He would have to create another entity.

Certainly, God is *not* a liar. He does *not* break His covenants and since the Abrahamic Covenant (as well as the Land and Davidic) is *unconditional* in nature, there is no way that these covenants could be broken unless God broke them. The many anti-Zionist voices to-day cry louder and louder at the humanity of lives lost in the Middle East conflict that has been boiling below the surface for decades. Un-fortunately, these same folks seem to have absolutely no feelings for the Israelis involved in the conflict, only for the Arabs, or Palestini-ans. This form of anti-Semitism is just as wrong today as it was dur-ing Hitler's day. Anti-Semitism is never right, yet for the anti-Zionist, what matters to them is that the *Palestinians* are treated fairly.

People can do all they can do for either side. The truth remains that ultimately, God has *already* decided. He certainly is not swayed by anyone to bring about His dictates. He has gotten the world this far, based on His prophetic council from the past. Will He continue to work in the midst of that situation, fighting for His people, His land and His Holy city, or will He allow it to take "its own course" (what-ever that means)?

If God has no further plans for Israel, then those who stand with her are wasting their time and breath. If, on the other hand, God *still* stands with Israel, then all those who stand against her are in actuali-ty standing against *God*. It is obviously important to know what the Bible teaches about Israel's future, if there is one at all.

Certainly, the Bible teaches one thing, and either those who believe that God is done with Israel are correct in their understanding, or those who believe that God still stands with Israel are correct. Time will certainly reveal all things. Regardless of how vociferous people get in their support for one side or the other, God is the final Determiner of what occurs in that area of the world, just as He is the final Determiner of what takes place in every other part of the world.

The United States now has a new president, one who seems to be fully enamored by the failed socialistic policies of other countries. He appears also to be a Muslim, fully in favor of those who fight *against* Israel. The reality, though, is that God placed President Obama in his current position. It appears that God has plans He will accomplish through our president. I pray that all of God's plans become a firm reality and I look forward to seeing how things will unfold.

2

Islam Will Dominate

(Blogged: 01/04/2010)

H ere is the situation: Radical Muslims believe that Islam will dominate the entire world, and they will make it happen through *force*, if necessary. Islam is waiting for the final "Mahdi," who, it is said, will usher in world peace. Muslims believe in a synopsis of the End Times that is similar to Christianity's, except the names are changed. Within Christendom, there are many (like Steve Wohlberg, Gary DeMar, Gary North and others) who pooh-pooh the idea of a literal End Times. Throughout the world today, many movements are afoot which await some type of End Times prophet.

The reality is interesting. On one hand, we have multiple groups of people who believe, to some degree or another, that the End Times is real and that it is upon us. We merely wait for things to come to fulfillment in order that the final "Christ" can appear on the religious landscape. Think about the fact that the following groups all believe that soon some momentous event will occur on this planet which will forever it change it:

UFOlogists – These believe that our salvation will come from outer space, in the form of aliens who will remove the people who continue to keep this planet from evolving to the next level and thereby allow those who remain (or who are LEFT BEHIND) to move to the next evolutionary plane. This new plane of existence will usher in the final and ultimate peace to which this world (both the populace and the earth itself) has been yearning.

New Age Practitioners - There are many varying beliefs within this loose-knit worldwide movement. Virtually all agree that this world awaits the final "Christ" *consciousness*, which will bring peace to this world as has never been experienced. Like UFOologists, this new peace will come only to those who are "enlightened" and not guided by the ancient, outmoded principles of Christianity or Judaism.

Islam - Though not one of the more *ethereal* or esoteric religions, Islam is monotheistic and dates back to A.D. 600s, with Muhammad. Followers of Islam - Muslims - await their final Mahdi, which will correct all wrongs and bring in world peace by making Islam the mandatory (and only) religion of the world.

Judaism – These people are still awaiting their Messiah, who will fight for them and provide justice for Israel.

Christianity – Authentic Christians await the return of Jesus, who will destroy the Antichrist, set up His kingdom, and reign for 1,000 years on earth. During this time, His monarchy will be established as the only rule and wrongs committed will be dealt with instantly.

There are also groups that believe that there is no End Times, no Armageddon, no Tribulation, or anything similar:

Atheists - (Includes agnostics.) This group, of course, denies God at all costs, believing that merely denying His existence makes it so. They have spent years convincing themselves of the truth of error-ridden evolution. They have also convinced themselves that they have proven God does not exist. Generally, atheists believe that this planet becomes better only as people free themselves from religious beliefs and work to *make* this planet better.

Preterists, Reformed, Covenant - These folks do not see prophecy *literally*. For most, the Tribulation and return of Christ already occurred in A.D. 70, with the destruction of Jerusalem. There is nothing left to occur except the physical return of Christ at the end of the age.

Seventh-day Adventists, Jehovah's Witnesses, Mormons, etc. - have varying viewpoints with respect to the End Times. Seventh-day Adventists fall in line with the above groups with respect to believing that the Tribulation and return already occurred.

Certainly, both sets of groups above are not all-inclusive, but it is interesting what they share regarding their beliefs about the End Times, specifically the Tribulation and the return of Christ. The important thing to note, though, is that Islam has made tremendous gains in the world. Most media will say nothing bad about Islam or Muhammad especially, for fear of reprisals. The sad fact of the matter is that even when no one says anything bad about Islam or Muhammad, Islamic extremists continue to rain terror down on people with suicide bomb missions, attacks by Taliban or Al Qaeda, or otherwise.

Just recently, the Danish paper Politiken exhibited no problem at all in glorifying President Obama, even lifting him up higher than Jesus. Yet this same exact thing would not have taken place had the comparison been Muhammad. Why? Because of the death and/or mayhem that would have resulted from such a comparison. Christians are not exempt from this type of slander and bigotry, simply because Christians do not as a group (or individually, for the most part) react with violence every time someone uses the name of Jesus Christ as an epithet. Can you imagine how many people would die daily if they did?

Islam is on the move and the world refuses to do anything about it. The Islamic world knows this and perceives it as *fear*. They are right. The world is afraid of Islam and because of this fear Islam is allowed to do anything. People unfortunately believe that if they hide their heads in the sand and do not utter a negative word about Islam they at least will be allowed to live without harassment. The truth is, though, that Islam, if left unchecked, will allow nothing to stand in its way. Their intention is to dominate the world - literally. They firmly believe this will occur, and because of this growing trend Islam is becoming a force to be dealt with throughout the world. It is this intention that will usher in the final Mahdi. This particular Mahdi is said to bring about peace, but at what cost? He will rule strongly, insisting on Islamic rule throughout the world.

Now, for many people (especially those who give no credence to the End Times) the above scenario is so far-fetched that it could not possibly occur. These people need to revisit history and see for themselves how quickly Islam has gained a solid footing in the world's society. Most religions - in one form or another - have a type of live and let live attitude. Most religions do not attempt to force their beliefs onto others through acts of terrorism. Islam is an exception. Many within Islam interpret "Jihad" in a variety of ways. However, it is clear that many Islamic extremists understand Jihad to mean *physically* destroying the enemy. That enemy is anyone who is not Muslim. In other words, Islam will have its day by violence. It does not matter if you are an atheist who firmly believes that no God exists. It does not matter if you are an agnostic who questions life, the existence of God or anything else and have come to no solid conclusions. It does not matter if you are part of the UFOology movement. Islam will have its say and is looking forward to having its day, when the entire world will be Islamic.

If this were to occur, then we can imagine major changes in society. Do I have to enumerate them? Women in Burhkas, Taliban-type law put in place and enforced to the letter, praying five times a day, facing Mecca, traveling to Mecca once in your lifetime, and much more. The world will go *backwards* if this takes place. Yet the world's leaders seem either oblivious to this oncoming threat or choose to ignore it for the time being. It may be they simply do not understand how to fight against its encroachment.

Meanwhile, Muslims have their way and are successful in shouting down (or maiming/killing) those who oppose Islam and those who would blaspheme it by presenting caricatures of Muhammad or writing/reporting negatively about it. However, Islamic extremists have no difficulty in characterizing religions other than Islam as born of Satan. The world just shakes its head and moves on, going about its business, apparently thinking that these knee-jerk protestors will go away in time. They will *not* go away, and with every day they increase the size of their collective voice.

Islam extremists strive to turn the planet into one in which Islam dominates. They are on their way to doing that, and once their Mahdi appears people will initially be taken in by his charm, sincerity, intelligence, and oratory skills. He will be a master manipulator, achieving his goals at first through the *appearance* of peace. It will only be after he has gained the world's attention and commitment that his true colors will come to the fore. The Mahdi that approaches through the collective voice of Islam will be the Antichrist. Unlike what people like Steve Wohlberg believe, this Antichrist will be an actual person and he will lead this world into a one-world government. Then we will see all of Wohlberg's ridiculously uneducated biblical guesses go down the drain. What will Wohlberg and others say then? "*Whoops, I guess I was wrong...*" That, of course, will not be good enough - but it also will not matter at that point.

It is interesting to watch as this world sleeps in the shadow of the approaching darkness. More than ever, people need Jesus as Savior. People need to repent, which means to change your opinion of Jesus Christ. Repenting does not mean, "*I resolve to turn from sin.*" Repenting means changing your mind about the identity and work of Jesus Christ as it relates to you. How do you see Him? He is one of the following to you:

- *a good man and a good teacher, but not god*
- *a myth, a legend, someone who never existed*
- *a lunatic, who suffered from visions of grandeur*
- *God the Son, Savior of the world for those who believe*

If you find yourself believing 1, 2, or 3, but not 4, then this is what you need to repent from believing. You must simply look at Jesus and decide that He is God the Son, who was born of a virgin, lived among us without sin, and died a brutally horrific death, shedding His blood for you and for me. Once you believe this about Him, you are on your way to receiving salvation. Repenting is only the first step in the process. It is what allows our eyes to open to the truth of Jesus Christ. From there, another step is needed. We must place our faith in Christ's finished work on the cross on our behalf. We must come to the point of realizing that we are in need of a Savior. Once we understand our *need*, we then GO to Him believing that He is who

He says He is and that He accomplished on our behalf what He is said to have accomplished. This believing is what faith is, as it allows us to *receive* His salvation. Without faith, it is impossible to please God and it is impossible to receive salvation.

Once we receive salvation, the Holy Spirit seals us unto the day of redemption, which is the day we stand before Him *after* our death. Christ says He will never leave or forsake us, and the Bible tells us that He is the Author and Perfector of our faith. We cooperate in the process by submitting ourselves to Him; however, we cannot and do not resolve to stop sinning *BEFORE* we come to Him. That is NOT repentance. Repentance is changing your mind about who Jesus Christ is, and this is exactly what the thief on the cross did. One moment he was ridiculing Christ and the next minute He had changed his mind about Jesus, believing Him to be a King. This is why the thief asked Jesus to simply "remember him" when He came into His kingdom.

Friend, you must change your opinion about Jesus Christ. You must repent of your denial of His deity and embrace Him. Repenting is not enough. Judas repented, realizing he had betrayed innocent blood, but it did NOT lead to salvation. Repentance is the first step, which CAN lead to belief in His work of salvation on our behalf. Without being able to believe that He actually accomplished salvation for us, we cannot hope to have that salvation. Ask Him to help you believe. This is *not* easy-believism, as many charge. It is how a person comes to know Jesus Christ as Savior. Once that occurs, then that individual's life will begin to change because the Holy Spirit within will start to make that person's life change.

The authentic Christian WILL exhibit good works. They will exhibit good works because the Holy Spirit will cause them to be an outward appearance of the new birth that occurred within. Growth will take place for the remainder of the person's life.

3

Obama Greater Than Jesus?

(Blogged: 01/01/2010)

N ot long ago, an editorial appeared in the Danish newspaper
Politiken citing, among other things, that President Obama is
greater than Jesus. The exact quote is, "*Obama is, of course,
greater than Jesus – if we have to play that absurd Christmas game.
But it is probably more meaningful to insist that with today's domestic
triumph that he has already assured himself a place in the history
books – a space he has good chances of expanding considerably in coming years.*"[1]

---

[1] http://politiken.dk/newsinenglish/article868683.ece

What is amazing about the Obama-phenomenon is that it is obviously *media-made*. It became somewhat the norm to refer to Obama in divine terms while he was running for president. The fact that he really said nothing, except for his desire to "*spread the wealth around*," which is synonymous with creating a Socialist regime in the United States, is power for his course. Obama is a great speaker...until the teleprompter goes off (or crashes to the ground). At that point, he often seems out of his element.

One can only wonder why people such as Sting would have been heard essentially stating that (prior to his election) Obama could very well be the answer to the world's problems - the divine answer. What makes Obama so uncharacteristically human, so that people see him as divine?

Jesus Christ lived, died, and rose again for the sins of humanity. Obama did none of these and he is quickly turning the whole of the United States into a Socialist regime. I am a Christian and an American, and Obama does not hold a candle to Jesus. What I find more troubling than someone's announcement comparing Obama with Jesus (with Jesus coming in second place), however, is the fact that it is highly doubtful that this very same comparison would have been made with Muhammad. Why? Because, generally speaking (except for the odd nut here and there), Christians do not strap bombs on themselves and blow up innocent people (or guilty ones for that matter), nor do they gun down or stab filmmakers to death in the streets. Beyond this, they do not wish ill will on cartoonists who dare to caricature Muhammad or other aspects of Islam.

Of course, *if* Christians did routinely participate in these things, then what was stated in the editorial would likely not have been stated for fear of reprisals. In fact, decisions are made today to avoid running a particular editorial or a political cartoon. This is due to the potential violence from Islam. These individuals know that threats of death to various parts of the world are enough to keep people from castigating or ridiculing Muhammad. It's funny how the threats of death and mayhem are enough to keep people from saying things that are asinine, spiteful and lacking in truth, isn't it?

This is not true of Christianity (and I am not saying that it should be). Christians should be respected for what they believe and for how they live their lives (bearing in mind that not all who claim to be Christian really *are* Christian). The idea that we can compare some human being with the Creator is absurd. The idea that people can complain and/or even attempt to take away the rights of Christians because we will not grab a gun or strap on bombs in retaliation is certainly something that should not exist. For the Muslim, there is little danger of this occurring, even to the point of governments, companies, and schools eliminating freedom of speech; do or say something that even appears to blaspheme Muhammad, and prepare for dire consequences.

Obama, in my opinion, is a test for the coming Antichrist. In spite of what people believe about the End Times, it is incredible to see that things continue to unfold as they do, with the world moving to become one, and yet people thoughtlessly repeat the mantra that the End Times "*already occurred,*" or "*the antichrist is an attitude,*" etc. Sometimes, I think that when this world divides into 10-kingdoms (as declared in Daniel), people will still deny the reality of prophetic Scripture. Interestingly enough, the Club of Rome published a document in 1973 in which every nation of that time had been categorized under 1 of 10 divisions. No country was left out; all were separated into one of the 10 kingdoms.

Whatever the author of the article in question believes, Obama is someone created by the media, and he catapulted to fame and presidential capacity by the same. What he ultimately accomplishes is already known by those of us who realize the road he is traveling in attempting to take the U.S. down. It will not be pretty, but in spite of what anyone thinks, God is in control, not Obama, and certainly not *Politiken.*

Yet, we have people like Steve Wohlberg, Gary North, Hank Hanegraaff, and a host of others either denying the reality of the coming one-world government or stating that prophecy should be taken symbolically. This means that most of it has already occurred. It makes me think that if Noah's Ark were actually located and excavated, people would still refuse to accept that reality. Faced with the undeniable reality of the Ark, other explanations would be offered as to why it was built and how it got near the summit of a mountain.

No; in truth, President Obama brings nothing special at all to the table. He is more socialistic than anyone prior. He is simply playing into the hands of those who put him in office, and they will use him until he is no longer useful to them. They will then find someone else, who will continue what they were able to accomplish through President Obama. This will occur until one particular leader steps away from the pack and with great charm, charisma, intellect, and believability, he will take this entire world down a primrose path that leads only to destruction. He will be the Antichrist, and unlike Wohlberg's version, this Antichrist will be a real person, with a real vision, and with the ability to make things happen.

The Antichrist is most certainly on his way, if not already on this planet. To those who consistently state that this type of "theology" breeds fear and sells books, I would remind them that those opposed to it sell just as many books. I would also ask: since when is something that breeds fear an untruth? Christ spoke of hell more than any other subject, yet we have "theologians" today who angrily protest this idea that hell is a real place. Frankly, my vote is with Jesus, who treated the subject as if it was real. He spent a good portion of His public ministry warning people about it, as did John the Baptist before Him.

For those who wish to deny the reality of hell, that does not make it so. For those who also wish to disavow the reality of the coming world leader, that also does not make it so. People like that are merely hanging onto a world that they will one day leave behind through the door of death. No one lives forever on planet earth, and once gone from this place, all opportunities to repent and receive salvation will be gone with it.

4

Ahmadinejad Cries Foul!

(Blogged: 12/07/2009)

Iranian President Mahmoud Ahmadinejad apparently has "documented evidence" that the United States is doing all it can to keep the hidden Imam from appearing. This Imam - the Mahdi - is believed to the "ultimate savior of mankind."

Ahmadinejad is quoted as saying, "*We have documented proof that they [U.S.] believe that a descendant of the prophet of Islam will raise in these parts [Middle East] and he will dry the roots of all injustice in the world.*"

That is interesting, isn't it? Here I was, thinking that the United States has lost its influence, but apparently, we are still strong enough to keep something supernatural from occurring!

Also according to the Iranian president, he has evidence that indicates both the east and west are planning to annihilate Iran. I'm not sure where he gets his information, but it would seem to be a bit off base. I mean, our government cannot even decide if we are going to remain in Afghanistan, and then when it does decide to remain by sending additional troops, the message is immediately followed with the decision to pull out all troops within 18 months.

A third and final (for now), accusation from Ahmadinejad is that the United States is nothing without Iran, and all of our government's rhetoric is merely meant to send up a cloud of fog to confuse everyone.

I have to ask: why is the United States being blamed on keeping the Mahdi from appearing? While Israel is the "little Satan" the United States is the "big Satan," and because of that it is Iran and every other hard-line Muslim nation that wants to see the United States overthrown.

Why has this not happened yet? Maybe it has more to do with the fact that without the United States, much of this world would not exist as it does. Think of the United Nations. Would the U.N. exist without the United States and the money that we pump into that organization? Iran has no foundation upon which to make her claims against the United States or anyone else.

Look, if the United States is in Iran's way - or anyone else's way for that matter - why has no one declared war against us? War *was* declared against us and it was clearly done on 9/11. That act of war dragged us into a situation that we did not want to be involved in, but

where we seemed to have no choice but to engage the enemy wherever we could find them.

I am always amazed at the rhetoric of people like Ahmadinejad. He is
a person who is likely possessed; certainly, he is not in his right
mind. Hatred can do that to a person. His hatred runs deep. He
hates Jews and he hates Israel. He also hates anyone who has ever
sided with Israel. That hatred of his blinds him to the truth. He does
not even realize how ridiculous he sounds. Right, the United States is
able to keep this alleged Mahdi from appearing. That makes a lot of
sense.

I thought it was the Muslim's job to join in the jihad against countries
like the United States. In fact, I was under the impression that Islam
will not be content until every person who is not a Muslim either becomes one or dies. This is their mantra. This is their belief. This is
what they live for and what they strive to achieve.

In the meantime, the world as one stands against Israel. The last
time this happened, Hitler slaughtered millions of Jews in his attempted ethnic cleansing. We are moving toward a time - and are
likely already there - when the truth will appear to be a lie, and lies
will become the new truth.

Whether it is Ahmadinejad lying about the alleged power of the United States to keep the Mahdi from appearing or the entire world attempting once again to make Israel the scapegoat for the world's
problems, it is all the same, and it all stems from the same source.
That source is absolutely the coming Mahdi; however, he will not be
the savior everyone thinks he will be. He is the Antichrist, coming to
destroy all semblance of loyalty to the only wise and true God of the
Bible.

There is nothing truthful about the coming Antichrist. Nothing. He
will do whatever it takes to gain leadership ultimately over the entire

earth. That's right - the *globe*, not merely a region on the globe. He will lie, cheat, steal and even kill to gain access to the highest position over all the earth, a position that belongs to God and Him only.

Once the Antichrist achieves that level of power his leadership will quickly become a dictatorship, an Absolute Imperialistic kingdom where he will rule with an iron fist, eliminating everyone who opposes him and his rule.

That time is coming and is here now. I cannot imagine that the Antichrist is *not* alive on this planet right now. Too many signs and signals have come into play and lined themselves up. They all point to him, and his public appearance cannot be far off.

Whether this coming "Mahdi" is the Antichrist or will merely act as his False Prophet remains to be seen. One thing is certain. The lies will continue to be fed to the masses until they are accepted as truth. Once this new "truth" takes hold, all bets are off and it will be every man for himself.

We are facing this reality. This path will lead to the climax of world history. This is what everything in the Bible leads to - Jesus Christ and His Second Coming, when He kills the Antichrist with the breath of His mouth and when He takes control of a world that has been, for too long, ignoring Him and His Word.

Even so, come quickly Lord Jesus!

5

Anti-Semitic Rant

(Blogged: 02/16/2010)

Anyone who has heard at least some of the pronouncements, accusations and rhetoric of Iranian President Ahmadinejad is aware of the fact that he has no love loss for Israel at all. In fact, the more he speaks, the more he begins to sound like a modern day Adolph Hitler.

While I realize that too many people make a distinction between Israel and the people of Israel, regarding Ahmadinejad's comments, I am not convinced that he does make a distinction. To him, it appears (at least to me) that he only wishes ill will for Israel and that obviously includes the people of Israel as well.

Let us take a moment to consider some of the things that he has been quoted as saying:

"Ahmadinejad quoted a remark from Iran's Ayatollah Khomeini, the founder of Iran's Islamic revolution, who said that Israel 'must be wiped out from the map of the world'."[2]

In the same article on CNN, he stated, *"Ahmadinejad is quoted as saying, 'Anybody who recognizes Israel will burn in the fire of the Islamic nation's fury'."*[3]

Interestingly enough, it is no surprise that this man denies the Holocaust ever took place, even going so far as to as to host a conference emphasizing those beliefs.

Here is what one British individual said about Ahmadinejad's rank anti-Semitism during one of his speeches (from 2008 to the UN): *"In the words of British politician and former Minister for Europe Denis McShane, Ahmadinejad's address was 'probably the most consistently anti-Semitic speech by any leader since the end of the Third Reich'..."*[4]

"Tuesday 23 September 2008 will go down in history as the day the United Nations General Assembly provided a platform for a head of state to spew unadulterated, vile anti-Semitism – and the assembled nations of the world clapped...." - Anne Bayevsky[5]

Regarding this same speech, Daniel Johnson stated, "This time he went too far. If a western head of state had echoed Adolf Hitler, as Mahmoud Ahmadinejad did this week, would Europeans have shrugged their shoulders and dragged their feet over sanctions?"

---

[2] http://www.cnn.com/2005/WORLD/meast/10/26/ahmadinejad/index.html
[3] Ibid
[4] Ibid
[5] Ibid

"Yet it seems that the Iranian President is now licensed to blame 'Zionists' for everything from the economic crisis to the 'whole world order', to threaten Israel's existence and to use words like 'cesspool' to describe its people. There was a deafening silence in Britain. Prime Minister Brown was too preoccupied with his own survival, making yet another 'life-or-death' speech at his Labor Party conference. The conservative leader David Cameron also ignored the scandal...."[6]

Other world leaders noted his obvious anti-Semitic rhetoric and were appalled, yet Ahmadinejad still stands as the president of Iran. The U.N., far from sanctioning him, applauded him during his speech.

The day after giving this speech at the U.N., Ahmadinejad met with ultra-conservative Jews who strictly follow the Torah and who believe that a Jewish state is forbidden prior to the coming of the Messiah. Apparently, they missed the fact that the Messiah already came and went once. He will be back though.

During his meeting with these ultraconservatives, Ahmadinejad said, *"Zionism has greatly weakened and, God willing, it will be destroyed soon and then all Jews, Muslims and Christians can live peacefully with one another."*[7]

These same Jewish rabbis stated this about Ahmadinejad: *"That we have the honor and privilege to meet with such a distinguished person who understands the difference between Zionism and Judaism is for us a tremendously happy occasion."*[8]

I am scratching my head a bit here. While at least some of the leaders in the world, as well as the news correspondents, noted that Ahmadinejad's rhetoric was nothing more than anti-Semitism, these par-

---

[6] http://www.cnn.com/2005/WORLD/meast/10/26/ahmadinejad/index.html

[7]

http://www.reuters.com/article/idUSTRE48O00E20080925?feedType=RSS&feedName=worldNews

[8] Ibid

ticular ultra-orthodox rabbis praised the man. They would probably be wiser to start studying the Qur'an, to find out exactly what drives the president of Iran. He cares nothing about Jews. He wants them out of the Middle East. He wants the state of Israel dismantled and the only way he is willing to allow individual Jews to remain is if they become subservient to Islam.

Interestingly enough, Muslim Adnan Oktar, who goes by the pen name Harun Yahya, is supportive of another Jewish Temple being built on the Temple Mount. He states that this area should be a place where Jews, Muslims, and Christians can come without fear of reprisals from anyone.

No Need to Destroy Dome of the Rock Mosque to Make Room for Jewish Temple

He firmly believes that the time of the coming Mahdi will bring peace to the Jews, Christians, and Muslims. He is one of the few Muslims that I am aware of who is not only working with Jews, but who seems to appreciate them genuinely as people.

Harun Yahya's Work with Jewish Rabbis

Far from hating and spewing anti-Semitic rants and rhetoric, Yahya's interest is to come to a fair and amicable solution to the problem of the lack of worship space for Jews on the Temple Mount.

If one considers the vast difference between Harun Yahya and President Ahmadinejad, the contrast is stark. Even Yahya's demeanor toward Jews is much more than merely "polite." He seems to genuinely enjoy being with them as evidenced in the photos seen on the Internet.

We read about Yahya's growing up years, his education, his adulthood, his work against the alleged science of evolution and even his stay in a mental hospital (on trumped up charges) where he was tortured and kept against his will on false charges. Throughout the narrative, one gains a strong respect for this man who understands freedom to practice religion and freedom from the unwanted forcing of religious values on someone.

While Ahmadinejad wants to promote nothing but Islamic jihad (at the expense of "Zionists") Yahya is interested in promoting peace - lasting peace. This is evidenced by any number of books and articles on his website. This particular article is noteworthy:

A Letter to Muslim, Christian, and Jewish Believers
The difference in approach represented by these two men stems from what is within them. Of course, looks could always be deceiving and only time will bear that out, but for now, it appears as though Harun Yahya is a man who, unlike Ahmadinejad, not only wants peace for Jews, but is willing to help them get there and still allow them to keep what they already have.

Both men are men to be watched in the coming years. Both men have goals for Israel and both men say they want peace. Ahmadine-jad wants it by wiping Israel off the world map. Yahya wants it by bringing people together based on a common bond.

In the long and short run, it may be that Yahya's version will be the one to play out, at least for a short period of time. Only time will tell and only God knows for sure what will occur. My suggestion is that we pay close attention to both individuals as time progresses.

6

Ezekiel 37 Fulfilled, says Netanyahu

(Blogged: 02/16/2010)

According to Netanyahu, Ezekiel 37 has been fulfilled. What makes him think so? For those unfamiliar with Ezekiel's vision of the Valley of Dry Bones, the prophet is shown a visual of a valley filled with bones. Ezekiel is told to walk around the bones and agrees that they were "very dry."

There has been any number of interpretations based on the alleged meaning of the passage. One camp believes the bones relate to the entirety of the invisible Church, while another camp believes that this is a vision of what will occur for Israel. Is there any way to know? Yes, but it all depends upon the hermeneutic a person uses during the interpretation process. It is of the utmost importance to understand that when approaching any area of Scripture, we need to seek *God's* meaning; not what we *think* He says, but what He actually says. Admittedly, it is difficult for most of us to approach Scripture without any biases whatsoever.

For instance, if we approach Scripture believing that God is completely finished with Israel, then passages like this one in Ezekiel will of necessity be understood to say something that is in line with our presupposition. Conversely, if we firmly believe that God is *not* done with Israel, but certain things await fulfillment, then we may also fail to understand important aspects of passages like these.

This does not mean that we come to Scripture with an empty head. It means we come to Scripture with the ability to be flexible and to learn. We will never come to the end of our learning in this life, so to be dogmatic about everything we believe may leave little room for the Holy Spirit to teach. If someone approaches this particular passage believing ahead of time that God is done with Israel, there is really only one meaning to gain from this passage. This is true of those in the opposite camp as well. The tragedy is that obviously only one position can be correct, and, just as obviously, God means one thing in this and every other section of Scripture. Depending upon how we view this particular passage, our assumptions will cause us to act and/or think a certain way about Israel the Land as well as Israel the nation.

In Ezekiel 37:5-6, the bones come to life in three stages:

- sinews will be placed on the bones
- flesh will be placed over the bones and sinews, and
- breath will come into them

This process is a *three-stage* process. When Ezekiel prophesies, first the bones rattle and come together, then Ezekiel sees the sinews cover the bones, and then he witnesses the skin covering the bones and sinews. There is no breath in them, though.

God tells Ezekiel to prophesy over the newly formed bodies so that breath could come into them. Ezekiel does so and breath comes into the bodies. These bodies, which were far passed being dead (the bones were completely *dry*) have literally been raised from the dead. Where there once was no life, life now exists.

When this is completed, God says to Ezekiel, "*Son of man, these bones are the* **whole house of Israel***: behold, they say, Our bones are dried, and our hope is lost: we are cut off for our parts*" (Ezekiel 37:11; emphasis added). It is important to understand the passage the way God means it to be understood. In this case, God specifically says to *Ezekiel* that the bones *ARE* the whole house of Israel. God says without equivocation that the bones are the entire nation of Israel.

People have some interesting ways of interpreting the passage. More and more people today are saying that this passage and particularly the phrase "whole house of Israel" represents not just Jewish believers, but the entire invisible Church of Christ; *all believers*. In order to get to that point, however, the "whole house of Israel" phrase must be viewed allegorically. The people who do this are then required to cause Scripture to jump through a number of interpretive hoops to make it all gel.

First, they say that the Church is revealed in the Old Testament, when it is *not*. This is normally based on the promise to Abraham where God tells him that through him (Abraham) all the people of the world will be blessed (cf. Genesis 12:1-3; 15; 17, etc.). This, say many, is God indicating that the Church would eventually come to fruition. Actually, the individual who believes this is hard pressed to prove it. We know without doubt from God's promises to Abraham that all the people of the world *would be blessed*, but it does not make sense to say that the Church is being *revealed* here.

What is likely being revealed here is that from Abraham would come forth a great nation, as God has revealed to him. God is saying that through Abraham (and ultimately through the nation created from Abraham) the world would be blessed. This could mean two things:

1) That God is referencing the fact that the Savior of the world would eventually be born into the nation of Israel, or 2) that Israel would be the light of the world and those who wanted to know Israel's God would have to come through Israel, which is the way it was done in the Old Testament.

It could also mean both of these things. It is impossible to dogmatically state that God was revealing the Church here, especially considering the fact that Paul tells us that he and he alone revealed the mystery of the Church. So, what am I to believe: God's Word or people's interpretation? To me, it seems perfectly clear that in Ezekiel 37, God is speaking about the nation of Israel *only*.

People constantly charge that normative Dispensationalists teach two modes of salvation. This is untrue. There is only one form of salvation. It is revealed to us in Genesis through Revelation, and that is faith in God's Word (written or spoken). There is no other method of salvation, in spite of what many Covenant and Reformed Theologians teach (that Adam and Eve were to have been saved by *obedience*, which is a work, but after Adam and Eve it switched to faith only).

Taking the text as it is - allowing it to speak for itself - it is difficult to understand God to be saying anything but what we read in the text: that the bones represent (or ARE) the entire nation of Israel. If we understand it to be saying something else, then we are in danger of changing God's meaning - and that is nothing to fool with.

Netanyahu said recently, "*Armed with the Jewish spirit, the justice of man, and the vision of the prophets, we sprouted new branches and grew deep roots. Dry bones became covered with flesh, a spirit filled them, and they lived and stood on their own feet."*[9]

The interesting thing here is that it appears that these bones did not realize *why* or *who* was raising them. It was not until God literally placed His spirit within them did they come to understand the reason.

If we consider Israel today, it seems clear enough, in spite of the fact that the majority of professing Christians disagree, that Israel came back from the dead in 1948. In spite of the obviousness of the situation, there are many who continue to deny this and look at this as an accident - either of nature or simply due to Israel's stubbornness. However, in spite of the all the odds, Israel once again became a nation. Not only this, but since that time the Hebrew language (also dead as a language prior to that point) was resurrected. This is unheard of that dead languages are resurrected!

Today, *continuing* against all odds, Israel exists. She has fought off many of her Arab/Muslim neighbors, leaving them scratching their heads. During the Six-Day War of 1967, the world expected Israel to be defeated in short order. Instead, after two weeks of fighting, tiny Israel, against the Goliaths of the south, took back the land she had lost in the past two weeks and then began to gain even *more* ground.

To this day, Syria, Libya, Jordan and others are extremely angry that Israel took what they believed was theirs. Because of this, there is no forgiveness and no willingness to participate in open dialogue to solve the problems in the Middle East. A deep-seated hatred of Jews forms the very reason these anti-Semitic and Anti-Zionist groups exist. They want Israel destroyed and they want the Middle East purged of Jews.

---

[9] http://www.onenewsnow.com/Culture/Default.aspx?id=898508

Here is the rub, though. The Land of Israel is *God's Land*. He owns it, just as he owns this entire planet. As far as God is concerned, Jerusalem is the center of our world (cf. Ezekiel 5:5). The idea that warring factions believe they can waltz in and either take or split up Israel into parts is the highest form of arrogance. In the past, God judged the people of Israel's disobedience and rebellion by expelling them from the Land. He always brought them back, *always*. Since 1948, God Himself has brought life to those "dry bones" by putting life in them and bringing them back to the Land (Ezekiel 37:14). God has done this. While the people of Israel may believe *they* did it, or that God is on "their side," the reality is that God is on HIS side.

The people who believe that God is done with Israel are, in essence, calling God a liar. They do not like to hear that, but if we understand the entire book of Ezekiel, God seems to be clear. He states on numerous occasions in that book that He will bring Israel back, He will make them a nation, and He will do this or that for one reason and for one reason only: *for the sake of His holy Name*, (cf. Ezekiel 36:23, 32; 38:23).

Throughout the entire book of Ezekiel, God makes His plans known. He tells us what He is going to do with Israel and with the heathen nations that surround her. There are many judgments upon Israel in this book, but there is also the time when God will lift them up from the grave. He did that in 1948. He promises to put His spirit within them, something He has not yet done. When He does that, they will know that He is their God.

However, something many people miss repeatedly is that the only reason God continues to have a plan and purpose for Israel is because of His Name, which the nation of Israel has *profaned*. If God were to leave Israel alone, and decided to deal with the Church and never even think of Israel again, then there is absolutely NO way that His Name would be restored to honor.

In other words, Israel received all the judgments due to their rebellion and their willful sin. It was because of that rebellion and sin that they brought disgrace to God's Name. In fact, His Name became an epithet because of the way the nation of Israel lived. They did not care if God was profaned. They did not care how He looked to the rest of the world. What they cared about was their needs and wants.

Since God created Israel, His Name has been made a joke throughout the world. His Name is routinely blasphemed by being used as a curse word. This is due to Israel's failure to live the life that God created them to live. Did this surprise God? Did it take Him by surprise? Because of it, did He have to go to Plan B, which was the Church? Hardly. Everything that God has ever done, is doing, and will ever do is for one reason only, His *glory.*

"And I will sanctify my great name, which was profaned among the heathen, which ye have profaned in the midst of them; and the heathen shall know that I am the LORD, saith the Lord GOD, when I shall be sanctified in you before their eyes," (Ezekiel 36:23).

"Not for your sakes do I this, saith the Lord GOD, be it known unto you: be ashamed and confounded for your own ways, O house of Israel," (Ezekiel 36:32; emphasis added).

"Then the heathen that are left round about you shall know that I the LORD build the ruined places, and plant that that was desolate: I the LORD have spoken it, and I will do it," (Ezekiel 36:36).

In chapter 38 of Ezekiel, God speaks of something He will do with respect to Gog and Magog. *"And thou shalt come up against my people of Israel, as a cloud to cover the land; it shall be in the latter days,* **and I will bring thee against my land,** *that the heathen may know me, when* **I shall be sanctified in thee**, *O Gog, before their eyes,"* (Ezekiel 38:16; emphasis added). Here God promises to create a situation where He will be glorified. Note that He refers to the Land of Israel as HIS Land and the people of Israel as HIS people. Yet, we have people today who say this is not what it means and that God is referencing the Church in an *allegorical* way. There is great danger in changing the meaning of God's Word to make it mean something else. If these folks are wrong, they are very wrong indeed.

In verse 18, even though God creates this event, with this alliance led by Gog (a title), God's fury is poured out onto that alliance because Gog and his armies dared to come against Israel. God's jealousy for His Land and His people will be so aroused that the Land will shake (earthquakes) and Gog and his allies will be wiped out by God Himself with fire, brimstone, earthquakes (which will also likely knock the Dome of the Rock mosque way off its foundations, allowing Israel to build the third Temple), civil war and more. Israel will not have to raise a finger to help here. God will do it because of His holy anger.

Verse 23 of chapter 38 states, "*Thus will I magnify myself, and sanctify myself; and I will be known in the eyes of many nations, and they shall know that I am the LORD.*" The only unfortunate part of this is that these nations will come to understand that God did what He did, but they will very quickly *forget*.

In chapter 39, God states unequivocally, "*So will I make my holy name known in the midst of my people Israel; and I will not let them pollute my holy name any more: and the heathen shall know that I am the LORD, the Holy One in Israel,*" (Ezekiel 39:7).

It should be clear that the ONLY reason God stands for Israel is because of His holy Name. He will have come to the end of His patience when this event occurs, and He will remove the pollution found on His Name, put there by Israel herself.

Too many people think that people like me support Israel *unconditionally*. They believe that we do not see Israel's faults and we have placed Israel on a pedestal. None of that is true. Israel is filled with fallen, depraved, corrupt Jews. They all need God, yet most will die without Him. Being a Jew guarantees *nothing*. Becoming a believer is the only thing that provides any guarantee.

We are coming to a time in this world's history when God will act to restore the beauty, splendor, and majesty of His holy Name, which has been and continues to be profaned by Israel. He has brought them back into His Land and He has done so in order to purge them of their sinful dependence upon themselves. The victories that Israel has gained since 1948 have come because God supports HIMSELF, His LAND, and His holy *Name*. Israel has much to go through yet before God is able to separate the Remnant from the rebels.

In the end, God will receive all the glory. In the end, His Name will be cleared. What a tragedy it is that the very human beings He created have responded to Him with treachery, deceit, hatred, and malice. This is true of all of us, unless and until God opens our eyes. God will have His way with Israel and He will have His way with this world as well. He will be the Victor and He will be fully *vindicated*. He will do all of this for the sake of His holy Name and for no other reason.

That is the reason I support Israel, because of what God is doing and what He *will* do. Praise to our heavenly Father for His love, His patience, His chastisement, His justice, His willingness to stoop, and for His *salvation*. May our lives reflect all of these things, as He endeavors to fill us with His Spirit, creating within us the image of His one and only blessed Son, the second Person of the Godhead, Jesus Christ.

7

Who is Adnan Oktar?

(Blogged: 02/17/2010)

I recently included information on Adnan Oktar (who goes by the pseudonym Harun Yayha) when I referenced Iranian President Ahmadinejad. While on one hand it appears that Mr. Oktar is a genuine person who seems to love the Jewish people, there may be more than meets the eye.

After doing some research on the Internet, it appears that Mr. Oktar may have a checkered past. In fact, he has been found guilty of a number of crimes in Turkish courts and awaits the results of his final appeal. If his conviction stands, he would begin serving a three year sentence. People have accused Mr. Oktar of being the leader of a cult in which women were allegedly conned into becoming part of his group and made to perform sexual favors for high-ranking officials, all of it surreptitiously filmed in order to convince the same officials that it would be to their best interest to provide political favors for Oktar's group.

I would like to stress that as far as I am concerned, this is all alleged; however, since he has been found guilty of certain crimes in Turkish courts (though awaiting his final appeal) it appears as though there may be at least a kernel of truth to some of the allegations.

What I find fascinating is that this man is described as a "megalomaniac." He has the ability to put people at ease instantly. He comes across as genuinely caring, but if the allegations of his misconduct are true, then it is obviously a facade in which he does so to carry forward his own plans. Of course, the information that Mr. Oktar includes about himself on his own web page is far from all of the above. According to him, he had a very difficult life; however, he only slept a few hours each night, voraciously reading everything he could get his hands on. His website boasts hundreds of articles and books (all free to download) written on numerous subjects from Islam to his favorite topic, exposing the lies of evolution. Some individuals claim that he did not write the articles and books but that he only attaches his name to them, taking all the credit for them. Who knows what the truth is about Oktar?

The reality is that in many ways, when the Antichrist makes his appearance on this planet he at first will appear to be *self-effacing*, diligently working with those in the Middle East to solve the problem of a lack of peace there. He will be seen as a friend of the Jew and of Israel, as well as of Islam, so that they will take him into their confidence. When he is finally able to produce a document that promises peace for at least 7 years, this will be all that the leaders of Israel need to sign onboard with him. This event - the signing of the cove-

nant - marks the beginning of the 7-Year period known as the Tribulation. This is clearly delineated in Daniel 9:27, where we read that
this "prince" shall make a covenant with the people for one week.
The one week here can only be referring to a period of seven years, if
context means anything. While I realize that some folks take this to
refer to Jesus (like Steve Wohlberg, who states he follows the rules of
grammar, but obviously does not in this case), it cannot be, if the
rules of grammar mean anything. There are three references using
the pronoun "he" and all of them cannot be referring to Jesus unless
the *rule of antecedents* is completely ignored. This is what Steve
Wohlberg, along with most Reformed or Covenant Theologians and
Preterists do here. It is convenient for them, but it is *wrong*.

Why is it that this particular event marks the beginning of the Tribulation period and not the Rapture? In my opinion, it is because when
Israel's leaders sign on with Antichrist, in spite of the fact that they
are not aware of his true motivation (or identity), they will have effectively signed a pact with Satan himself. This move that Israel
makes signals the beginning of the end. Of course, let's also understand that the timing of the signing of this covenant is also in God's
hands, meaning it will not happen until the foreordained time comes
to fruition.

What will it be about this coming man of sin that deceives the leaders
of Israel? Obviously, it will be his demeanor, which will include a willingness to see "justice" occur where Israel is concerned. Seeking to
befriend Jews, this man of sin will be seen as so genuine and so con-
genial, wanting nothing but peace between Judaism, Christianity and
Islam, that too many will fall in line behind him, allowing him to lead
them unflinchingly wherever he chooses to go.

At first, this man of sin will play the part of a great humanitarian, loving all people with a love that goes beyond the bounds of religious
dogma. He will be gladly received by most because of his alleged
knowledge of the Bible and the Qur'an. He will help people under-

stand that all faiths can and should worship side-by-side in peaceful co-existence while retaining their *differences*. This coming man of sin will fool most of the people, though obviously not all. The text of Daniel states that Antichrist will enter into a covenant with the "many," for a period of seven years. The text infers that not all people will accept him with open arms. A faction of individuals will be wary of him and with good reason, though they may not be aware of that reason at first. Nonetheless, the coming Antichrist will successfully broker a deal with the major parties in the Middle East, and when he accomplishes that, the entire world will take notice. His rise to fame and infamy will have begun in earnest. After all, the man who can bring peace to the Middle East, even if for only seven years, must have ways of eliminating other world problems.

According to Daniel 9:27, in the middle of the week, this same man of sin (referred to as "*a* prince" in Daniel), will break the covenant. Again, here is where theologians part company, with some believing that this references Christ who died on the cross "in the middle of the week." Unfortunately, though, to find a way to get the text to mean some specific "week" in which Christ died is strained at best. Moreover, contrary to the belief that Christ broke any covenant (by His death, or by any other means), He actually *fulfilled* all the tenets of the Law and the major prophecies surrounding His death. Christ came to fulfill the Law, not to break any covenants. The Antichrist *breaks* covenants. For more information, the reader is encouraged to purchase *Between Weeks*, which fully explains this section of Daniel. Beyond that, there is any number of extremely well written and easy-to-read books on this same subject.

The reality for the world, though, is that in many ways the Antichrist may appear just as men like Oktar appear; strong, yet genuine; loving, yet hating evil; speaking words of religious comfort and desirous of peace. Behind the veil may be nothing more than megalomania, which ultimately demands that people do things his way. In the end, as these megalomaniacs build their kingdoms, they break more of the rules, but since they are gaining fame and power, many of those rules do not seem to apply to them. They come to a point where they believe that *none* of the rules applies and that they will make their own rules. They mark out their own path and they blaze their own trail. Because of this, they become even more attractive to people based on their apparent ability to be the true "Renaissance man:" one who does not cater to those in power but presents himself as one who is equal to all in power, if not superior to them. He is able to do this in a way that, at least outwardly, bears no resemblance to ego, while at the same time offers nothing that would put people on the defensive - unless within his very close, inner circle. To the public, he is a man to admire on all counts.

I am NOT saying or implying that Adnan Oktar is the Antichrist and I would like to make that clear. What this article is saying is that if everything that is alleged about Adnan Oktar is true, then we can know that this same type of situation will exist with the coming Antichrist, except ten times greater. If the allegations against Oktar are true, then his public persona is far different from his private one. The Antichrist will also be a master deceiver and may not even realize his close alliance with his father, Satan, until he finds himself at the zenith of his power. Whether he knows it or not, the Antichrist will be fully empowered by Satan as he casts all of his power and purpose into this last chance to defeat God. Israel will be, as the rest of the world will be, merely a pawn to obtain control of the Land that belongs to God and His holy city, Jerusalem – and, ultimately, the world. Satan firmly believes this planet belongs to him and he is not willing to give it up, and certainly not without a fight.

The prophetic Scriptures point to the fact (if literal meaning of the text along with context means anything) that Jesus will reign physically from David's throne in Jerusalem. From there, He will rule the world, *physically*. Is it any wonder then that the Antichrist will do all that he can to set his headquarters up as close to Jerusalem as possible? Antichrist will also know the prophecies concerning Christ and His coming kingdom, in spite of the fact that many others either do not or attempt to negate them.

Antichrist's entire life and rule will be an attempt to fulfill by imitation the prophecies that apply to Christ. Those who view Scripture allegorically are at an obvious disadvantage, simply because they cannot see these things as they happen, nor can they read the signs of the things that will happen. Because of that, Antichrist will have the element of surprise. If the Tribulation is scheduled to occur in this lifetime, then it follows that the Antichrist is likely alive now. He is rising to power and setting himself up as a man who has already amassed some power, riches, and fame. He bides his time working in what appears to be situations that will show him as a man of genuine concern for the plight of the Jew, the Arab, and the Christian. He wishes to unite all of them, not necessarily into one religion (at first), but to make it possible for them to all worship at the same place (the Temple Mount) without fearing any reprisals of any kind. The Antichrist *needs* the Temple built so that he can desecrate it!

As Antichrist continues his rise to Absolute Imperialism, this facade will slowly melt away until all that is left is the raw, unadulterated power of Satan himself, who seeks the only thing he has ever sought - to be worshiped *as God is worshiped.*

There may be many men like Adnan Oktar who come and go before we get to the last man of sin, the Antichrist. This last man will be the consummate chameleon, able to present himself as the man of the hour with the answers to the world's problems. He will prove it by brokering peace in the Middle East. With all the talk of the coming Mahdi from Islam, the return of Christ, and the need for peace in the Middle East, this man of sin cannot really be that far away.

The world waits for a man that will ultimately be evil incarnate while the Christian looks to God, who controls all things and will use all the coming events of the future, including all that the Antichrist seeks to achieve, to bring Himself glory. For God, there is no greater purpose for anything He does than to bring glory to Himself. All people - Christians and non - will ultimately give God glory. They will all bow the knee, declaring that Jesus Christ is Lord of Lords and King of Kings. The only difference, of course, is that those who know Christ - those who are born from above and who are authentic Christians - will bow the knee *gladly* and *gratefully*. All the rest will bow because they are *forced* to do it.

The Antichrist will be Satan's man and he will strive to dethrone God. His puny attempts will only wind up fooling humankind, as he will be destroyed with Christ's breath as He returns in victory to reclaim the planet that was taken when Adam and Eve sinned, thereby giving their allegiance to Satan. This one act of sin gave this world into the hands of Satan who is the ruler of the air. Though vanquished through the cross of Christ, his sentence has not physically been carried out. God will allow him to go as far as he can go, in order that sin might go to the uttermost to be sin. In other words, sin will play itself out and be seen for what it actually is...*lawlessness*. No matter, as God in Christ is not deterred from His purposes and no sin can overcome God or His purposes.

Praise to the God who rules this universe with justice and holiness, love and patience!

8

Israel Has Rights Too

(Blogged: 02/20/2010)

I have recently been considering the situation in the Middle East and how so many people are against Israel and the Jews, believing that they literally have NO right to have their own land and country. This has come upon them repeatedly, in spite of the concessions that Israel has made. What the media tells us is how much the Palestinians suffer at the hands of the Israeli state, yet rarely if ever do we hear of what the Palestinians perpetrate *against* Israel. When we do hear anything, it is seen as retaliation for something Israel has done. The truth of the matter is that what the world hears via news bureaus is not really the truth. That should surprise no one, but it does.

A few months ago Marv Rosenthal reported in a special bulletin the truth regarding the situation in the Middle East specifically as it relates to Israel and the Arabs around her. *"Today's inhabitants of Gaza are Palestinian, a name given to the land by the Romans almost fifteen hundred years after the Jews settled the land. The Palestinians living in Gaza are separated by about 45 miles from the larger Palestinian community in the West Bank of the Jordan Valley."*[10]

Rosenthal continues by stating, *"Today, Syria refuses to speak to Israel about peace without the precondition that Israel give to Syria the Golan Heights – the very mountain range from which she shelled Israeli farm communities near the Sea of Galilee almost daily for nineteen years (1948-1967) while it was under Syrian control."*[11]

Rosenthal speaks of Yassar Arafat's climb to power and how his actions clearly indicated a complete lack of concern for his own people. He was more intent on gaining and keeping the power he sought through the PLO.

Yassar's PR Scam Has Fooled the World

The area that Israel occupies (as well as people known as Palestinians) goes back to biblical days of the Old Testament. *"When the children of Israel under Joshua entered the land of Canaan, the tribe of Dan was to capture the area of Gaza. Instead, the tribe of Dan moved north and settled near the base of Mount Hermon. As a result, the Philistines became a major "thorn in the flesh" to Israel for centuries."*[12]

Today's Palestinian people have no clear origin. Scholars have determined that they do not descend from the ancient Philistines, who gave Israel so many problems during and beyond the time of King David.

---

[10] Marvin Rosenthal, Truth Siege (Zion's Fire 2009), 1
[11] Ibid, 2
[12] Ibid, 3

If we segue to modern day we see the beginnings of new groups, and their stated purpose is essentially the destruction of Israel. Rosenthal comments, "*In 1987, Hamas was founded by Sheikh Ahmad Yasin. Hamas is an Arabic acronym for "The Islamic Resistance Movement." Its stated purpose is to establish an Islamic state in Israel, the West Bank, and the Gaza Strip. To achieve its purpose, Israel and the Jews must be destroyed. And therefore, peace with Israel is not an option to be considered under any circumstance.*"[13]

In 1993, Hamas began carrying out unprovoked attacks on Israeli civilians and opposed any agreement between the PLO and Israel. At the time, the agreement would have included the complete withdrawal of Israeli troops from the West Bank and autonomy "*in both the Gaza Strip and the West Bank for the Palestinians.*"[14]

In 2007, Hamas seized full control of the Gaza Strip, which created problems for PLO, Israel and other neighboring people. "*After more than fifty years, the West Bank leadership wanted to move toward peace with Israel; while at the same time, the concept of peace with Israel was not even an option to be considered by the Hamas leadership who now controlled Gaza.*"[15]

Because of Hamas' new position in the West Bank, they lobbed thousands of rockets into Israeli territory over the past eight years. The number of rockets launched is near the 6,000 mark. Interestingly enough, the rockets, along with other military hardware and weaponry, were being smuggled into Gaza through tunnels. These tunnels were on the Egyptian border and were approximately 70 feet or more below ground, with at least some of the tunnels being a half mile or longer in length. So far, 90 such tunnels have been located

---

[13] Marvin Rosenthal, Truth Siege (Zion's Fire 2009), 3
[14] Ibid, 3
[15] Ibid, 3

and destroyed, although some place the full number at over 300 tunnels remaining.

It is generally accepted knowledge that Hamas is funded in large part by the Iraqis and Syria, and that Hamas itself is safely headquartered in Damascus among the civilian population. This situation grew to the point of becoming intolerable for Israel, and she launched an offensive against Hamas. When Israel went on the offensive, there were three goals ahead of her: *"first, to stop the rockets; second, to destroy the Hamas infrastructure that makes their launching possible; and third, to make certain that after her troop withdrawal, the rockets will not be reintroduced into Gaza to again harm Israel."*[16]

Had Israel wanted to do so, she could have destroyed the entirety of the Gaza Strip within hours. Because Hamas was certain of an Israeli strike, they (Hamas) deliberately used women and children to shield themselves by placing them on the rooftops of Hamas buildings. Prior to Israel launching their attack they dropped thousands of leaflets to the people in the targeted area, warning them of the upcoming attack. By doing so, Israel lost the element of surprise, but saved untold lives in the process, which was her aim.

The Palestinians of Gaza are not innocent. They voted in Hamas during a democratic election and gave them their full support, knowing their stand against Israel.

We have all of this going on in the world, yet anyone who supports Israel is considered a Christian Zionist (which is not a compliment) working against God. People who refer to those of us who support Israel's right to land and autonomous rule as Zionists apparently believe that Israel has no right to land or autonomous rule in the Middle East.

---

[16] Marvin Rosenthal, Truth Siege (Zion's Fire 2009), 3

What is more surprising is the fact that many of those who oppose what Israel is trying to accomplish are Jews themselves; Christian Jews, or Messianic Jews, or whatever they prefer to call themselves. The trouble is, not only have they been blinded by the absolute error of Replacement Theology, which is normally part of Covenant Theology, but they have also become part of something else that is becoming more and more insidious.

Think about something for a moment. Forget religion for a minute and simply think about what it is that the world is saying. In a purely secular world, what everyone seems to be saying is that the Jews have NO right to have any land at all, nor should they be allowed autonomous rule. This is patently absurd, yet this is what the world is saying, loud and clear!

In the Middle East, Israel is surrounded by Arab nations. The Palestinians themselves are Arab, passing themselves off as "Palestinian" as if this represents a separate culture, language, or ethnicity. It does not, with no thanks to PLO leader Yassar Arafat (you know, the guy who looked like Ringo Starr, and allegedly died of AIDS), who created one of the best sleight of hands ever. He created a situation in which the Arabs living in the West Bank were seen by the world as a unique species of people. However, it is clear that the Arabs who call themselves Palestinians are so simply because they live in the area referred to as Palestine. Yet, so did many, many Jews - but they are not called Palestinians. They are still called Jews.

I support Israel's right to have land and I support their right to be autonomous. The Arab world has plenty of land and countries that surround Israel, yet they are not satisfied with that because they want more. They have stated repeatedly that they will not be happy until the Jews are pushed into the Mediterranean Sea. Therefore, the reality for the Arab is that they want the Jews gone, out of the land entirely. They do not want a two-state solution. They want to eradicate the Jews. Frankly, I am sure they will not be happy until they see every last Jew dead, and they have stated as much. This, of course, will never occur.

Though the world seems to disagree vehemently, from a secular standpoint Israel has every right to exist as a nation. It does not matter that the world's opinion is stacked against them. In fact, to see how much oppression they have suffered and yet still maintain what they maintain is remarkable. They keep pushing on in spite of the odds against them.

It is also remarkable when you stop to consider how much the world is against the Jew and Israel being their own nation and ruling themselves in general. From a purely pragmatic point of view, it is an unfair position that the world has put Israel in. Israel has every right to fight back, push for autonomy, and press on against a world that is attempting to force them to do it their way.

It is interesting how the world does no such thing against the Arab world. Interesting indeed. For decades, they have lobbed rockets into Israel space from Jordan. They have dug tunnels from their countries into Israel, tunnels which they have repeatedly used to smuggle in weaponry used against Jews. The world does nothing. It blames the Jews and Israel for their own problems.

The absurdity of this position is seen when placed against the backdrop of the world's opinion and resultant actions.

I will continue to support Israel's right to land and autonomous rule, if for no other reason than they are the underdog. I will also support those rights for Israel because of biblical reasons as well.

Ultimately, I believe that what occurs in the Middle East is in God's hands. I believe it will work out according to God's timetable, His will, and His purposes. Certainly that remains to be seen; however, for the time being, Israel should have its own land and nation solely because it currently has it and the Arab nations are plentiful. They do not need another nation on the West Bank, or anywhere. Nevertheless, don't tell the rest of the world that, because it appears they believe Israel has too much already and the poor Arab has nothing.

Wake up, world! Israel has rights too.

9

Israel Squeezed Again!

(Blogged: 02/25/2010)

In a recent development, the European Union (EU) has now decided that Israeli goods made in Judea and Samaria are open to EU import duties, because they say that both of these territories are not considered part of Israeli territory.

It is clear that the world stands against Israel, and for many their response to this decision is to cheer loudly. The problem, of course, is that while many believe that Israel is the worst nation on earth, and that no other nation compares with their alleged "bloodlust," all other countries are just that - their own countries - and they seem to enjoy a sovereignty that Israel does not, in spite of the fact that Israel became a nation again in 1948. This does not seem to matter to the rest of the world, though, because the Israelis are seen as interlopers.

The fact that the world is NOW saying that there is NO room for Israel as a country, especially in the part of the world that has defined Israel for generations, is ridiculous. Yet, there it is.

It is interesting that when Hitler walked this earth and led his anti-Zionist Nazi troops into World War II, his attempt to exterminate ALL Jews was all but ignored by most people of the world. Most did not want to risk being executed themselves. A few people like Corrie Ten Boom (who also spent time in a concentration camp and lost several family members) went out on a limb to save who they could save.

How could the entire world allow one man, with millions following his lead, to treat one specific ethnic group of people as though they are worthless and deserve death? As far as God is concerned, ALL of us deserve death. There is no one righteous, no not one. Yet even God, who spared not His own Son, gave Him in death that we might have life. Not even Hitler, and certainly not the coming Antichrist, of which Hitler was merely a shadow, are righteous.

Very few see where this world is heading, and it will make the Nazi death camps look like parks compared to what the Antichrist is going to mete out, especially on Jews. The despicable part is to hear professing Christians side with the rest of the world against Jewish people and the state of Israel, because they believe that "the Jews" are responsible for all the major problems of this world!

I have heard it repeatedly. It is stated so often that no one blinks at it anymore. Black leaders have stated it, Arabs and Muslims have stated it, and professing Christians have stated it. Yet if all the ills of the world were blamed on African Americans, or some other group, you can bet there would be an outcry so loud that all the windows in the world would shatter, with Jesse Jackson and Al Sharpton leading the parade.

People who stand against Jews and Israel need to ask themselves WHY. Why is it they harbor such unmitigated ethnic bias against a group that, in spite of the fact that they have survived attempted extermination on more than one occasion, these same professing Christians and others see the Jews as the problem?

Could it possibly be that Satan is instigating them to do, say, and feel what *HE* feels for the Jews? After all, if not for the Jews there would be NO salvation, since Christ was born into Israel, as a *Jew*, lived as a *Jew*, was crucified as a *Jew*, rose again as a *Jew* and continues to exist in full humanity (while being God), as a JEW.

I have to wonder how those who hate Jews separate the facts that Christ is a Jew, Jewish individuals wrote the Bible, and the culture within the Bible reflects *Judaism*? How is that possible, especially when Arabs and Muslims (Jihadists) train their children from near *infancy* to hate Jews, and much of their literature (including places in the Qur'an) reflects that hatred? There is something extremely wrong with picking Jews out of the line up, so to speak, while letting everyone else off the hook.

The Jews then were not seen as people, but as objects, and those objects were seen as worthless, requiring nothing less than full extermination. The world is quickly rising to that same point again. There is no concern for the fact that every nation on earth is now against Israel, including the United States under Team Obama. While people continually come back to the supposed "terror" that Israel has created in the Middle East, these same people are completely blind to the fact that Israel, surrounded by Arab/Muslim nations, has continued to do whatever is necessary to ensure a Middle East sans Jewish people and certainly without a Jewish state.

I see few protesting Iran or Iraq because of those country's atrocities. I see few coming out against Ahmadinejad, who, along with Khadafi, should have been arrested when those men appeared at the United Nations. Instead, dictator Ahmadinejad was applauded, in spite of the fact that a number of other high-level diplomats and leaders of other countries condemned his speech as one of the most virulent, anti-Semitic speeches since Adolph Hitler.

In the end I believe God will be victorious, since the Land spoken of in Scripture (originally the Palestinian Land Covenant, but shortened to simply the Land Covenant because of Arafat's coup) is *God's* Land. While the Gentiles continue to trample it, the appointed time will come when God will stand and will direct Michael the Archangel to come *against* the enemies of Israel.

As Ezekiel repeatedly states throughout the book bearing his name, God will do what He does in the Middle East for the sake of His holy Name. People continually forget that.

In fact, in Ezekiel God *clearly* states that it is *not* for Israel or for the Jewish people that He does what He will do, but *solely* for the sake of His Name. The world (including Israel) will answer to that.

The remainder of the article from IsraelNN.com is reprinted here:

"The ruling determined that Israel has no standing in the Biblical heartland and opens the door to EU import duties on Israeli goods from Judea and Samaria, which would make those products less competitive. The EU has signed accords with both Israel and the Palestinian Authority and presently does not levy customs duties from either.

"The court said the EU's agreement with Israel 'applies to the territory of the State of Israel' while the one with the PA applies to 'the territories of the West Bank and the Gaza Strip,' according to Associated Press.

"Thursday's ruling stems from a German case filed by Brita, a German company that imports soft-drink-making machines from Soda-Club Ltd., an Israeli company based in Mishor Adumim, in the Binyamin region. Brita had asked German customs authorities not to charge it import duties, but the authorities rejected the request. On appeal, a Hamburg appeal court asked the Court of Justice of the European Union for its opinion.

*"**Political Decision***
Industrialists' Federation President Shraga Brosh said that the EU decision to levy customs on goods made in Judea and Samaria is more political than economic in nature. He added that it would be better if the EU focused on advancing economic cooperation between Israel and the PA, instead of being dragged into 'disputed legal-diplomatic interpretations,' as he put it.

"The court decision 'surprised nobody,' IDF Radio quoted a Foreign Ministry source as saying Thursday. 'Israel regrets that the ruling legitimizes the campaign against Israeli products made in Judea and Samaria, and is a continuation of the political European campaign against the settlements,' the source added."[17]

---

[17] http://www.israelnationalnews.com/News/News.aspx/136207

10

Israel at the Hands of the Media

(Blogged: 03/01/2010)

I t was revealed that letters from schools in Spain were sent to the Israeli Ambassador in Madrid. "*'The letters, addressed to the Israeli ambassador in Spain, ask, 'Mr. Ambassador, how many Palestinians did you murder today?' The letters are apparently all from the same school in the Valencia region. Israeli officials believe that the children – who are in elementary school – were put up to the 'project' by school officials and teachers.*"[18]

---

[18] http://www.israelnationalnews.com/News/Flash.aspx/181476

It is fascinating, isn't it, that the world views Israel as the *culprit* and the *problem* not only for what is going on in the Middle East, but essentially throughout the world. People blame the 9/11 World Trade Tower attacks on "Jews." Why? Because there is one particular man whom people believe had a great deal of money to gain from that incident, and so because of that the entire 9/11 was set up - with the collusion of our government. Oh, and the man in question is *Jewish*.

The "Rev." Jesse Jackson can call New York City "hymietown" and, along with Al Sharpton (another "Rev"), can make other condescending and anti-Semitic remarks about Jewish people and it's not a big deal because he's Black. Therefore, he understands what it means to be held down by "the man." Apparently, "the man" is the Jew.

It is funny, though, how everyone believes Jews control the world's affairs. Interesting. They apparently control all major corporations, including the Media. However, let us stop and consider for a moment that if this is true, then their PR campaign is obviously *failing*. If the Jews actually run everything as people charge that they do, then either the Jews are not as smart as everyone gives them credit for being or they are simply *masochists*. If they *do* run the Media, then you would think that the world would be swayed in *favor* of Israel and the Jews. Not so. In fact, to hear the Media tell it, only Jews are creating casualties in the Middle East. It is due to their apparent bloodlust that they need to continue to slaughter Palestinian after Palestinian. Does anyone else notice the problem here?

Who knows, though; maybe it IS true. I shop at a men's store in my area when I am in need of a new suit. The store is owned by a Jewish family. There you have it! Obviously, the Jews run the men's suit empire as well. I guess I should look for another place to shop. Oh wait, I can't, because any place I shop is either owned or controlled by Jews. Gosh Wally, I guess you just can't win for losing. I have no choice but to buy my suits from Jews. Oh, the horror!

There are many, many gullible people in this world who actually believe that the Jews have conspired together to create Socialism, as well as a continued problem in the Middle East. This is in order that the world would look at the Jews as the *victim*, when in truth, they are not only not the victim, but also the perpetrators, and the real threat to freedom. This is what people believe. Yet their beliefs do not fall in line with reality.

If the Jews have somehow banded together to form these elite coalitions in order to gain control of the world, they are obviously doing it all *wrong*. They need to go back to the drawing board and consider where they have failed to gain the opinion of the public in favor of them and their motives. Jews throughout the world are looked down on. It is generally believed that they have no right to be in the Middle East at all, and especially not as a nation.

The plain fact of the matter is that *if* Jews are the problem, then they have completely forgotten to unite as *one*. If it is then merely a few Jews who "run the world," so to speak, why are all Jews badmouthed, criticized, and targeted as the "bad guy"? Somewhere along the lines, *if* the Jews are running things (especially the Media) they have failed miserably to gain world support. So, either the Jews are not as smart as everyone gives them credit for being, or this belief that they are running the world is a fantasy - a mirage - put in place by individuals who have so much power that they are simply manipulating the players of this world, like one huge chess game.

Are all Jews "good" by humanity's standards? Of course not, but neither are all Jews "bad" by those same standards. Are all white people "good" by humanity's standards? Of course not, as there are plenty of "bad" white people (and black people, and Latin people, etc.). Yet it is becoming increasingly more fashionable to blame Jews for the world's ills. Anyone who does this, instead of being criticized, actually receives accolades! Today, what the Media cares to share with us regarding the problems in the Middle East is how often Palestinians are allegedly killed or brutalized by Jews. What the world *never* hears about, though, is what the Palestinians are doing to these same innocent children, turning them into Jew-haters almost as soon as they are born. It is tragic, but there it is...and the worst thing about it is that it goes *unnoticed* by much of the world because the Media (controlled by Jews apparently) never lets us see these images. Does that make sense to you?

Look, as far as I am concerned, *all* Jews - just as *all* Gentiles - need salvation. They need Jesus, as He is the only one who offers true salvation. If God judges each one of us by *His* standards (the Ten Commandments alone), not ONE of us would stand before Him and be declared INNOCENT. Not one of us. We have *all* broken God's Laws. Interestingly enough, while the Mosaic Law, including the sacrificial system, was given to Israel, it was given for a higher purpose than for simply covering over sin, allowing Jews to reestablish fellowship with God. It should be completely obvious that sacrificing bulls, calves, rams, sheep, doves, and whatnot has no *lasting* effect. That system cannot and never did remove sin permanently. If that were the case, Moses would have been able to offer *one* sacrifice for Israel with finality.

The sacrificial system was put in place to point to something much higher. That something was found in the *Messiah, Jesus Christ*. He came, He lived a perfect life, and He followed every part of the Law perfectly, down to the last jot and tittle. It was because of this that He was able to become a sacrifice for our sin, and His sacrifice lasts *forever*. His one sacrifice allowed God the Father to pour out His wrath on Jesus instead of on *us*. This and this alone is what allows God to redeem those who believe in Jesus' act of propitiation. Without Christ, we have nothing. The only reason the Mosaic sacrificial system worked at all was that it merely pointed to something much greater than itself: Jesus Christ.

The sacrificial system under the Mosaic Law has no merit in and of itself. In fact, long before it was put into place, God was redeeming people the same way He has always redeemed people: through *faith*. Because Abraham believed God, that belief was counted for righteousness (cf. Genesis 15:6; Romans 4:3; Galatians 3:6). God was able to credit Abraham's account with God's own righteousness (made possible by the death of Christ). That righteousness for Abraham is the exact same righteousness that we receive when we believe that Jesus Christ came in the flesh and died on the cross with the shedding of His blood. Without the shedding of blood, there is no remission of sin (cf. Hebrews 9:22). Christ rose from the grave three days later because the grave could not hold Him. All people, regardless of race or ethnicity, need the salvation that only comes from Jesus. The Jews are included in this invitation.

Those of you who are angry with the Jews because they "crucified" Christ obviously do not get it at all. Christ *came* to die. As a Gentile, I am *just* as guilty of killing Jesus as any Jew. MY sin placed Him on Calvary's cross as well as yours. For that I am and will be eternally grateful - and so should you.

You folks that blame the Jews for everything need to wake up and wake up quickly. You are a *pawn*, used by the media to further their efforts to eliminate a Jewish state. Oh, sure, you've got all your reasons, but they are merely fed to you from the same media that you believe is owned *and* controlled by the Jews. Think again, folks. If the Jews (as a whole) owned and controlled the media, it seems to me that what we would be hearing and seeing from that same media are stories and images that *support* Jews and the state of Israel, while coming down on the Palestinians, Hamas, Hezbollah and all the rest. This is certainly not the case, though, is it?

You can live for only so long with your heads in the sand. While your head is there, the rest of your body is exposed, and one day you will be run over by the same media that you swore is owned and controlled by the almighty Jew. Something is wrong here. Either the Jews are absolute morons (though they are smart enough to purchase and own controlling shares in the very media that hates them, apparently) or YOU have it wrong. I vote for the latter.

11

Muslim Mafia Infiltrates America

(Blogged: 03/01/2010)

For those people who think that it's the "*Jew, Jews, Jews!*" who have banded together to take over the world and destroy society as we know it, it might be a good idea for these folks to shift their gaze to another group that literally began infiltrating America roughly 40 years ago. Their intents and purposes are extremely dangerous and sinister, yet many within these United States view their presence and work in America as altruistic.

The **Muslim Brotherhood**, based in Egypt, is often likened to the Italian Mafia. They are organized and are connected one with another throughout the world and, more specifically, throughout the United States. In fact, it has been largely easy for this group (and its many offshoots) to set up shop in America, due to the fact that, *"'We can have as many organizations as we want,' no questions asked, thanks to America's tolerant and pluralistic society."*[19] The previous statement, made by **CAIR** official, Omar Ahmad, indicates how easily our own laws of the land can be used against us. This is exactly what this **Muslim Mafia** has done and continues to do.

Many of the organizations that were alive and kicking in the United States prior to 9/11 were shut down after the Feds determined that many to most of these organizations were simply money laundering fronts, working in order to take in cash and get it over to terrorists throughout the world. Many of their charities were seen by our government as criminal enterprises and were shut down. The fact that groups like CAIR qualify for non-profit status means that they are required to report virtually nothing to our government.

Therefore, what does the Muslim Mafia want (and it should be noted that not ALL Muslims are involved here, nor do they wish to be. We are speaking of those Muslims with Jihadist mentalities that believe the United States should be *overthrown*, violently if necessary)? From their own documents (confiscated during an arrest of one of the leaders in the U.S.-based organization), our government has learned:

"It has stated clearly in its recently declassified U.S. charter that it considers the United States to be its enemy."[20]

"The long-term goal is to destroy the United States from within, by using its freedoms and political processes against it.

"Their ambitious plans include a complete U.S. takeover, replacing the Constitution with Shariah, or Islamic Law."[21]

---

[19] Gaubetz & Sperry Muslim Mafia (WND Books, 2009), 232
[20] Ibid, 230

It is obvious that these groups take their job seriously. They have been working toward that end since the early 1970s, and continue to this day. The Roman Empire was destroyed from within by its own citizenry in part. They thought they were too powerful and too well protected for anyone to successfully come against them. They were wrong, as history has shown. Marauding bands of Germanic tribes, who swept in when Rome was actually at its weakest - though the citizens felt their empire was impenetrable - overcame them.

Is this what America is coming to? While people focus on the "Jew" and "Israel," we have groups right here within the borders of the United States who seek nothing less than the complete overthrow of our great nation. The attitude of most people in this country mirrors that of Rome's people. We believe we are strong. We believe that if we just stop "antagonizing" Bin Laden, Hamas, Ahmadinejad, and others, they will leave the United States *alone*. That is a pipe dream! As long as groups like the Muslim Brotherhood exist, they will not stop *voluntarily*. In fact, that they will not stop until they are completely quashed.

Their intent is not to simply overthrow the United States. Their intent is to overthrow the world, turning the entire planet into one that is governed by Sharia, and all of it done for *Allah*. Ahmadinejad recently made comments about how the United States is keeping the last Mahdi from appearing on this planet. What is the solution to that? Simply to take out the United States. Of course, it seems highly improbable and unlikely that this could be accomplished, yet undercover and with the protection of our own laws, splinter groups and branches of Muslim Brotherhood have made huge inroads into the fabric of America. It is happening under our noses.

They spend their time blackmailing large corporate banks, deciding whom they will help and who they will work against during every

---

[21] Gaubetz & Sperry Muslim Mafia (WND Books, 2009), 230

election that is held in the United States, all the while presenting themselves as nothing more than a social network for Muslims here in the United States.

Oh, but wait! This can't be true! Behind all of this there just has to be a Jew somewhere, *perpetrating* this evil. It has to be, because Jews pull the strings and hold all the cards! My, oh my, where can we turn for truth?

The reality is that the Muslim Brotherhood has been in the sights of the FBI and other federal agencies since 9/11 (it is too bad it was not before!). Our government has been working to dismantle the groups here which are directly or indirectly associated with the Muslim Brotherhood. If you do not believe that, then I would suggest you purchase your own copy of *Muslim Mafia*. Fact after fact is listed - their infiltration, their rise to power, and what they are doing now.

You need to focus on the *real* problem and stop hating Jews, believing them to be the source behind every problem. It is time for *logical-thinking* people to wake up, focus, and take back our country. However, the reality is that it simply may be too late for that.

12

Earthquakes and the Earth's Axis

(Blogged: 03/02/2010)

I t was reported that the Chilean earthquake was so catastrophic that it altered the earth's axis. In fact, scientists are saying this shift has actually shortened the normal day by 1.26 microseconds.[22] Sure, that does not appear to be a great amount of *time*, but the fact that *any* earthquake could have such an effect on earth and its axis actually says a great deal. The fact that the earth day's 24-hour period has been altered is immense, in spite of the fact that that amount of time is not noticeable by people.

For years, we have had all types of naysayers regarding the End Times. Preterists, Covenant and Reformed Theologians and others

---

[22] http://www.space.com/news/chile-earthquake-earth-days-100302.html

have all had one good laugh over the alleged signs of the times. They have more than pooh-poohed the idea that the end is really coming.

These theologians have pointed to the individuals whom they charge with being egotistical enough to put specific times to days (regarding the Lord's return), when Scripture clearly warns against that. I had a good laugh at the rigmarole that Richard Abanes goes through in his book End Times Vision. In it, he defines the First World War as the *War of the Spanish Succession* and, lo and behold, he found *two* historians (both now deceased) who espoused it. Let us ignore the fact that virtually everyone else sees the war that was labeled *World War I* as the actual First World War.

Of course, we remember how many "theologians" today point to the destruction of the Temple and Jerusalem in A.D. 70 by the Roman troops as not only God's judgment for rejecting Jesus Christ, but also the point at which Jesus apparently *returned...spiritually*, of course. This is in spite of the fact that that no one saw Him, yet He said that every eye would see Him (in Acts 1; Matthew 24). I don't know, whom should we believe?

So, here in 2010 we see an increase in the frequency of earthquakes as well as the intensity of them. In the past few years we have seen earthquakes which have destroyed towns, cities, and villages. If that was not enough, at least two of these major earthquakes have created tsunamis which have further devastated these same areas. Who can forget the Thailand earthquake/tsunami, which destroyed homes, villages, port towns and took thousands of lives?

Nature has run amok. It is not what it used to be. In spite of the dire warnings of Global Warming, we have discovered that not only is the earth *not* heating up, but it is actually getting *colder*. Makes you wonder why anyone listened to Al Gore at all. Oh wait, didn't he invent the Internet? No, that was the military, *decades* ago.

We are in the midst of the earth's birth pangs. It is clear because it is happening all around us. The naysayers continue to "naysay," while those of us who seem to think that prophecy marches on are still ridiculed and laughed at.

Eschatology is not an exact science, unfortunately. The only One who has all the answers is God Himself. We are left to study and *attempt* to put the pieces together the best way that we can. More than anything, what prophecy *should* do is create a passion for getting the Gospel of Jesus Christ to the lost of this world. In Thailand, the world lost over 200,000 people! In Chile, the number is around 1,000 and growing. However, with every day that passes, 150,000 people actually die. They are gone - poof! Were they presented with the Gospel?

Besides the fact that nature is going whacko (as foretold by Jesus Himself in Matthew 24's Olivet Discourse), there is another aspect of the End Time that is heating up. It is *anti-Semitism*. Apparently, in France the incidences of hate crimes toward Jewish people have risen dramatically, over 75% since last year. Interestingly enough, there has also been a tremendous rise in the Muslim population in France as well. Hmmm, wonder if there is a connection?

In England, we have already seen that there is a connection between increased Muslim population and an increase in *protests* and *crime*. Of course, this is not to say (or suggest) that *all* Muslims are of the mind that Jihad is the best way to go, or even the only way to go. Many Muslims simply want to live in peace and worship their god. Too many Muslims create violence where none existed before. This will not stop, either, because these people believe that the world must be converted to Islam, and all laws replaced with Sharia.

We are living in interesting times. As I stated in a previous post, Nephilim demons are creating havoc *through* human beings. We are seeing Paul's prophetic utterances happen right before our eyes.

In spite of this, many appear to be either blind, asleep, or both. No matter. What happens in the world will happen, and it will happen because God has *foreordained* it. Authentic Christians need to be spreading the Gospel, not arguing about this aspect of Eschatology or that one.

If you are an individual who believes as Preterists do, that the Lord returned in A.D. 70, good for you. The big question, though, is: are you out there *evangelizing*? Are you evangelizing the *lost*? Are you introducing people to Jesus Christ, who is the only Person who can truly save? If not, *why not*?

Enjoy your Eschatological opinions. No one is saying you cannot have them. However, when those opinions get in the way of the Great Commission, then something is obviously wrong.

I remember speaking with one well known Preterist not long ago. He has a radio station on the internet and has produced a number of books promoting his views. I asked him directly why he spends all of his time talking about Eschatology and completely ignoring discussion of the Gospel of Jesus Christ on his radio program. He did not respond. He simply *avoided* the question altogether. That says a lot. It says Eschatology has more weight than anything does, and evangelizing the lost comes in second, or maybe last, place for him.

When we stand before Christ, He will not be asking our view of Eschatology. He will be asking about our concern for the lost and how that concern worked itself out in this life. Too many Christians are sidetracked. We need to get back on track and we need to do it now.

13

Muslim Aggression

(Blogged: 03/05/2010)

It was recently reported that two Muslims in Egypt, who, on October 19, 2009, viciously shot 61-year-old Farouk Attallah 31 times in broad daylight - and then beheaded him - were *acquitted* of all charges. This was done in a very busy market place not far from Cairo, while horrified people looked on.

The judge in the case did not believe the evidence against the two accused Muslim men was enough to warrant life in prison, or execution. Because of it, both men were completely acquitted as shouts of

"Allah is Great!" filled the courtroom. Muslim aggression toward Copts (Christian Orthodox Coptic Church of Egypt) has been on the rise of late.

"What prompted the killing of Farouk Attallah was an alleged illicit sexual relationship between his son Romany and a local Muslim girl, Hagger Hassouna. A rumor that intimate photos of Hagger together with her lover Romany were circulating on cell phones in Dairout lead four members of the Hassona family to kill Romany's father, after failing to locate his son, who had fled.

"Besides the killing of Farouk Attallah, the arrest of the Hassouna perpetrators sparked on October 24, 2009, Muslim riots and collective punishment against all Copts in Dairout. Christian-owned shops, pharmacies, and homes were looted and burned."[23]

The story continues: *"The majority of Copts believe the reason for the acquittal of Muslims is that although Egypt claims to be a secular state, in reality it applies the Sharia law which dictates that a Muslim who kills a non-Muslim must not be killed, because it is not reasonable to equate a Muslim with a 'polytheist' (a Christian).*

"Commenting on the acquittal, Dr. Naguib Gobraeel, President of the Egyptian Union of Human Rights, said: 'What is the solution? The same happened with regards to Al-Kosheh Massacre [21 Copts were slaughtered in 2000 and not one Muslim was indicted], the attack on the Copts in Alexandria were blamed on a mentally unstable person; even the assailant who beheaded Abdo Goerge Younan in Menoufiah is now in a mental hospital. Heavenly Justice is our last resort.' He stated that he will appeal this week's verdict."[24]

Sharia Law is *Islamic* Law. This law turns the hands of the clock back thousands of years, where people are executed for the simplest of

---

[23] http://www.aina.org/news/20100303215642.htm
[24] Ibid

things, all because Allah is allegedly offended. Muslims like the ones in this article are narrow and myopic. They have no sense of dignity, nor do they value human life. This type of law is what Islam wants to impose on the entire world. This is the main goal of Islam and the Jihadist Muslim.

Though these murderers literally got away with murder in a human court, they will obviously face THE God of the Universe and beyond, and unfortunately for them, it will NOT be Allah.

14

Zionists Continue to Support Israel

(Blogged: 03/09/2010)

Realizing all the acrimony in the world against Israel, it seems clear that V.P. Biden is a professional at speaking out of both sides of his mouth, as are most politicians. Earlier, in a meeting with Perez, he confirmed that the United States stands with Israel. When asked by Perez to take a tougher stand against Iran's potential encroachment, Biden also assured him that the United States has and will continue to take a very tough stand.

Apparently, Biden believes that the average individual is a *moron*. Even if we leave Israel completely out of the picture, it becomes clear that the United States has *not* done enough to eliminate the threat that Iran brings to the world with their developing nuclear program.

I guess President Obama believes that because he outwardly and obviously supports Muslims over Jews, President Ahmadinejad will leave the United States alone if they ever get to a point of pushing the button to launch nukes in our direction. The absurdity (or is it naiveté?) of this belief smacks in the face of everything that Ahmadinejad stands for, based on his posturing and verbal assaults on the sovereignty of the United States.

It seems clear (and has seemed clear for some time) that Iran has no incentive to back down and every incentive to keep going. What they want to see - along with multitudes of Muslims worldwide (though certainly not all) - is a world that is guided by Islam, and in which Sharia is *the* law.

The people that believe this is merely wishful thinking or a pipe dream on the part of Ahmadinejad and others have not been paying attention. Regarding Israel, in spite of the fact that most of the world is opposed to Israel being a state anywhere, much less in the Middle East, Christian Zionists *are* having an impact for them.

Let's be clear here - Israel has every right to be a sovereign nation. The fact that Jews of Israel (as well as the MAJORITY of the world) are in complete rebellion against God is obviously an important fact to be considered. At the same time, the world places no constraints on any other nation regarding their alleged relationship with their god, or whether they are in rebellion against it. Somehow, this only applies to Israel, and it is completely unsupportable by any document in the world that relates to the sovereignty of nations.

The fact that the Jews of Israel are in rebellion to God is *their* problem, and it is a problem that God Himself *will* correct, which is why I believe, based on numerous passages from Ezekiel, that God is drawing

Jews back to the Land. He is doing it with an "*outstretched arm and with wrath poured out,*" (cf. Ezekiel 20:34).

In spite of the way things look, God has everything under control. The people who are constantly accusing and attacking Zionists obviously have *very* little faith in the sovereignty of God. THEY need to get their act together and find out who God truly is, because their opinion of Him is exceedingly small.

This is from Israel Today Headline News:
http://www.israeltoday.co.il/default.aspx?tabid=178&nid=20712

Israeli Prime Minister Benjamin Netanyahu on Monday addressed a Christians United for Israel (CUFI) summit in Jerusalem and encouraged Christian Zionists around the world to stay the course in their defense of the Jewish state.

Netanyahu reiterated the amazing turn of events that the presence of Israel-loving Christians in the Jewish state represents after centuries of Christian persecution of Jewish minorities.

"Your presence here today represents a profound transformation in the relationship between Christians and Jews," said the prime minister. "This transformation has its roots in the 19th century when the early Christian Zionists came to the Land Israel and when they began exploring the land of the Bible, when they began to yearn for the Jewish restoration in this land, the restoration of our numbers, the restoration of our sovereignty."

Netanyahu noted the Christian Zionism actually preceded modern Jewish Zionism, and acted as a stepping stone for the reestablishment of Israeli sovereignty. In the same spirit as those 19th century Christian Zionists, Netanyahu said leaders like CUFI Director John Hagee are continuing to hold Israel aloft in both prayer and advocacy.

"Time after time, through thick and thin, you have stood shoulder to shoulder with our state, and I have come here tonight to thank you for your unwavering friendship," said Netanyahu. "I salute you, the people of Israel salute you, the Jewish people salute you."

The summit was attended by 1,000 Christian delegates and led by Hagee, who took the opportunity to reaffirm his support and the support of tens of millions of American Christians for Israel.

15

Biblical Perspective on Illegal Immigration

(Blogged: 03/11/2010)

L ast March 21, 2010, liberal bleeding hearts headed to Washington, DC to protest the fact that America's borders are not open for all people from all countries to merely *walk in.*

Mark Tooley stated, "*Joining with groups like ACORN, a wide coalition of religious left groups will march on Washington, D.C. on March 21 on behalf of eventual amnesty and largely open borders under the rubric of Comprehensive Immigration Reform (CIR). The National Council of*

Churches (NCC) is even hailing CIR as a 'divine mandate' and a 'patriotic act.'"[25]

The interesting thing, of course, is that there are multitudes of *illegal* immigrants in our country. They are not registered, they do not pay taxes, and yet there are people like this living in our country, sending their children to schools and receiving medical aid when they need it. In essence, while they are giving *nothing* back to America, they are mainly taking.

I simply do not understand how some people think, honestly. According to Tooley's article, spokespeople for the march on Washington demanded that the broken immigration problem in our country be fixed. Their solution is to throw open the borders - wide open! How does that fix anything? It solves no problem at all.

The article goes onto say that "*the march's co-sponsor is the decidedly less religious 'Reform Immigration for America,' whose members include ACORN, CodePink, National Council of LaRaza, National Gay and Lesbian Task Force, and People for the American Way, among many others, including labor groups, like the AFL-CIO. Plus, of course, the Council on American Islamic Relations and Muslim Public Affairs Council are signed on. The church groups are specifically urging support for Illinois Democratic Congressman Rep. Luis Gutierrez's Comprehensive Immigration Reform for America's Security and Prosperity Act.*"[26]

Essentially - as unbelievable as it sounds - there are groups in this country who simply want to see America *fall*, and they are hastening it along with their beliefs. Though America has given them all they have in most cases, they are not content with that. They want - like our current President and many within Congress - to turn America into a Socialist state, one in which everyone (except the ultra rich) share and share alike.

---

[25] Mark Tooley on Immigration
[26] Ibid

Unfortunately, there is no country in history that has succeeded with Socialism in place. Like Welfare, Socialism can and often does create laziness in people, though it is not meant to do that. People get used to getting something for *nothing*, which can often take away from them the motivation to go out and work. Granted, a percentage of those on Welfare actually need those services and it is good that our government created that system. The problem is that there are too many who are on it and have learned how to beat it. Obviously, that is not why that system was created.

My wife spent time in Europe a number of years ago. She went through a country that was largely Socialistic. The government of that country owned businesses. There was absolutely no incentive for the employees (in the shoe store where my wife was attempting to buy a pair of shoes) to wait on my wife. They got the same money whether they sold any shoes or not. After a long time of waiting and receiving no help at all, my wife walked out.

Why, for goodness sakes, would we want to turn America into a country of "state workers"? While that may sound insulting to some, I spent one summer working for a state government. I quickly learned that things were done one way - *slowly*. If you went faster than your co-workers did, you received dirty looks. If you did not "get it," someone eventually pulled you aside and explained the way the system worked. Working slowly created job *security*, which was the name of the game - not doing your best job.

At least with state workers, they do *some* work. Those on Welfare do nothing - and most like it that way. Where illegal immigrants are concerned, most are hard working individuals who are simply trying to provide for their families. The difficulty, though, is the drain they often unintentionally place on the services of this country.

In states near the Mexican border, it is very common for pregnant women to come from Mexico into neighboring states and give birth.

Obviously, they do this because the care is better, but they also do it because their child will then have *citizenship* of the United States. This, of course, means that as the child's mother, she is entitled to receive services from the state and local governments, even though she is an *illegal* immigrant.

The large question is, what does the Bible say about this whole situation? We know that during Jesus' day, a common practice, which started with Moses, was to leave some of the crop standing unharvested. This small bit of crop was leftover for the poor and widows. They would be able to come through and take as much as they could carry in their hands to eat. They were not allowed to use implements to harvest the leftover crop (that would have been stealing), but taking enough to assuage their hunger was permissible, and the crop was left for that reason.

Nations that have borders seem to be something that God Himself ordained, which goes back to the Tower of Babel. Joseph Farrar states, "*Nation-states are an invention of the Creator – a deliberately chosen device to serve His purposes.*"[27]

If God ordained the nation-state, then it must be for a good reason. "*Ultimately, the purpose of nation-states seems to be to restrain Satan's efforts at creating his kingdom on earth. That will happen eventually – only when God Himself permits it in His timing, as shown in Revelation 17:17: 'For God hath put in their hearts to fulfill his will, and to agree, and give their kingdom unto the beast, until the words of God shall be fulfilled.' But nation-states serve another purpose as well – to be God's instruments on earth for meting out justice and providing protection for the people. (Deuteronomy 17:14-17)*"[28]

The problem, of course, is that with the Clinton Administration and the North American Trade Agreement (NAFTA) we saw a large first

---

[27] Joseph Farrar on Illegal Immigration
[28] Ibid

step in *eliminating* borders between the United States and Canada. It was the first step in blending people of neighboring countries together. Farrar comments, "*This agreement, which was supposed to stem the tide of illegal immigration by stimulating the economy of Mexico, had the exact opposite effect. It wrecked it beyond all recognition, stimulating, instead, a massive exodus of Mexican workers to the U.S. trying to provide for their families.*"[29]

Farrar continues, opining: "*this was no accident. It was not just a mistake. It was, I believe, an effort to "harmonize" the two countries – to begin integrating them, erasing the differences between them, mixing the populations to such an extent that discussions of merging the three major North American nations along the lines of the European Union would no longer seem inappropriate.*

"*In other words, what is happening in North America and Europe and Africa and Asia – breaking down the barriers of nation-state sovereignty – is not that much different from what happened back in the days of the Tower of Babel.*"[30]

It seems that at every turn there are people who simply want to throw the United States under the bus. They are doing whatever they can to move this country rapidly toward *Socialism*. They do not care how the average American feels about it, either. The only reason President Obama recently decided to start listening to Republications over the health care issue is because of the fact that when Sen. Kennedy died, a long shot Republican was voted into his vacated seat! All of a sudden, it became important for President Obama to consider the Republican opinion. Could it also have had something to do with the fact that he knew that without Republicans at that point, his health care dream was dead in the water?

---

[29] Joseph Farrar on Illegal Immigration
[30] Ibid

It does not seem to matter how much the United States helps other countries in need. It does not seem to make any difference how quickly people from our country are on the scene in places like Chile or elsewhere. As far as the world is concerned, the only time the good ol' U. S. is needed is when they need our money and our resources.

This does not mean that we should take a "*talk to the hand*" approach with respect to the needs of other countries at all. What it means is that we need to begin looking at where the money is coming from to help everyone else when, in fact, unemployment in this country is higher than it has been since the 1929 crash.

There is a biblical way to meet needs, and, obviously, God is in control even when it looks like He is not in control. There is biblical evidence to support the fact that Satan - prior to his fall from grace - was the highest created being in the universe under God Himself. It appears from Isaiah 14 and Ezekiel 28 that one of his jobs included directing the heavenly choir. It also appears - because of what he wore - that he was actually king (small "k") of heaven (again, *under* God).

When Satan fell, he lost direct control of all that God had created. When he saw that God had created a human being in the form of Adam and that Adam had been put in charge of Eden and the Earth, Satan realized that God had created another king (small "k") to rule over His Creation. This galled Satan, and he knew the only way he could gain direct control was by causing Adam to fall. He would not stand by and allow this created upstart to do the job that he (Satan) had done!

Since the Garden of Eden, Satan's goal has been to rule the world - to take back what he lost. We can see the definite beginnings of this in the Tower of Babel (Genesis 11). It was then that God confounded languages and created various cultures. However, since that time, Satan has never stopped attempting to bring the world together as one. He knows that *if* he is able to accomplish this, the world will literally be his oyster - at least for a time.

The world is moving toward that end. It has been happening and it continues to happen. One day, the world will be one, with a one-world ruler and the one-world religion he will be pushing. Eventually, that one-world religion will become the outright worship of him. Since he will be the son of Satan, the world will be worshiping Satan unknowingly. Satan will get his wish to be ruler of that which he did not create and lost, but only for a time. It is amazing how quickly things are moving along, as preordained by God.

All the folks who are pushing for America to eliminate her borders are simply pawns in a much larger game. They see nothing but their own selfish gain (though they believe they are altruistic) and though they are using the "religion" card on this very heated topic of illegal immigration, all that matters is that they get what they want.

They will get it eventually, but woe to them through which that comes. They will have gotten far more than that for which they bargained.

16

Philip Gulley Says the Church Is Not Christian

(Blogged: 03/14/2010)

Y ou know, you have to appreciate how fast and often we are hearing about how terrible the church is, how pharisaical her people are, and essentially how far we have come from the values that Jesus apparently taught.

Philip Gulley was raised in a home with a Baptist father and a Roman Catholic mother. He spent a good deal of time in the Roman Catholic Church, and then walked away from it. He eventually wound up as a Quaker minister, and his latest book presents his reflections on the church and its alleged separation from the One who is building it.

Gulley's book is filled with stories, anecdotes, and accusations. He speaks of his struggles with a variety of situations that face every minister. He also speaks of his solutions to these same situations and how often he was met with animosity, anger, and, in some cases, hatred for the particular stance he took.

Like Brian McLaren, Gulley comes down hard on those who oppose same-sex marriages, believing that this type of bigotry has no place in Christ's church of *love*. He also has problems with the church for its unwillingness to offer some type of public ceremony for those going through divorce.

Beyond this, Gulley believes that the virgin birth of Jesus is nothing more than a *myth*, as is the *Trinity*. What is odd here, though, is that *if* Jesus Christ *is* God (as is the Father), then that is already *two* individuals who are God, so why not *three in one*? However, I guess if Gulley cannot wrap his brain around the concept of the Trinity, then it just must not be true. How dare God try to be larger than any conceptualization of him that humankind can consider.

It also should be noted that since Gulley rejects the virgin birth of Jesus *and* the fact that Jesus is God (he rejects the Trinity), then he has essentially rejected the Jesus of the Bible. With it, he has rejected authentic salvation.

Gulley's book is just under 200 pages, and it boasts a total of 14 Scripture references. In fact, what is extremely noticeable is the *lack* of biblical discussion. Gulley arrives at his conclusions based on what he *thinks*. He rarely refers to Scripture, and the Bible holds no real place in the process he goes through in arriving at his doctrinal positions.

It is a shame that there are individuals like Philip Gulley purporting to be shepherds of the flock. One statement he made - which floored me - was that apparently, the church should *not* be concentrating on the fact that Jesus came and died a substitutionary death on Calvary's cross. No way. Instead, what the church should be doing is focusing on how to *imitate* Christ. So, like many within the Emergent Church, Gulley's focus is *external*, with nothing at all connected to the internal - the new birth that Jesus took the time to explain to Nicodemus in John 3. There, Christ spoke of a *spiritual transaction*. Gulley mentions none of this that I could locate in his book. Like McLaren, Campolo, Warren and a host of other Emergent luminaries, the emphasis on Christianity is on the *external*, although the internal is there as a factory for making me feel good about myself. Here is simply another proof that Gulley is not an authentic Christian - from his own lips.

For Philip Gulley, witnessing or evangelizing people is not really important. What is important for Gulley is that people should be ministered to, and this should be accomplished by meeting their needs, both *socially* and *judicially*. To hear Gulley tell it, Christians have never been involved in soup kitchens or organized mission trips to out of the way third world countries. They have certainly never died for their faith.

Philip Gulley says to forget the *atonement*. That is not important. What is important is turning the gospel of Jesus Christ into something *social*. Christianity is measured by our action, not our new birth. Of course, Philip Gulley can take this view. Do you know why?

At the end of his *If the Church Were Christian* book, there is an excerpt from another book in which Gulley shares with us something he believes to be so profound that it has changed his life. It has changed the way he views himself and the way he views and deals with other people. It has given him hope, joy, peace, love, and a high view of God. It has enriched and enhanced his life.

What is this profound truth? Simply that he believes that *all people will eventually be saved*. Did you hear that? If you are a Universalist, then you are probably clapping right now, ecstatic that someone else "gets it." If you happen to read the Bible, you probably already know that Jesus talked about hell more than He did about any other subject. Apparently, it is a real place, and it is *eternal*. Gulley does not believe that, though. No, he prefers to go by how something makes him feel. I guess he also does not realize that he is calling Jesus a *liar*.

It is tragic that there are people like Philip Gulley in ministry at all. They do nothing for people except provide them with platitudes and a smile. He really has nothing else to offer anyone that has any lasting value. He itches the ears of those who have rejected the truth.

In some ways, Philip Gulley reminds *me* of a Pharisee, although he says in his book that I am one. Bill Slabaugh and Philip Gulley should get together some time and share quips and anecdotes about all the Pharisees that have ruined churches.

Gulley's Pharisaism stems from the fact that he in all likelihood does not have salvation, and because he is so liberal with respect to the narrowness of God's decrees. No one who sits under his ministry will probably gain salvation, either. How could they, since he believes it is more important to *socialize the gospel* than to *evangelize people*?

People's needs *are* being met, and the church has been at the forefront of those endeavors for centuries. Gulley needs to get off his high horse, stop determining doctrine based on his feelings and spend some time in God's Word. Maybe, just maybe, the Lord might take the time to remove the blinders from his eyes long enough for him to see his error.

People like Philip Gulley need our prayers. I cannot imagine how dreadful it will be for those who have changed God's Word, making Him to be seen as a liar. No wonder the statement rings so true: how dreadful it is to fall into the hands of the living God (cf. Hebrews 10:31).

God is loving, patient, and forgiving. He is also just, holy, and righteous. Beyond that, He is very jealous for the honor due His Name. People like Gulley (and all of us teachers) will most certainly come under the greater condemnation because we teach people. It is for that reason alone that people who teach need to be as sure as possible that what we credit God as saying is what He is actually saying, not what we would *like* Him to be saying, or what we *think* He is saying.

Woe unto those of us who are too cavalier about the tremendous responsibility we have before us.

17

Speaking for God

(Blogged: 03/15/2010)

I f you have been following my blog posts, you'll note that I have recently posted reviews of three books, in all of which the authors believe they speak for God. Anyone who teaches theology or anything biblical is essentially speaking for God (including me; cf. James 3:1). In a previous post, I alluded to the fact that because those of us who teach speak *for* God, we also come under greater condemnation if we are wrong.

The Word of God - the Bible - is either God's Word, or it is not. Though written by men (cf. 2 Peter 1:21), their thoughts were most certainly guided by the Holy Spirit, so that ultimately what we have is a book in which God is the final and absolute Author. Because of this, whenever we preach or teach from the Bible it is important to realize that we are then disseminating the meaning of God's Word to those who are listening and/or reading what it is we are saying.

Because of this, the responsibility is great, and we cannot afford to be cavalier in the handling of God's Word. If more pastors and teachers would stop to realize that we are representing God, whenever we stand in the pulpit or in the front of the classroom, maybe - just maybe - we would think two, three, and even *four* times before we stated something that we attribute to God.

As I was reading to the end of the book of Job this morning, I was impressed with a number of things. Of course, we are familiar with all that Job suffered, all because Satan wanted to sift him as wheat and watch him fall by cursing God. If we look closely at the opening dialogue between God and Satan, *God* first brings the subject of Job up, *not* Satan (cf. Job 1:8). Satan took the bait and proceeding to bring accusations against Job. God *allowed* Satan to do whatever he wanted, but he was not given permission to touch Job at all. The tragedies that occurred were *around* Job and only indirectly affected him. Yet, in spite of the fact that he lost his children and his herds and flocks, he did not curse God but actually *thanked* Him because He gives and He takes away.

The next step was God granting Satan permission to do whatever he wanted to do to Job - except take his life. Following this, we see a multitude of horrific things that Satan inflicts on Job. His teeth fell out, his skin turned black, and he became covered with painful boils from head to toe. He developed insomnia, yet he had terrible nightmares while awake, and he suffered other things as well. In all of this, he did not curse God.

His so-called friends - Eliphaz, Bildad, and Zophar - came to Job to try to comfort him. One by one, they all said what they believed God was doing with Job. They were sure they were right. Ultimately, they agreed that all of this was happening to Job because of unconfessed sin, resulting in Job's hypocrisy. While Job obviously went through the motions of doing all God wanted by sacrificing and praying, these - to his friends - were clearly only *outward*, and did not come from the heart. While he did these things, he must have been sinning, and while other people could not see his sin, it was not hidden from God.

Elihu comes along and his words are filled with wisdom. Yet even he too was slightly arrogant, because there was too much self-assertiveness on his part. Yet it is interesting to note that when God finally does respond to Job, while He accuses Job's friends of wrongdoing, He leaves Elihu alone.

This brings us to the crux of the problem. Many people - in fact, all people - who preach, teach, or write books that have anything to do with God, are stating that *their* view is God's view. Of course, this cannot be true of everyone, simply because there are so many opposing sides to every theological debate. It is not wrong to believe something about the Bible, unless it denigrates God's attributes. Gulley (as mentioned in a previous post) does just that, unfortunately, as does Brian McLaren. These men speak their words and they firmly believe that they are speaking truth, which they in turn believe to be reflective of God's thoughts.

Job's three friends also believed they spoke the truth, but as it turns out, they were far from the truth. In fact, in Job 42, God makes it perfectly clear that these three men had sinned. God says to Eliphaz the Temanite, "*My wrath is kindled against thee, and against thy two friends: **for ye have not spoken of me the thing that is right**, as my servant Job hath*," (Job 42:7b; emphasis added). Did you catch the full meaning of that? God was angry against Eliphaz, Bildad, and Zophar because they gave a *false representation* of God. In effect, they told *lies* about God, who He is, and the nature of His attributes. Because of this, they were required to offer a hefty sacrifice (7 bullocks and 7 rams), and even then it would not be enough. On top of the sacrifice, it was only after Job prayed for them that they would be forgiven.

The tragedy is that too many people claim to speak for God, but do so in a way that attributes *lies* to Him. His character is maligned on a daily basis throughout the world; every Sunday, on Wednesdays, and at any other time that the Bible is either opened or spoken about from a pulpit. What should this realization cause to occur within us? Well, obviously, it should make us think soberly about what we believe the Bible to be saying. We should approach God's Word with complete humility, praying that God will keep us from an egotistical outlook.

Even after arriving at opinions about what we *think* God's Word is teaching, we need to humbly and fearfully realize that we could be wrong. If we understand that in this life we will never have perfect knowledge of God or His Word, this alone will make it easier for us to appreciate the importance of speaking for God with some hesitation. This does not mean that we cannot be *emphatic*. It means that we should always recognize that God through the Holy Spirit will always be teaching us.

I have noticed two things about the way people approach doctrine and wind up arriving at conclusions that are not necessarily biblically based:

First, for many the mode of interpretation is purely *allegorical*, in which it is possible to make the Bible say just about anything someone wants it to say. There are far too many who approach situations in life with no thought of considering the Bible, but instead rely purely on how they feel about a situation.

Allegory as a standard form of interpretation is simply not the way to approach Scripture. Even in those areas in which prophecy *appears* to be allegorical in nature, it should be clear that God would have only one meaning.

Second, there are those who look to themselves to determine what God would do in any given situation; they are elevating themselves to a higher authority than God's Word. They believe that if they come to believe that same-sex marriage is fine, then how much more does God, since He loves perfectly? The problem is that these individuals, far from understanding God's position against all forms of sin, resort to a type of emotional, sympathetic "love" that is no love at all. It is purely *sentimentalism*.

God has spoken, and it is in *His* Word, the Bible. Those who believe that the Bible was written by men, put together by men, and ultimately defined by men, have an extremely low view of God, and it certainly shows in their "exegesis" of God's Word. They routinely come up severely lacking. They have no fear of God at all.

When God spoke to Job out of the whirlwind, his mouth was stopped. Job said of himself, "*I have heard of thee by the hearing of the ear: but now mine eye seeth thee. Wherefore I abhor myself, and repent in dust and ashes,*" *(Job 42:5-6)*. Job abhorred himself at the sight and sound of God, yet this man was considered "*perfect and an upright man, one that feareth God, and escheweth evil,*" (Job 2:3b) by God.

Too many of us have become excessively familiar with God. Because God loves us, and because this was proven to us by God the Son and His bloody and brutal death on Calvary's cross, we believe that if Jesus were physically here we would go up to Him, slap Him on the back, and say, "*What up?*" We have taken God for granted, and by doing so have brought Him down to our level. We have left His holiness, righteousness, and justice behind Him because we prefer to see God only in a loving sense.

God *is* love, but He remains holy, just, righteous and all the other attributes. Because of this, it is incumbent upon each one of us who deigns to speak for the Lord to think again before attributing our thoughts and beliefs to Him. Beyond this, even when we arrive at a specific belief after carefully searching the Scriptures, we need to understand that humility is the path of learning, not arrogance.

In my opinion, many individuals today should *not* be preaching, teaching, or writing books. Of course, that sounds arrogant, but it is not meant to be. Too many today are presenting their beliefs and opinions about God as if God Himself were presenting them. The trouble is that these beliefs do not stand up under the scrutiny of God's Word. Again, this may sound arrogant, especially to those who are fond of using the "*judge not, lest ye be judged*" card, which of course has absolutely nothing to do with using the discernment God gives us as we approach His Word in humility. We should never judge the motivations of another individual, but we are also called to discern what is right and true. This can only occur by comparing the espoused beliefs and doctrines of others to the Word of God. The Bereans of Acts did this with respect to Paul, and Paul had no problem with it at all (cf. Acts 17:10-12).

We are all called to be like the Bereans, who *"received the Word with all readiness of mind, and searched the scriptures daily, whether those things (that Paul was teaching - ed) were so,"* (Acts 17:11b). It is our obligation to compare *all* teaching to the Bible. This is not judging. It is *discerning*. Do we want to know what God is saying? It is in His Word. Do we want to teach what God is saying? We had best look to His Word, allowing His Word to interpret itself.

If no one discerns what is right and true today, then error abounds. The reason there is so much error today is that there is little discernment. When someone steps forward in an attempt to discern, they are quickly shouted down, called names, and heckled. This should not be, but, unfortunately, it is. "*But there were false prophets also among the people, even as there shall be false teachers among you, who privily shall bring in damnable heresies, even denying the Lord that bought them, and bring upon themselves swift destruction. And many shall follow their pernicious ways; by reason of whom the way of truth shall be evil spoken of,"* (2 Peter 2:1-2).

This is what is happening today, folks. Good is bad and bad is good. Right is wrong and wrong is right. More than anything, we need discernment. We need to be like the Bereans, who searched the whole Scriptures to determine *truth*. They did not merely pull a proof text here and another one there. They viewed the entirety of the Scriptures to determine God's truth. How much more should we?

18

Obama and the Middle East

(Blogged: 03/16/2010)

P resident Obama has continued to make it abundantly clear that he holds no real favorable position toward Israel, because all of his favor has and continues to reach out to Arab nations. This is in spite of the fact that these same Arab nations not only couldn't care less about the United States, but too many of them see to us as the *"great Satan."* I find it frankly unconscionable that this administration persists in demanding a complete stop to Jewish settlement construction in and around the parts of Jerusalem under

Israel sovereignty. This has never *ever* been part of the equation in prior years with prior U.S. administrations, but because of President Obama's favoritism toward Islam, this situation has been added to the mix.

The reality is that one can only wonder why/how the United States believes it has the power to tell *any* country what to do; but because it is Israel, and they are our allies (or *have* been), apparently that gives us the right to place conditions on our alliance. That is like saying to a friend, "*You need to do things my way, or I am going to be better friends with your enemies.*" Does that make sense? If it makes sense to you, then my suggestion is that you are not really friends with the person you have just given the ultimatum to, but that your friendship is merely a *con*.

The people of Israel are not stupid, for as many people as there are who cannot stand the Jews. Netanyahu has most recently determined that all construction in Jerusalem will continue. Good for him. The idea that a nation can dictate to another nation where, when, and *how* to build anything is ridiculous. Yet we offer no real protests against Iran and its search for the "*bomb.*" Supposedly, it is because Israel continues to build in Jerusalem that everything may one day explode. Uh...okay, *sure.*

The plain fact of the matter is that every day we see more and more of President Obama's desire to be found favorable in the eyes of the Arabs. The question is, *Why*? They have shown us no favors. They are constantly referring to us as something evil that needs to be eliminated. They deign to want to destroy us, either from without or within; it really does not matter, as long as the United States is destroyed.

This is also the first president we have had, that I can recall, who has ever literally *bowed* to other dignitaries or leaders of other countries! What is *that* about? By doing so, President Obama is immediately saying to these leaders that the United States comes *under* their sovereignty. At every turn, President Obama seems to want to toss the United States under the bus. He is constantly ignoring the will of the people, his ratings have plummeted, and yet he persists in attempting to bring *his* socialistic plans to fruition. This nation cannot afford the type of health care bill that the socialists in congress want to see passed. Will it affect *them*? Of course not. They will have their own doctors, they will still be limo'd from place to place, they will continue to have their expenses paid, and, in short, they are already living the socialist lifestyle because they are essentially on the public doles and have been since they were elected.

Of course, the problem is that any socialist system developed in this country will be at least two-tiered, one for the über-rich and one for the rest of us, with those of us who work paying for the *rest* of the populace. You don't think the richy-rich congress people will be paying their own way out of their own pockets, do you? That would deplete their own storehouse of wealth. It wouldn't be prudent. Best to place *more* burden on the already overburdened taxpayer.

President Obama (before he was elected) indicated that he would prefer to be a great one-term president than a mediocre two-term president (my paraphrase). Unfortunately, with the way things are going it does not appear that he will get his wish. He will most likely be a one-term president who was not even *mediocre*. Of course, if you listen to people like Minister Farrakhan, it is the "white right" which is trying to ensure that President Obama will not be re-elected (I love how the race card can be pulled out when it is time to put a "dare" in front of the American people. This same card was played while President Obama was running for office; "*This country will NEVER elect a black man to the presidency*," etc.).

Actually, it is President Obama himself who seems to be ensuring his own career as a one-term president only, because since he took the oath of office he has been bent on bringing his own values, beliefs, and ideologies to the fore. Those of us who saw those things knew where we were headed. The folks who were fooled into thinking that this man was really a messiah were really let down. It was not long before the protests began from the very people who voted him into the highest office of the land. Where was the media, however, when the recent "Tea Party" protests took place? Dutifully ignoring it until it was claimed that there were racists among them. It would be a terrible thing if people's complaints were actually aired on national television, wouldn't it? However, we know that the media is fair and unbiased, correct? What was I thinking?

As for this blogger, I am so glad that Israel is standing up to the ridiculous and unfair demands of this Oval Office. We have no right to insist on anything where Israel is concerned. If we were truly their ally, we would be doing all that we could to ensure their safety and that they received fairness. For the United States, being an ally of Israel now is simply lip service and nothing more. I believe that if President Obama had his druthers, he would like to see come to fruition what President Ahmadinejad is aiming for, which is a world, or at least a Middle East, without the Jewish "problem."

It is nice to see some of the GOP standing publicly against President Obama's decisions and stance against Israel. Even some of the Democrats are becoming concerned about President Obama's posturing.[31] It is obvious, when Biden goes to the Middle East and speaks out of both sides of his mouth, and when his wife completely ignores Israel and the Jews during her recent visit, that the United States is not at all concerned with the welfare of their "ally," Israel. Even the *Euro-Med* partnership is now focusing only on the projected PA state (The *Euro-Med,* for those of you who do not know, is President Sarkozy's [France] baby. In 2008, he came up with the *Mediterranean Union,* which, remarkably, looks almost exactly like the Old Roman Empire

---

[31] http://www.israelnationalnews.com/

and whose first secretary-general is a *Muslim*. It is fascinating for those of us who take the Bible literally).

I say to Netanyahu, "*Press on and continue to stand up to the bullying of the United States!*" Of course, by saying this, am I ignoring the fact that most of Israel is liberal and wants little to nothing to do with Judaism? No, I am not ignoring that at all. These are two different issues. Israel's political statehood is separate from any beliefs they may have, especially considering the fact that *no other* country in the world is allowed to exist (or not) based on its religious beliefs (or lack of them). Apparently, this condition is only for Israel...[rolls eyes].

We shall see what continues to develop in the Middle East. However, those of us who *do* understand the Bible in literal terms (that's *literal*, not *literalistic*) already know the outcome of the story. It is the people who view prophetic discourse in allegorical terms who have issues and problems. They do not see that because they are too busy blaming Zionists for bringing about the upcoming Armageddon. Sure; and God is impotent, too, completely unable to bring His plans and purposes to completion. I do not know about you, but I am certainly glad I do *not* worship that type of God. The God I worship is *all-knowing, omnipotent, just, holy, loving, patient* and all the rest that coincides with His holy character. The idea that God is *not* in control of what takes place in this world is one of the most heinous doctrines ever born in hell. The people who believe that need to take a good look at themselves and understand that the god they have created is *not* the God of the Bible.

My suggestion would be to humble yourselves, confess your weaknesses and sins in having other gods before you, and get *right* with God by asking Him to develop the right attitude within you. Either He is in *full* control of everything that transpires in this world, or He is not. If the latter, He is no more worthy of worship than a wooden idol. If the former, there is *none* greater and no one more worthy of worship. The God of Abraham, Isaac, and Jacob is the same God of all authentic Christians. I pray that He be pleased to continue to work in and through us in order that the perfection of His will and purposes will be brought to realization.

19

President Obama Anti-Semitic?

(Blogged: 03/17/2010)

I nquiring minds want to know. This is what people are saying - specifically, Netanyahu's brother-in-law, who said, "'*The time has come to tell the truth.' Dr. Ben-Artzi told Arutz-7 radio (Hebrew) 'I understand the Prime Minister's reaction to me, but the truth must be told. Obama is an anti-Semite.' He said that Israel is dealing with 'a president who was educated by anti-Semitic preacher Jeremiah Wright.'*"[32] I cannot imagine that statement coming as a surprise to anyone, except possibly President Obama himself, who likely has operated under the belief that he has successfully pulled the wool over

---

[32] http://www.israelnationalnews.com/News/News.aspx/136571

everyone's eyes. Then again, that belief is merely an insult to those of us who have any semblance of intelligence.

Another group has declared that President Obama is nothing but a PLO Agent masquerading as the President of the United States. The article states, "*A group of far-right activists on Tuesday announced their plan to hang hundreds of posters across the country depicting U.S. President Barack Obama under the headline 'agent of the PLO.' The banner is already on display in the office of National Union MK Michael Ben Ari. 'The poster is within the limits of the country's freedom of speech act,' said Ben Ari's aide, Itamar Ben Gvir. 'I pity those who clapped during [U.S. Vice President] Joe Biden's speech,' said Ben Gvir, referring to Biden's address to the Israeli people at Tel Aviv University last week.*"[33]

I am all for diplomacy - not that it will do any good in the Middle East, because the situation demands that *sides be taken*. What is appallingly absurd, though, is to hear Biden, President Obama, Hillary Clinton and others parrot the sentiment that the United States stands behind Israel when, in point of fact, everything they are *doing* tells a different story. Israel cannot make a move without Broomhilda Clinton coming down on them. Biden can look Netanyahu straight in the eyes and state that the United States wants a strong Israel, yet everything this administration is doing is undercutting that statement. It simply shows how adept politicians can be at lying while showing no signs of lying and how stupid they believe the average person to be.

I for one am glad that Netanyahu has stood up against Clinton's demands and calmly reiterated (for the umpteenth time) that Israel will continue to build homes in the part of Jerusalem that has been under Israeli sovereignty since 1967. No such demands are made of the Arab nations. In fact, *have* there been any demands made of the Arab

---

[33] http://www.haaretz.com/hasen/spages/1156844.html

nation? I can think of no real demands. Suggestions, yes; demands, no.

I do not like the fact that our Administration thinks it speaks for everyone. Even those in congress are now starting to wake up to the fact that President Obama's administration is overtly *pro-Arab* and *anti-Israel*. Of course, this does not surprise me at all, because for anyone who was actually paying attention to Obama's life and work PRIOR to running for president, it was clear that he supported Arab nations then and was decidedly against Israel, in spite of the fact that the entire media, it seems, refused to bring these facts to light.

Frankly, if Iran or anyone came against Israel right now, I do not believe the United States would lift a finger to help Israel. The administration might offer a few words of encouragement to Israel and condemnation to those who attack her, but it would do nothing. Even though we are sending 387 bunker busters to the Indian Ocean area, this simply seems like posturing more than anything. It is trying to show the world that "see, we *do* care about Israel's safety." The fact is that if this administration does *nothing*, it *will* be seen for what it is - fully supportive of Arab nations, and fully against Israel. That would not do, so it is better to play the political game instead. Then this administration can at least say, "We tried."

Isn't it amazing to anyone else that in spite of all odds, Israel *remains* Israel? In spite of the fact that I cannot think of one country in the world that is actually *for* Israel, Israel continues to exist. That is incredible, and, as Ezekiel states, it is not for Israel that God is doing what He is doing. It is for the *sake of His holy Name* that He is doing what He is doing. While I do not blindly support Israel with their decadence, their immorality, or their lack of fear where God is concerned, I support their political right to exist, and I without equivocation support what I believe God is doing in that region of the world.

Time, of course, will tell what is what - but for those who understand the Scriptures *literally*, the answer has already been given. For those who view prophecy in *allegorical* terms: well, they are in for a huge surprise. Even then, however, they will admit nothing. It is a shame that they are so blinded with *anti-Semitism* that they are unable to see the truth even when that truth unfolds right before their very eyes.

20

Quartet Urges Israeli Settlement Freeze

(Blogged: 03/19/2010)

M iddle East mediators called on Israel to freeze all settlement activities and denounced Israel's aim to build new housing in East Jerusalem Friday.

United Nations Secretary General Ban Ki-moon read a joint statement by the members - Russia, the United States, the U.N. and the European Union - following a meeting of the group in Moscow which welcomed the prospect of "proximity talks" between Israel and the Palestinians.

"'The Quartet believes these negotiations should lead to a settlement, negotiated between the parties within 24 months, that ends the occupation which began in 1967 and results in the emergence of an independent, democratic and viable Palestinian state living side by side in peace and security with Israel and its other neighbors,' the statement said."[34]

You know what? Who cares what this or any other "quartet" thinks about what Israel is doing? Can you imagine someone coming together to condemn the United States action of rebuilding the area of the Twin Towers? I have to wonder why these same individuals are not banding together to *condemn* Iran's nuclear armament? Apparently, it is much more dangerous for Israel to build some homes and buildings in the area that they *already* control than to tell Iran they need to stop moving toward having their own nuclear bomb.

This whole situation is completely absurd. Why does the world think that it has the right to tell Israel what to do? I will tell you why. It is because Satan is the prince of the power of the air (cf. Ephesians 2). Because of this it is clear that the *air* is where he accesses total control of all that takes place on the earth. Of course, this is under God's complete sovereignty; nonetheless, the ruler of this world *hates* Jews. Why? As Paul explains in Romans, salvation *comes* from the Jews and from Israel. Whether or not they recognize this is beside the point.

Satan has tried numerous times in history to destroy the Jews. He has tried in the Old Testament, he has tried in the New Testament, and he has tried since the New Testament. His hatred for the Jews knows no bounds, and the world has fallen into the trap of believing the lie that Jews are the cause of all that is wrong in this world. What absolute garbage. They must be exceedingly powerful individuals to have withstood all of his attempts to destroy them utterly, yet not

---

[34] http://www.msnbc.msn.com/id/35944997/ns/world_news-mideastn_africa

only do they insist on continuing to exist, but they also apparently control the world! The people who believe this type of rubbish have brains that do not properly work. Certainly, they are devoid of logic.

Now the world deigns to tell Israel where they can and cannot build, even to the point of telling them that they must *cease* building in the areas of Jerusalem and Israel that they sovereignly control! These people — Blair, Clinton, Ki-moon, and others — have the temerity to believe that their position is *just* and *righteous*. No such demands are made of the Arabs. In fact, it is perfectly fine for the Arabs ("Palestinians") to attack the Jews if they even *berate* near the Temple Mount because the rest of the world says, "*See? The Jews are trouble makers.*"

There are TWO issues at hand here:

1. The world is blind to the truth about what God is doing in Israel and the Middle East, and
2. The Jews are blind to the fact that Jesus is their Messiah

What is interesting, though, if one takes the time to actually *read* Ezekiel, Isaiah, Jeremiah and other biblical books from ages past, is that God has *foreordained* what is happening and what will happen for one purpose and one purpose only: so that the honor and glory due His Name will be *restored*. This is why the world hates Jews: because when they do wake up to the fact that their actions are nothing but "politically correct" anti-Semitism, the result will be their abject horror at the fact that what they believed was not only wrong but was in direct *defiance* to God.

I find it remarkable that in spite of *all* the odds Israel continues to exist. The liberal Jews of Israel believe that they exist because of their own strength, their own willpower, their own "calling." In truth, the Jews continue to exist because of God, whether they would like to admit that or not (and they *will* admit it one day). They do not see that God protects *them* as He continues to protect *His Land.* He does not do this for any reason other than the fact that He will bring honor to His Name and the entire world will one day *finally* recognize that and submit to Him. Of course, by then it will be way too late. At that point they will be *forced* to submit to Him, not willingly.

The truth remains that God is in control of the Middle East, but woe to those who believe - like this "quartet" - that they have the answers and they have the power. They are nothing, yet they talk as if they are all-powerful. The world awaits delivery from this Middle East "problem." When the Antichrist shows up, ready, willing, and able to provide a solution, there will be celebrations in the streets! It will be a no-brainer - everyone a winner!

Only a few years later, the hammer will fall and the Jews of Israel will realize they have been deceived. It will be *then* that the Remnant of that generation will *finally* see that Jesus is Lord, Messiah and God. There is no other.

It cannot happen too soon.

21

Middle East "Peace" Quartet Rebuked

(Blogged: 03/19/2010)

I t looks like, in spite of their best efforts, those folks who just want peace in the Middle East are receiving a thumbs down from Foreign Minister Lieberman. It seems that the impression the Quartet of the Middle East wants to give is that if *only* Israel would stop its *aggressive* acts of construction, and if they would give up land, and if they would give up any claim to the Temple Mount, *then* peace talks could resume. Of course, this denies two things:

Never have any peace talks in the Middle East been predicated on Israel's construction - *never*. It was a condition largely introduced by

President Obama's Administration, in agreement with complaints by the Arab populace. Unfortunately, in spite of the fact that this condition has never been part of the peace process, now that it is on the table it will not be rescinded. In fact, it would really be impossible to rescind it. Of course, no such demands are made against any Arab nations in the surrounding area.

Israel has consistently made tremendous gestures of good will by removing themselves from specific areas demanded by Arab leaders and *not* returning fire in spite of the fact that *Israel* has been fired upon (and still is to this day) off and on since the Six Day War of 1967.

For anyone who can really see what is happening, it is absolutely clear that the Arab nations which surround Israel prefer that Israel was not there at all. That is their preference, and Ahmadinejad (as well as others) has consistently reiterated this fact, which has been shared in various media outlets. The fact that this man - the president of Iran (modern day Persia) - can make malicious, anti-Semitic remarks (presenting them as fact; i.e. the Holocaust never happened) and the world continues to treat him with kid gloves, is unconscionable.

As I look back over the last 20 year history of problems in the Middle East, it is clear that the Arab nations have given *nothing*. Everything that is wrong is said to lie squarely at the feet of the Jews and Israel. The world nods and looks on. On one hand, it is absolutely hilarious that such a tiny nation can not only continue to exist, but can create such problems in the Middle East! I mean, my goodness, you would think any one of those nations which surround Israel would be able to squash her like a fly. Instead, they posture, puff themselves up, smear Jewish people, and discharge anti-Semitism as fast as an automatic weapon.

Ahmadinejad's speech at the recent U.N. gathering is a case in point that has already been discussed. His remarks would have been approved of and appreciated by Adolph Hitler and there were those who stated such after that speech was given. Yet the world turns a blind eye to all of that because all the world wants is *peace* and peace at *any* cost. They want the Jews and the Arabs to live in peace. That cannot happen, because *both* groups claim that *they* are the chosen people; the Jews through Isaac, and the Arabs through Ishmael. So tell me, who is going to be able to step into that arena and *make* peace happen?

The historical problem dates back to Muhammad and the offering of himself to the Jews as their Messiah. He was roundly rejected, and because of that, he became determined to vilify the Jews. He successfully created a religion in which the Jews are seen as being worse than Satan and should therefore be eradicated. Islam is a religion of peace *only* when Islam is the ruling religion of the entire world.

People think they want church and state separated *now*. Wait until Islam gets what it wants - control of government. This is beginning to happen in Great Britain as well as other places, which heretofore did not have the difficulty of having to bow to Islamic pressure. Great Britain is now learning what that means...the hard way.

Those who honestly believe that individuals from around the world can actually create peace in the Middle East are not only kidding themselves, but they are nothing but *pawns*. For some reason the Arab nations opposed to Israel give nothing, yet continue to demand that Israel give everything, while complaining that Israel has given nothing - even after she *has* given up territories.

It is like a dog chasing its tail. The Arab nations howl and the world weeps. Israel gives and the world says it is not enough. It reminds me of the coverage of the presidential campaigns leading up to the election. I cannot recall one network or media outlet (not including those of a highly conservative nature) which gave McCain any benefit of the doubt. The great hope was in Obama. He would bring change. He would bring reform.

So far, with a democratically-controlled Congress, he has done nothing. Besides health care reform, the only other thing he seems interested in achieving is peace in the Middle East; however, it is a peace with the Arab nations getting what *they* want, leaving Israel with virtually nothing.

With respect to the Middle East, here is a solution: Why can't Israel be allowed to build her Temple alongside the Dome of the Rock Mosque? If people *really* want the peace that they *say* they want, why is this not an option that is being considered? Because the Arab nations will not allow it, in spite of the fact that, on paper, Israel *controls* the Temple Mount. If Israel were allowed to build her Temple, peace would be at hand. It is absolutely *that* simple.

Will it happen?

The article below is from Prophezine.com:

"Foreign Minister Avigdor Lieberman responded Friday to the Quartet of Middle East peace mediators' call to relaunch Israeli-Palestinian peace negotiations, saying that peace is not something which can be created artificially and with unrealistic timetables.

"'Peace will be established through actions and not by force,' Lieberman told Belgium's Jewish community ahead of his scheduled talks with the ministers of several European nations.

"'The Quartet is ignoring the last 16 years of Israeli attempts, and is giving the Palestinians the impression that they can achieve their demands by continuing to refuse direct negotiations under false pretexts,' Lieberman said.

"'The Israeli government has made many significant gestures. Now it's the Palestinian's turn to prove that they are really interested in negotiations,' Lieberman added.

"The Quartet, which comprises members from Russia, the United States, the UN and the European Union, called Israel and the Palestinians to renew peace negotiations in order to achieve a two-state solution within 24 months. The members met in Moscow on Friday in an effort to defuse the latest crisis in peace efforts between Israel and the Palestinians.

"'The Quartet believes these negotiations should lead to a settlement, negotiated between the parties within 24 months, that ends the occupation that began in 1967 and results in the emergence of an independent, democratic and viable Palestinian state living side by side in peace and security with Israel and its other neighbors,' said a joint statement read by UN Secretary-General Ban Ki-moon.

"The mediators also called on Israel following their meeting to freeze all settlement activities and denounced its recent decision to approve construction of 1.600 new homes in East Jerusalem.

"U.S. Secretary of State Hillary Clinton, in Moscow, discussed steps to improve the outlook for Israeli-Palestinian peace by telephone with Prime Minister Benjamin Netanyahu on Thursday.

"Netanyahu's spokesman Nir Chefetz said the Israeli leader had proposed some 'mutual confidence-building steps' that both Israel and the Palestinians could take in the West Bank. He declined to spell these out.

"Clinton met her Russian counterpart Lavrov, UN Secretary General Ban Ki-moon, EU foreign policy chief Catherine Ashton and Quartet Representative Tony Blair over a closed dinner on Thursday evening before Friday's formal meeting.

"No details of that meeting were disclosed.

"*Moscow had originally hoped to organize a full-scale international conference on the Middle East this year but the lack of progress on Israeli-Palestinian peace talks has forced Russia to settle instead for hosting a quartet meeting.*

"*Meanwhile, U.S. Vice President Joe Biden has called Israel's decision to approve 1,600 new homes in East Jerusalem week 'provocative,' adding that it was 'obviously designed by some in Israel to undermine a peace process George Mitchell - our negotiator - finally got back on track.'*

"*In an interview with ABC's Nightline which will air on Friday night, Biden reiterated that 'Israel's security is undeniably in our interest to make sure it is absolutely secure' and Washington and Jerusalem to 'get over' the recent tensions that flared in response to the announcement.*

"*'And so the message is: We've got to get over this,' Biden said. '"Granted, I condemn the announcement made by that planning council. ... The irony is even that planning council acknowledging not a single new unit can be built at least for a year and maybe never will be built, it was provocative.'*

"*In the interview, Biden denied reports that he had told Prime Minister Benjamin Netanyahu that Israel's policy on settlements puts U.S. troops at risk.*

"*'No, I never said that,' Biden told ABC.*

22

Intifada in the Middle East?

(Blogged: 03/23/2010)

As tensions continue to heat up in the Middle East, Israel is not only feeling the heat from Washington, but now "*Palestinian Authority Chairman and Fatah leader Mahmoud Abbas hinted Monday during his meeting with United States Middle East envoy George Mitchell that a third intifada may be in the making.*"[35]

For those who are not familiar with the term, an intifada literally means "*a shaking off*" or "*uprising against,*" and as it applies to this situation it means that the PA may move toward another "*shaking*

---

[35] http://www.israelnationalnews.com/News/News.aspx/136670

off" of Israel. During 1987-1993 there was an intifada, or uprising against, Israeli rule over Palestinians. It bears noting that for the purposes of historical correctness, the term "Palestinians" came to be applied *only* to Arab individuals who lived in Israel (mainly near or in the West Bank area) through the political efforts of Yassar Arafat, who is alleged to have died of AIDS November 11, 2004. Prior to his usage of the term, "Palestinian" meant anyone - either Jew or Gentile - living in the area known as Palestine. At that time, Jewish individuals far outnumbered Arabs; however, Arafat's political coup successfully assigned the word "Palestinian" to mean only those of Arab descent.

Returning to Abbas' comments, it was also noted that others within the PA indicated that they would not return to the use of violence to meet its demands. However, with the continuing tone of violence on all sides in the Middle East it is difficult to believe that violence is going to be eschewed by parties involved.

The article continues: "*During the course of his conversation with Mitchell in Ramallah, Abbas condemned the killing of four PA teens in two separate incidents last week. Two died after being hit with rubber bullets during a massive riot in the village of Iraq-Burin and two were killed while attempting to attack IDF soldiers on patrol near Shechem.*"[36]

This situation, coupled with the demands that Obama's Administration is placing on Israel, seems to be moving in only one direction: *to cower Israel into submission.*

If history means anything, though, every time Israel gave into the demands to give up land, as a for instance, shelling of Israel never stopped as was promised by her enemies. In effect, what occurred was that Israel's enemies simply moved into the land that Israel had

---

[36] http://www.israelnationalnews.com/News/News.aspx/136670

just given up and took up those positions to continue to shell Israel. Though this is historical fact, the powers that existed then never came against Hamas, or the PA, or any other group which violated the terms of the agreement with Israel.

Israel *gave*, the other party *took*, and they continued with their un-warranted and hostile attacks against the people of Israel, not caring if they hit or killed innocent civilians in the process. If we consider what has been happening, it seems a consistent whittling away of Israeli land has been occurring, in the ultimate hopes of returning Israel to the land she had *prior* to the 6-Day War of 1967. This oc-curred because Egypt simply attacked Israel on the *Sabbath* day, when they knew she could not return fire. Though casualties and great portions of land were lost during the first two weeks of the bat-tle, by the end, Israel had not only regained the land she had lost, but gained *more* land besides.

Israel was attacked and defended herself. She took the land in what started out as an unfair fight. Since then, the demands to return the land have not abated. Yet it is assumed that had Israel lost the land and demanded it back, the world would have been against Israel as they are against her today.

The point of this whole thing is that it is fascinating the way the world looks at Israel as essentially a thorn in everyone's side, deserv-ing no rights whatsoever. The world seems to side with the Arabs over the Temple Mount, over the Jerusalem situation, over the land situation, and over every aspect of the Middle East problem, believ-ing that Israel has no right to *anything* essentially.

The Obama Administration wants to divide Jerusalem, giving the part with the Temple Mount to the Arabs, in spite of the fact that on paper the Temple Mount is legally controlled by Israel. Of course, a legal document means little to nothing to the world today. What the world wants is to make sure that the Arabs are happy, and that is what they will certainly get - eventually.

The Obama Administration has shown *prior* to his election and proved *since* the election that favor lies with the Arabs regarding the problem in the Middle East. President Obama couldn't care less what anyone thinks about it because he has his own agenda. That should surprise no one because he said as much during his run for office. In spite of that, an overwhelming majority of people who voted him into office for the change he would bring are now angry with him for making that change happen.

We see this especially with the new Health Care package. Nearly 75% of people polled (out of just fewer than 700,000) are angry about the Health Care passage. It seems that Washington couldn't care less what the majority of people want in this country. The minority believes this is a good thing, yet the question of who pays for it has not really been answered. While people *believe* it will place ceilings and caps on insurance company expenditures and demands, it really will not. What the insurance companies will do is find a way to circumvent any legislation that does become law. Ultimately, of course, the taxpayer will wind up paying for everything. The idea that we are to believe that the new Health Care bill will provide health care for 3 billion people *without* raising taxes is the highest form of fantasy that the U.S. government has ever tried to sell to the American people.

All we need to do is look to Canada and Great Britain to find out exactly how many additional taxes the citizens of these countries pay in order to have health care. In Great Britain alone, their VAT tax is more than 17%. Granted, some of that goes to the Monarchy, but a good percentage of that is for country-wide health care.

Democracy in America is *dying*. We have a president who is pushing his agenda and it makes no difference what the American people want. Of course, there is a minority of people in the U.S. supporting Israel and Obama knows that; yet there is a newly created governor's group, made up of 30 U.S. governors, who are opposed to President Obama's position on the Middle East. Many more are opposed to the Heath Care legislation and states have already begun filing lawsuits to derail the Health Care process.

As the United States moves toward the precipice of Socialism, and as the world moves to destroy Israel's legal presence in the Middle East, we are also moving to a time when one individual will stand up and be recognized as leader. He will actually bring about peace in the Middle East, to the satisfaction of Israel and the surrounding Arab nations. Right now it is just people who think they have power, posturing. The man who is yet to come will bring about the real deal: peace. Yet the peace will be short lived, lasting only three and a half years (he will have promised 7 years, though).

The Great Apostasy is here and it is guiding the world's leaders, with the majority of citizens following in behind like lambs to the slaughter. Most will never wake up until it is too late. If you are one who believes that what is occurring in this world is right, good, and the only logical course to take, then it is not too late for you to understand that you may, in essence, be working *against* God and *for* the enemy of our souls. I pray for your understanding, that the Lord will open the eyes of your heart in order that you might know the truth.

If you believe that you are following the truth, and the truth is found in President Obama and those who are attempting to create a peace in the Middle East, then you are likely laughing or smirking at these words. No matter, because it will all come out in the end.

23

Obama's Churlish Behavior

(Blogged: 03/25/2010)

It boggles my mind (though it probably shouldn't) to think of President Obama's behavior toward Prime Minister Binyamin Netanyahu at the recent politically *undiplomatic* shindig at the White House this past Tuesday.

When Barack Obama was running for office, rumors and murmurings of "narcissism" and "egotism" could be heard in the poorly lit outer corridors of those who were forced to the outside of the circle. Of course, this was never even hinted at in the media, and why should it be? The media wanted to be able to say "President-elect Obama" as much as the next liberal, and the only way to ensure that this would become a reality would be to ignore anything that even smacked of negativity towards the "hope" of the United States.

Because of that, whenever a rumor actually made it to the forefront of the campaign trail -that Barack Obama was pro-Arab and anti-Israel, or that he loved himself inordinately and tended to have a god-complex - these things were not only pooh-poohed, but normally the tables were turned on the individual making the accusations. It just would not do for the media to have people think that their choice for next president had faults or chinks in his armor. Wouldn't be prudent.

Because of this, we now have a president who is not only *pro*-Arab and *anti*-Israel, but one who thinks America is better off if it became a true Socialist country. Never mind that Socialism has never really worked any place else in the world or that where health care is socialized to include all the population taxes go sky high. Beyond this, let's not worry that we have an individual sitting in the Oval Office who believes that acting like a three-year old is the way to get things done. Forget politics. Ignore diplomacy. Treat other leaders in the world as if they *owe* you their allegiance, in spite of the fact that you have given them absolutely nothing at all.

In essence, President Obama is telling Netanyahu to do it Obama's way, or else. In the end, this is a man who apparently believes that people answer to him. It does not matter that Israel's capital has been Jerusalem for the better part of 3,000 years. What matters is that President Obama has intended to embarrass and humiliate Netanyahu and his government.

"For a head of government to visit the White House and not pose for photographers is rare. For a key ally to be left to his own devices while the President withdraws to have dinner in private was, until this week,

unheard of."[37] Yet that is how Binyamin Netanyahu was treated by President Obama on Tuesday night, according to Israeli reports, on a trip viewed in Jerusalem as a humiliation.

"After failing to extract a written promise of concessions on settlements, Mr Obama walked out of his meeting with Mr Netanyahu but invited him to stay at the White House, consult with advisers and 'let me know if there is anything new', a US congressman, who spoke to the Prime Minister, said."[38]

I am sorry, but this type of behavior from the president of the United States is not only rude and churlish, but also inexcusable. There is no reason for a leader of one country to treat another like they are scum. This type of behavior was not even evidenced toward Ahmadinejad.

The article continues, "*'It was awful,' the congressman said. One Israeli newspaper called the meeting 'a hazing in stages,' poisoned by such mistrust that the Israeli delegation eventually left rather than risk being eavesdropped on a White House telephone line. Another said that the Prime Minister had received 'the treatment reserved for the President of Equatorial Guinea'.*"[39]

I am hoping that Israel will finally wake up to the fact that they do not need anyone except God. Why should Israel (or any country for that matter) have to kowtow to the United States?

While the U.S. is busy treating Israel as if they are the scum of the earth, all the while pandering to the Arabs (and of course, ignoring the fact that Iran is doing all they can to build their first Nuke), the world's animosity toward Israel continues to grow. Because of this, President Obama believes he has world support - and he does. The reality, though, is that what happens on Earth is controlled by God

---

[37] http://www.timesonline.co.uk/tol/news/world/us_and_americas/article7076431.ece
[38] Ibid
[39] Ibid

alone. Though people are fully responsible for their own actions, those actions occur because God allows them to occur.

Whatever the ramifications are of this latest situation between the United States and Israel, we can be sure that it is not over. How bad will it get? Only God knows for certain, but an educated guess would say that it could very likely get to the point of the United States severing ties with Israel. That too would be allowed by God.

Is God positioning Israel so that they will be all alone, with no other country to rely on for support? It is very possible, and what the world means for *evil*, God means for *good*. In spite of this, there is no excuse for our president to behave in such a manner toward the leader of another country.

24

Obama Lied and Clinton Foamed

(Blogged: 03/28/2010)

S hould it come as any type of surprise that the Healthcare bill touted by President Obama includes what he said he would avoid for the American people? In a recent report, President Obama was quoted from the days of his campaign: "*I can make a firm pledge. Under my plan, no family making less than $250,000 a year will see any form of tax increases,' the Illinois senator told a crowd in Dover, N.H. on Sept. 12, 2008. 'Not your income tax, not your payroll tax, not your capital gains taxes, not any of your taxes'.*"[40]

---

[40] http://www.eutimes.net/2010/03/obama-breaks-no-tax-pledge-to-american-people-with-12-new-ones-in-healthcare-bill/?utm_source=feedburner&utm_medium=email&utm_campaign=Feed%3A+TheEuropeanUnionTimes+%28The+European+Union+Times%29

His comments certainly seemed straightforward enough. I believe it is safe to assume that Barack Obama - at the time - meant no new taxes.

He repeated these sentiments later, saying, "*'If your family earns less than $250,000 a year, you will not see your taxes increased a single dime. I repeat: not a single dime.*"

Did you read that? He said "not a single dime." As it turns out, though, the new Healthcare bill includes numerous taxes. The article we refer to goes on to say, "*The bulk of the $500 billion in tax increases in the new health care law targets households earning $250,000 and individuals earning $200,000 — for example, the increase in the Medicare payroll tax. But many of the taxes hit the general public at large.*"[41]

In fact, by 2014, barring any legal delays and snafus, once this Healthcare plan goes into effect, it "*will require all legal U.S. residents to purchase a government-approved health insurance plan beginning in 2014. Once the reconciliation bill is voted on in the Senate to amend the law signed by Obama this week, the individual mandate **will require a single person to pay 2.5 percent of their income or $695 if they do not purchase health insurance.***"[42] (Emphasis added)

So, if you are a legal resident of the United States, you *must* purchase a government-approved insurance plan. But wait a minute, I thought the Healthcare bill was simply going to be given or extended to everyone. Now, not only are we being told that each person must purchase one, but we are being told that we will also be taxed to support the plan. Hmm, that is interesting. Should that come as a shock? Of

---

[41] http://www.eutimes.net/2010/03/obama-breaks-no-tax-pledge-to-american-people-with-12-new-ones-in-healthcare-bill/?utm_source=feedburner&utm_medium=email&utm_campaign=Feed%3A+TheEuropeanUnionTimes+%28The+European+Union+Times%29
[42] Ibid

course not, considering the high taxes people in Canada and Great Britain must pay in order to receive "free" healthcare. No mention is directly made regarding the requirements of all illegal residents of the United States. It can be assumed, then, that there will be no additional financial impact on these individuals.

When Obama ran for president, it was on the "hope and change" platform. Maybe it should have been on the "take and take" platform, since this is what it is amounting to for the United States. All those folks who were tricked into voting for President Obama have now put this country on the fast track toward Socialism. I hope they are proud of that fact. They were "dared" from numerous quarters and they took the bait. Oh, come on, you have all heard the dares:

"This country will never elect a black man to office"

"Prove you're not prejudice and vote black"

Numerous other slogans were touted as well. It was just like the O.J. Simpson trial, which ultimately became about race, not whether Simpson committed the murders or not. Of course, we are not prejudice, so O.J. Simpson was *not* guilty. Really? It all comes out in the wash and God has the final say, because He is the only one who judges correctly. So, the liberal whites fell for the "dare" so they would not be seen as prejudiced. The blacks, of course, had to vote for Obama or they would have been seen as an Uncle Tom. The media got behind Obama because they like to create problems rather than simply report on news.

In the end, we have another politician who is rather well skilled at the art of lying with a straight face. Who knows what President Obama will try next? Maybe he will attempt to turn the presidency into a monarchy. He seems to have taken on that persona already, considering his demagoguery with respect to Israel, so he is getting close to considering himself to be the king of the United States. So, that "hope and change," is it good for you? Excellent.

Oh, and by the way, while it causes great concern that the American people are going to face more taxes to get this Healthcare bill up and running (some estimates running as high as 1 *trillion* dollars!), apparently President Obama is now demanding another 2.8 *billion* dollars for Haiti. It just keeps getting better and better. It makes one wonder whether or not President Obama even realizes that the American economy is not only in the toilet but also on the verge of being flushed down that same toilet.

It also seems that Hillary Clinton, appointed by the Obama Administration to Secretary (so that she would not hold a grudge against President Obama for winning the election and shoving her to the side), has ramped up her criticism of Israel and Netanyahu (taking her cue from President Obama, who remains blissfully in the background for the most part while she does his dirty work).

The problem with this administration's posturing with regards to Israel is that it is what the minority of people in this country want and approve. The rest of us believe that this type of demagoguery and chicanery is not only uncalled for, but that it is deeply disturbing for our elected officials to treat leaders of Israel as they are doing.

In fact, with all the rhetoric that Clinton alone has used in the past - in which she promised unwavering and unswerving support of Israel - her new position against Israel has not gone unnoticed. Many within her former constituency of New York have demanded an apology for the fact that she - like President Obama - has outright *lied*.

The Zionist Organization of America wrote a letter to Clinton, which stated in part:

"Your shocking words about Israel building in east Jerusalem is especially perplexing in light of the fact that you have ignored Congress

passing the 'Jerusalem Embassy Act of 1995' by a margin of 93 to 5 in the U.S. Senate and 347 to 37 in the U.S. House of Representatives.

"The Act which is U.S. Law stated:

(1)   Jerusalem should remain an undivided city.

(2)   Jerusalem should be recognized as the capital of the state of Israel."

It also stated,

"(1) Each sovereign nation, under international law and custom, may designate its own capital.

(2) Since 1950, the city of Jerusalem has been the capital of the State of Israel.

(3) The city of Jerusalem is the seat of Israel's President, Parliament, and Supreme Court, and the site of numerous government ministries and social and cultural institutions.

(4) The city of Jerusalem is the spiritual center of Judaism, and is also considered a holy city by the members of other religious faiths.

(5) From 1948-1967, Jerusalem was a divided city and Israeli citizens of all faiths as well as Jewish citizens of all states were denied access to holy sites in the area controlled by Jordan.

(6) In 1967, the city of Jerusalem was reunited during the conflict known as the Six Day War.

(7) Since 1967, Jerusalem has been a united city administered by Israel, and persons of all religious faiths have been guaranteed full access to holy sites within the city.

(8) This year marks the 28th consecutive year that Jerusalem has been administered as a unified city in which the rights of all faiths have been respected and protected.

(9) In 1990, the Congress unanimously adopted Senate Concurrent Resolution 106, which declares that the Congress "strongly believes that Jerusalem must remain an undivided city."

(10) In 1992, the United States Senate and House of Representatives unanimously adopted Senate Concurrent Resolution 113 of the One Hundred Second Congress to commemorate the 25th anniversary of the reunification of Jerusalem, and reaffirming congressional sentiment that Jerusalem must remain an undivided city."[43]

The article continued by quoting ZOA National President Morton A. Klein, who stated, *"It took only a few months to confirm that Secretary of State Clinton bears little resemblance to Senator Clinton on Israel issues and was apparently misrepresenting her true views and beliefs on Israel to her New York constituents. From having once loudly proclaimed support for an undivided Jerusalem, upon becoming Secretary of State, suddenly, parts of an 'undivided Jerusalem' became places where Jews may not move or build, even though Jews were a majority in eastern Jerusalem from the mid-1800s until 1948, when Jordan forced Jewish residents to flee, and are now a majority once again."*[44]

Even many within the United States House of Representatives got involved, drafting and submitting a letter to Clinton regarding her negative views on Israel. *"Signed by 327 Representatives, out of 435, the letter calls on Clinton and the Obama Administration to settle its disputes with Israel in a non-public and friendly fashion. The current*

---

[43] http://www.eutimes.net/2010/03/obama-breaks-no-tax-pledge-to-american-people-with-12-new-ones-in-healthcare-bill/?utm_source=feedburner&utm_medium=email&utm_campaign=Feed%3A+TheEuropeanUnionTimes+%28The+European+Union+Times%29
[44] Ibid

tensions 'will not advance the interests the U.S. and Israel share,' the letter states, as 'above all, we must remain focused on the threat posed by the Iranian nuclear weapons program to Middle East peace and stability.'[45]

It appears that without the checks and balances, anti-Semitism easily becomes all the rage. The naive liberal will continue to believe that both President Obama and Secretary of State Clinton really have everyone's best interests at heart. The problem, though, is that both believe they can belittle, shun, and generally treat Netanyahu like trash because they obviously favor Arabs over Jews. This is no surprise, since this is exactly what Satan has been doing for centuries. Why should *godless* politicians be any different? The fact that politicians have been telling people what they want to hear for as long as there have been politicians should not be shocking to anyone.

What makes it odd, though, is when no real "spin" can be placed on their own verbal twists and turns. In both cases - President Obama and Hillary Clinton - their lying is obvious, weighty, and severely damaging. Left unchecked, they will continue to do what seems right in their own eyes. Hopefully, the will of the House of Representatives and the letter from ZOA will have some effect in slowing down the growth of hostility within each of these two leaders, toward Israel and their right to build in their own capitol city. If not, we will see what happens...

---

[45] http://www.israelnationalnews.com/News/News.aspx/136758

25

Invisible vs. Visible

(Blogged: 03/29/2010)

S ince it *may* appear as though I am referring to individual local bodies of believers, I would like to clarify this article. When I refer to the Church throughout this particular article, I am referring to *Christ's Body*, the *invisible* Church. I am *not* referring to individual bodies of believers, which contain *tares* and *wheat*. This particular post is specifically addressing the subject of whether Christ's *Body* (the *invisible Church*) can become *impure*, or *corrupt*. My position on this is that it *cannot*. My sin - done in the flesh - does *not* stain Jesus, *or* His *Body*. My sin breaks fellowship with Him until such a time as I confess my sin to Him, whereby fellowship is res-

tored. As you read through this article, please keep this in mind.
Thank you.

I have grown tired of all the claims that the Church is corrupt, filled
with sin and in need of some good ol' purification. Many believe that
the coming persecution (or make that the *growing* persecution) is
designed by God to create this purification of Christ's Body, His
Church.

I have a huge problem biblically with that line of reasoning. Aside
from this, Paul tells me in the book of Romans that I am:

- *justified*
- *righteous*
- *glorified*
- *being sanctified*

The problem as I see it is that those who consistently mix Israel and
the Church believe that just as God had to purify Israel in the Old Testament numerous times, He must do the same thing to the Church
now. The difficulty, though, is that God always dealt with Israel as a
nation. In other words, when there was a problem in the camp of the
Israelites, the entire nation suffered. Beyond this, does anyone actually think that a "tare" or unsaved individual can actually *stain* Christ's Body?

For instance, in Numbers 14, we are familiar with the situation in
which many individuals in the camp of Israel complained against
Moses because of the report of the 12 spies. Ten of them did not believe the Lord. Why? Because they were rebels. They did not have
God's heart. They lived in unbelief and never believed the Lord.
While they enjoyed the bounty of God's provision time and time
again, they resolutely refused to acquiesce to His reign. They went
along for the ride with an *unbelieving* heart. It was because of this

that they were unable to believe that God would give them the victory. They had no ability to believe that because of their unbelief.

Two of the spies - *Joshua and Caleb* - believed that the Promised Land *could* be taken because God *would* give the victory. This did not matter to the people because they became convinced (or at least did not argue) by the complainers. It was because of this that God denied the entire camp access to the Promised Land, even though not all people sided with the complainers. Nonetheless, the entire camp wandered for 40 years until every last man of that generation who had complained against God died in the wilderness. When Israel did finally enter the Land, Joshua and Caleb were there with them.

Later on, in Joshua 7:1-15, we read of the sin of one man which caused the entire camp to suffer. Despite the command not to take any spoils of war, Achan takes a few items and hides them in his tent, unbeknownst to Joshua or anyone else in the camp. The entire camp wound up losing their battle against Ai because of this sin.

Please note the very first verse of Joshua 7, which states, "*But the children of Israel committed a trespass in the accursed thing: for Achan, the son of Carmi, the son of Zabdi, the son of Zerah, of the tribe of Judah, took of the accursed thing: and the anger of the LORD was kindled against the children of Israel.*"

Note that in this verse, God holds the *entire* nation of Israel guilty, even though it was one man - Achan - who committed the trespass. The camp suffered the loss and was on the receiving end of God's anger. After the loss, Joshua rent his clothes and sought the Lord. Joshua spent all day with his face before the Lord, beseeching the Lord for an answer. Eventually, God responds with this: "*Joshua, Get thee up; wherefore liest thou thus upon thy face?*" (v. 10b) God continued saying, "*Israel hath sinned, and they have also transgressed my covenant which I commanded them: for they have even taken of the ac-*

cursed thing, and have also stolen, and dissembled also, and they have put it even among their own stuff." (v. 11)

Do you see how God holds the entire camp of Israel responsible for what one individual did? This is not the case with the Church for any number of reasons, and the idea that the Church needs to be purified creates an insidious form of *false-piety*. In other words, what is ultimately being stated is that Christ's blood sacrifice neither was nor is good enough to cleanse His Bride; therefore, we as Christians need to *help* Christ by rending our clothes, sitting in ashes and dressing in sackcloth, and we must be willing to beat ourselves up emotionally in spite of the fact that Christ does not. We need to spend extended periods of time on our knees repenting of the many things that have apparently kept God from blessing us.

What I have found is that the majority of people who espouse this seem to be Covenant or Reformed individuals. They fall into this trap because of their inability to see a difference between the nation of Israel and the Church. In spite of the fact that my sin - *past, present,* and *future* - has not only been forgiven, but is completely gone, too many people believe that those within the (*visible*) Church are corrupt and therefore have corrupted the (*invisible*) Church. This is insane! The only thing my sin can do is break any fellowship that I should be enjoying with God.

Let me be exceedingly clear here so that there is no misunderstanding. I should *never* have a laissez-faire attitude about my own personal sin, because it was that sin that put Jesus Christ on the cross. Because of that, I am to see my sin as *reprehensible* because of what it prompted God to do for me.

I can never look at my sin as if it is no big deal, because it *is* a big deal. It is nothing short of *lawlessness*. It is allowing self to be glorified instead of God, who deserves *all* the glory. Whenever I sin - either knowingly or unknowingly - God is grieved. At that instant, the fellowship that I enjoy with Him is temporarily placed on hold until I confess my sin sincerely from the heart. It is at that point that God applies His forgiveness to me, and once again fellowship is reestablished. This continues until I sin again. This is the unfortunate aspect of being a Christian but continuing to retain the sin nature (which is true of *all* believers). Though God has given me a completely new nature, which has made me a new creation, my sin nature is ever-present. Because it is ever-present within me, it continues to try to force me to do what I do not want to do. It is because of this situation that sin is always at the door, always seeking its way, and always trying to get me to do what it wants me to do instead of what God wants me to do.

Even in spite of this, we are referred to as "*saints*" throughout the New Testament epistles from Paul, Peter and others. The first chapter of Ephesians explains that we were chosen to be holy. If this is read wrongly, it will be taken to mean that there is a choice made by us - to be holy or not to be holy. The reality is that as authentic Christians, we *already* are holy. Why? Because the new spirit that God has placed within us is holy and completely *sinless*. That new spirit within me can *never* sin. However, I can choose to follow the dictates of my sin nature, thereby committing sin. Though I commit sin, the new creation that God has made me does *not* sin. This is exactly why Paul can say in all truthfulness that "*Even when we were dead in sins, hath quickened us together with Christ, (by grace ye are saved;) And hath raised us up together, and made us sit together in heavenly places in Christ Jesus,*" (Ephesians 2:5-6).

He also teaches this to us in the book of Romans. When we become Christians, we are baptized into *His* Body. How is it possible for His Body to become contaminated by sin? It is *impossible*. The new spirit that God placed within me is already seated with Christ in the heavens. It is incapable of sinning, yet as I have *clearly* stated, in my flesh I *can* and *do* follow the dictates of my sin nature from time to time. But my sinful flesh is *not* part of Christ's Body. It is the flesh, which means it *is* corrupt, dying, and *will* die. The new spirit that God gave me will *never* die.

Based on this, how is it possible that the Church can ever be considered *unpure*? To believe that is to believe that Christ's sacrifice was not good enough, that His blood could not cleanse completely, and that as believers who are still able to sin, we are capable of making Christ's Body *impure*. This is so far off base that it is difficult to react without annoyance or anger or to remain emotionally detached from this error.

The people who clamor for, yell for, and demand that we as believers need to spend time on our knees in repentance, pleading with God to forgive us (something He has already done), do not, in my opinion, understand the doctrine of eternal security, or unmerited grace, or salvation through faith alone, by grace alone, in Christ alone - though they *say* they do. I also believe that these same individuals are constantly confusing *tares* with *wheat*. They see the *tares* in the visible Church and they believe that because of that, the visible Church needs to purify itself. This is a joke, because the *tares* are not part of the invisible Church (which is Christ's true *Bride*).

Believers are required to keep a very short list of sins. As the Holy Spirit brings our individual sins to our attention, we are to immediately agree and confess our sin, not with our lips, but from the heart. We should never want to sin or ever believe that "small" sins are okay with God. We should never wink at sin, nor should we take our standing before Christ for granted. Sin is sin and it is *never* acceptable to God. I cannot make that any clearer.

However, we as Christians, unlike what some evangelists teach, do not need to wallow in morose feelings for ourselves over our sin. The natural tendency of fallen human beings is either to think that sin is not a big deal or to fall into the trap of believing that unless we feel *terrible*, and unless we beat ourselves up emotionally (or even physically!), we have not truly repented. This borders on heresy in my opinion, because it attempts to *add* to the existing purifying reality of salvation. We are to live in accordance with our purified salvation, not give into our sin nature.

All authentic believers understand that salvation cannot be earned, yet too many have fallen into the mistake of believing that we must work to maintain our salvation, as if God is incapable of doing that Himself. Folks, if we have to help God maintain our salvation, then we do not actually have salvation at all.

Yes, I am *obligated* to confess my sin. I am also *obligated* to keep my eyes on Jesus. Focusing on my sin takes my eyes off of Jesus and puts them squarely on me, where they do not belong.

We read in 1 John 3:3-4, "*Beloved, now are we the sons of God, and it doth not yet appear what we shall be: but we know that, when he shall appear, we shall be like him; for we shall see him as he is. And every man that hath this hope in him purifieth himself, even as he is pure.*"

So what is it that actually purifies the believer? Beyond this, what exactly does it mean to purify ourselves? Does it not seem clear that when we have our thoughts on Jesus, we cannot be thinking of fulfilling the sin nature's demands? The two are *incompatible*. We cannot be focusing on Jesus while at the same time focusing on ways to fulfill the desires of the flesh. It is impossible. It is the focusing on Jesus that causes purity of *thought*, *word*, and *deed* in our lives.

Focusing on how terrible I am, how worthless I am, or how much of a worm I am is nothing but *self-aggrandizement* in the guise of externalized religious piety. That does absolutely no good. In fact, what it does is create a *false* sense of spiritual maturity, born of pride. Yes, while we come to believe that we are growing in our faith, because we think of ourselves as scum, all we are doing is spending time endorsing the evil inherent in the sin nature and the flesh.

If we truly believed that Christ's redemption was all in all, and that He is the Author and Perfector of our faith, we would not be trying so hard to drum up feelings of worthlessness within ourselves. Instead, we would be determined to focus on Him and His life within us. Doing this does more to bring about spiritual maturity than wallowing in the false sense of worthlessness that comes by focusing on self.

God has freed me from the Law of sin and death. He lives within me, and because of that I *can* overcome sin. Because I will never do it perfectly in this life does not negate the fact that I am a Christian, nor does it somehow sully Christ or His Bride. That is absurd, and the quicker believers get to the point of realizing that beating ourselves up is wrong because it denies the full efficacy of Christ's redemption, the quicker we begin focusing on the reality of our new birth and His presence within us. It is nothing but a form of godliness without the power.

As a final point, remember this from 1 John 3: "*but we know that, when he shall appear, we shall be like him*"? What does *that* statement mean? Doesn't it mean that when I die, I will *instantly* become *as* He is? If so, then that means that in the instant my soul leaves my body and stands before Him, I will become like Him. Funny, but John does not say that we have to repent and experience moroseness over our sin. He says we will BE like Him. In other words, it will happen apart from us. It will happen because *He makes it happen.*

Christians need to listen and understand that truth. There is a huge difference between *tares* and *wheat.* The *tares* will *never* be believers (*wheat*), and the *wheat* will *never* be *tares* (unbelieving frauds).

We cannot see the invisible Church. We can only see the *visible* Church, and that includes all the professing Christians along with the *tares.* It is the *invisible* Church that consists only of *wheat*, no *tares* - no professing Christian, just *wheat*.

While some Christians firmly believe that persecution is what cleanses and purifies the Church, I disagree vehemently. It is *not* persecution which purifies the Church because the Church is already pure. What persecution *does* is separate the sheep from the goats. The *tares* cannot handle persecution, while the *wheat* cannot nor will not run from it.

26

Nuclear Arms, the United States, and President Obama

(Blogged: 04/07/2010)

Apparently, President Obama is under the impression that by *reducing* our armaments buildup, not only will other nations follow that lead, but there will be a greatly reduced problem of terrorists being able to ultimately possess nuclear warheads.

Unfortunately, this flies in the face of the fact that Iran has nuclear capabilities. Iran *wants* nuclear capabilities so they can wipe Israel off the map, along with virtually anyone else who gets in their way. Does anyone really believe that the countries with dictators (and Iranian "President" Mahmoud Ahmadinejad certainly qualifies as a dictator) are interested in playing nicely with the rest of the world?

Yesterday at a press conference, "*U.S. Defense Secretary Robert Gates said the focus would now be on terror groups such as al-Qaida as well as North Korea's nuclear buildup and Iran's nuclear ambitions.*"[46] He also stated that the U.S.'s new rules on nuclear engagement would apparently force these groups to play by the rules. I cannot help but wonder if Gates actually believed what he said. More importantly, does he actually believe that the people of the United States (or the world) believe what he said?

Today, Ahmadinejad's reaction was announced. "*American material- ist politicians, whenever they are beaten by logic, immediately put their finger on the trigger like cowboys,*" he said. *Mr. Obama, you are a new- comer (to politics). Wait until your sweat dries and get some expe- rience. Be careful not to read just any paper put in front of you or re- peat any statement recommended,*" Ahmadinejad said in the speech, aired live on state TV. (American officials) bigger than you, more bul- lying than you, couldn't do a damn thing, let alone you.*"[47] Take that, President Obama!

It seems that no one is buying the President's new strategy, yet he continues to do everything he can to seemingly dismantle this coun- try, piece by piece. In spite of everything that President Obama has done to gain the support of the Arab nations, the only one who seems really interested in his overtures is Hamas, and that is only due to the fact that President Obama has come out against Israel on nearly every front. Others such as Ahmadinejad obviously prefer to do things on their own, and whether there appears to be a Muslim in the Oval Office or not, there seems to be no trust regarding what Presi- dent Obama's motives are for everything he is doing.

Whether true or not, it seems clear that President Obama is deter- mined to recreate this country into something it was not originally

---

[46] http://www.msnbc.msn.com/id/36212348/ns/world_news-mideastn_africa
[47] Ibid

founded to be: a Socialist nation. I cannot help but think what our
Founding Fathers would say if they could see what was happening to
the United States. Once known as the bastion of freedom for all, it
has become a nation overrun with political strategists, lobbyists, and
liberals who, if given the chance, would burn the Declaration of Inde-
pendence *and* the Constitution in favor of a Socialized dictatorship.
The ramifications of this are absolutely tragic, yet it progresses in
spite of the fact that President Obama's rating is at its lowest point
(44%), the majority of citizens in this country are up in arms over the
new Obamacare (which will likely cost trillions in *new* taxes), and
other things as well.

Some individuals are seemingly blind to the problems, preferring to
blame previous administrations for our current economic mess
(which administration actually *avoids* blaming current woes on past
presidencies?), and believing wholeheartedly that our current president and his administration is the change needed for this country.
This blogger certainly disagrees with that assessment, since the
proof is in the pudding.

President Obama has stated that he would prefer to be a great one-
term president than a mediocre two-term president (my paraphrase). I do not think he will get his wish on either count. No matter,
because God is in control anyway. He allowed President Obama to
become the first president in the history of this country to push so
hard for Socialism. He has become the first president who, while
having stated that he is a Christian, removed any reference to Jesus
Christ during his Easter speech. I guess no one has told him that
without Jesus Christ, there would actually be *no* Easter. He has become the first president of the United States who has bowed reli-
giously to leaders in the Arab and Asian world, and he has become
the first president who has openly wooed the Arab nations and de-
fied Israel. It will be interesting to see how the history books remember President Obama. Of course, if the liberal news outlets have

any say he will go down as the greatest president in the history of this country. After all, they are the ones who really rigged the election by creating the mantra of "hope and change." We are certainly getting change, and one can only hope that the end of his term as president will mean that someone else replaces him in the next presidential election...and I don't mean Biden either.

27

President Obama Born in Africa, Says Kenyan Official

(Blogged: 04/12/2010)

That's what a Kenyan Official says in this report from WND. Of course it makes sense, then (if this is true), that the Governor of Hawaii absolutely refused to provide the *real* birth certificate, since there would be none showing that Obama was born in any part of the United States, much less Hawaii. The story is from WND here:

http://www.wnd.com/index.php?fa=PAGE.view&pageId=139481

"*A Kenyan lawmaker told the nation's parliament last month that Barack Obama was born in Africa and is therefore 'not even a native American.'*

"During debate over the draft of a new Kenyan constitution, James Orengo, the country's minister of lands and a member of parliament for the Ugenya constituency, cited America's election of a Kenyan-born president as an example of what can be accomplished when diverse peoples unite:

"'If America was living in a situation where they feared ethnicity and did not see itself as a multiparty state or nation,' Orengo posited, 'how could a young man born here in Kenya, who is not even a native American, become the president of America?'

"Orengo held up the U.S. as a country no longer 'living in the past,' since Americans elected a Kenyan-born president without regard to 'ethnic consideration and objectives.'

"Debate is then recorded in the Kenyan government's official March 25, 2010, hansard – a traditional name for printed transcripts of a parliamentary debate – as continuing with no other MPs mentioning or attempting to correct Orengo's comments about Obama.

"As WND has reported, several other sources – including National Public Radio – have claimed Obama's birthplace as Kenya prior to his election as president.

WND also reported when a video appeared in which Michelle Obama said her husband's "home country" was Kenya, though her comments did not specifically suggest his birth there.

The video, posted April 3 on YouTube and forwarded by a score of Internet e-mails, shows Michelle Obama saying, "*When we took our trip to Africa and visited his home country in Kenya, we took a public HIV test.*"

"The reference drew attention because of the claim made in numerous lawsuits and other challenges to Obama's occupancy of the Oval Office that he is not eligible to be president under the requirement of Article

2, Section 1 of the Constitution that the president be a "natural born citizen."

"But the NPR reference and Michelle Obama's comment are far from the only ones of their kind.

"At one point, there were reports that even Obama's grandmother claimed being in attendance at his birth in Africa.

"According to a compilation of images at a military forum, another reference was made in 2008 in the Nigerian Observer.

"Under a byline from Solomon Asowata and a Washington dateline, the report says, "Americans will today go to the polls to elect their next president with Democratic Party candidate, Senator Barack Obama largely favoured to win. The Kenyan-born Senator will, however, face a stiff competition from his Republican counterpart..."[48]

A commentary at The Post & Email website said, *"It is no wonder that many doubt Obama's claim of a Hawaiian birth.*

"It cited another report from African Travel Magazine that said, "As Kenyan born U.S. Senator Barack Obama jets into Kenya today as part of his African tour, concerns have once again been raised on the security preparations for other visitors and residents. ....

"The Post & Email commentary also cited a report from Indonesia Matters that includes similar references."[49]

WND documented several other statements linking Obama and Kenya. These included the apparently archived article from the Sunday Standard in Kenya.

The report begins, *"Kenyan-born US Senate hopeful, Barrack (sic) Obama, appeared set to take over the Illinois Senate seat after his main*

---

[48] http://www.wnd.com/
[49] Ibid

rival, Jack Ryan, dropped out of the race on Friday night amid a furor over lurid sex club allegations.

"The article is credited to the wire service Associated Press at the bottom of the page. However, the article could not be found in either the AP archives available to the public online or the archive on the newspaper's website. WND telephone calls and e-mails to the newspaper did not generate a response.

"Last year, an African news site and an MSNBC broadcaster referred to President Obama's birthplace as being outside of the United States.

"Network correspondent Mara Schiavocampo was reporting on the celebratory atmosphere in Accra, Ghana, immediately prior to Obama's visit to the West African nation.

"Interviewing a person who appeared to be a shop operator, [Mara] stated, "Barack Obama is Kenyan ... but Ghanaians are still proud of him."[50]

Also, a report at Modern Ghana posted in advance of the president's visit cited his birthplace on the continent of Africa:

"For Ghana, Obama's visit will be a celebration of another milestone in African history as it hosts the first-ever African-American President on this presidential visit to the continent of his birth," the report said.

"WND has reported on dozens of legal challenges to Obama's status as a "natural born citizen." The Constitution, Article 2, Section 1, states, "No Person except a natural born Citizen, or a Citizen of the United States, at the time of the Adoption of this Constitution, shall be eligible to the Office of President.

"Some of the lawsuits question whether he was actually born in Hawaii, as he insists. If he was born out of the country, Obama's American

---

[50] http://www.wnd.com/

mother, the suits contend, was too young at the time of his birth to con-fer American citizenship to her son under the law at the time.

"Other challenges have focused on Obama's citizenship through his fa-ther, a Kenyan subject to the jurisdiction of the United Kingdom at the time of his birth, thus making him a dual citizen. The cases contend the framers of the Constitution excluded dual citizens from qualifying as natural born.

"Complicating the situation is Obama's decision to spend sums exceed-ing $1.7 million to avoid releasing an original long-form state birth certificate that would put to rest the questions.

"WND also has reported that among the documentation not yet availa-ble for Obama includes his kindergarten records, Punahou school records, Occidental College records, Columbia University records, Co-lumbia thesis, Harvard Law School records, Harvard Law Review ar-ticles, scholarly articles from the University of Chicago, passport, medi-cal records, files from his years as an Illinois state senator, his Illinois State Bar Association records, any baptism records and his adoption records.

"Because of the dearth of information about Obama's eligibility, WND founder Joseph Farah has launched a campaign to raise contributions to post billboards asking a simple question: "Where's the birth certifi-cate?

"WND also reported previously when Michelle Obama contradicted Obama's story that he lived with his mother and father for several years in Hawaii after he was born before his father left to pursue a graduate degree.

"Michelle Obama said her husband's mother, Ann Dunham, was "very young and very single" when she gave birth to the future U.S. president.

"Her comments undermine the official story as told by Barack Obama – that Dunham was married to his father, Barack Obama Sr., at the time of birth.

"Michelle Obama made the remarks during a July 2008 round table at the University of Missouri. Obama was responding to criticism of her husband's presidential campaign speeches about fatherhood and faith-based initiatives."[51]

---

[51] http://www.wnd.com/

28

Another Sign of the Times

(Blogged: 04/15/2010)

Recently, I discovered that Jennifer Knapp, a music artist who claims to be a Christian, came out of the closet to announce that she is not only a lesbian but has been living with another woman for eight years. Frankly, I find it shameful that people who claim to be Christians, see no problem with homosexuality nor do they see any contradiction between that lifestyle and God's Word.

Homosexuality seems to be all the rage, with more and more people coming out to disclose their sexual identity - as if I really want to know what people do in their bedrooms. I do not want to hear about my friends' sexuality or what they engage in. When someone says that they are a homosexual or a lesbian, the picture that is instantly created in one's mind is two people of the same sex having sexual relations. It is impossible to think of a homosexual relationship without the sexual aspect of it. This is part of the problem that the Gay community would like to wipe out, and they hope to do so by bringing homosexuality to the forefront and keeping it there as much as possible.

The thought is that over time homosexuality will be seen as normal, and once seen as normal it will then be viewed just as heterosexual relationships are viewed. I disagree. I've studied the problem for a long time and read many books by people on both sides of the issue, and it is clear that the prevalent behavior within the ranks of homosexuality is to have as many sexual liaisons as possible per year. It does not matter with whom, but just doing it is the point. I am sorry to be crass, but it is the homosexual community, which is crass.

The Gay community will do anything to find a way to rewrite the Bible to mean something other than what it truly means. In order to accomplish this, homosexuality must be seen not as an *alternative* lifestyle, but a *God-ordained* one. In other words, just as God is said to have made me heterosexual, the Gay community wants us to believe that He has made some individuals *homosexual* (they would like us to believe it's around 10% of the entire population, which of course makes one instantly ask, if homosexual is normal, why did God relegate it to such a *paltry* percentage? It is also fact that the actual number is far less than 10% of the entire population).

So not only does the Gay community want to be accepted as normal, but they also want to be seen as God-ordained. If they are accepted as God-ordained, then how dare anyone attempt to vilify what they do and who they are?

In his book *The Gay Gospel?* Joe Dallas states, "*I don't find gay and gospel to be compatible. The gospel is the good news of God's love expressed in the person of Jesus Christ and His atonement. The gospel is not homosexual or heterosexual, though its invitation is extended to both groups, and [his books'] title isn't mean to imply otherwise. But God's good news to all people is being revised and presented as God's approval of all people, and this is what I consider the 'gay gospel' to be about. It's a revision of the basics on human sexuality, with broader implications for the way we interpret the Scripture and approach Christian living.*"[52]

Dallas spent years as a homosexual himself before being freed from it. He understands what it is about and the goals associated with the movement. He speaks of the fact that with the "*ongoing pressure to change her views, the church has no choice but to argue. If we fail - if we find it too difficult or too intimidating - then I believe there are at least three general and drastic consequences we'll face:*

- *The denigration of biblical authority*
- *The sexual exploitation of children*
- *The loss of a coherent definition of family*"[53]

Dallas explains the history of the Gay movement to the present and how it has successfully burgeoned into a community of people from all walks of life, including those who call themselves Christian. Of course, this all revolves around the way Scripture is interpreted, most of the time in an allegorical or completely confusing textual criticism, which ultimately has no basis in fact or scientific interpretation. The key verses are those found in Genesis 19, in which the destruction of Sodom and Gomorrah takes place, preceded by the attempted forceful gang-rape of two angels sent to these twin cities to remove Lot and his family from the danger.

---

[52] Joe Dallas *The Gay Gospel?* (Harvest House Publishers 2007), 33
[53] Ibid, 41

Every possible template has been placed over this scene by Gay pro-ponents seeking to tone down the obviousness of the situation. Re-cently, in a bit of a debate on a forum with another person discussing this same subject, a woman responded and explained her view of the attempted gang-rape.

"Yes [Jesus] did Fred. But it was not a direct reference to homosexuali-ty. If one reads the story of Sodom and Gomorrah in translations done from the Hebrew, the sin was one of trying to force alien customs on people who found them abhorrent. For that matter, Lot offered his two daughters to the crowd to keep the visiting strangers safe, something I'm sure no real Christian would do today. Yet in that time it was seen as righteous, because he was trying to protect his hospitality toward the visiting strangers.

"In the Jerusalem Bible, the only English translation done from direct ancient Hebrew sources, it reads: They had not gone to bed when the house was surrounded by the men of the town, the men of Sodom both young and old, all the people without exception. Calling to Lot they said, 'Where are the men who came to you tonight? Send them out to us so that we may abuse them.'

There are, of course, a couple of problems with her understanding of the situation. She first states that the problem in Sodom/Gomorrah was that they had alien customs that they inflicted on strangers and this made God angry. She then states that the men were not interest-ed in sex, but simply abusing the two angels. What kind of a custom is this - alien or otherwise? This is a custom? You visit a strange town and the first thing that the entire town wants to do to you is gang-rape or abuse you?!

Then again, the Jerusalem Bible (the *only* one she uses) is not gener-ally known for its quality translation, but that's another story. Above all, though, the individual I have quoted is completely missing a very important point. God did *not* decide at the point of the two angels nearly being gang-raped (or abused) to destroy Sodom and Gomorrah. He had already decided, which is why the two angels were in the town. The attempted gang-rape of these two angels was not the final straw for God. That straw had already come and gone. The angels were there to escort Lot and his family out of town so that the towns could be destroyed. It is clear, then, that this event nearly perpetrated against the angels has absolutely no bearing on God's decision to destroy these twin cities.

Our friend is wrong on another point. She says, "*Lot offered his two daughters to the crowd to keep the visiting strangers safe, something I'm sure no real Christian would do today. Yet in that time it was seen as righteous, because he was trying to protect his hospitality toward the visiting strangers.*" She fails to understand that what Lot did was not considered righteous at all. She gets the idea that Lot was righteous from Peter, "*And turning the cities of Sodom and Gomorrah into ashes condemned them with an overthrow, making them an example unto those that after should live ungodly; And delivered just Lot, vexed with the filthy conversation of the wicked: (**For that righteous man dwelling among them, in seeing and hearing, vexed his righteous soul** from day to day with their unlawful deeds;),*" (2 Peter 2:6-8; emphasis added).

What our friend does not realize is that all authentic Christians are declared righteous by God the moment we receive salvation (cf. Romans 1ff). This is our *standing* or *position* in Christ. It is not based on what we do or how we live. It is based solely on God's declaration that we are righteous, because *by* faith and *through* faith He imputes Christ's righteousness to us when we receive salvation.

Lot was *not* righteous for offering his virgin daughters. He was not thinking clearly, and he certainly did not think about what he was offering. However, the fact that Lot pointed out that his daughters were *virgins* means that the men who had encircled his house wanted the two angels for *sexual* purposes, otherwise there would have been no need for Lot to offer his daughters at all.

There is no such thing as a Christian who is a practicing homosexual or lesbian. In fact, that aside, we have plenty of warnings and admonitions against *impurity, fornication*, and *adultery*. Yet Jennifer Knapp, who has been living with a woman for eight years, apparently believes that not only is it all right to be a lesbian, but it is also fine to have sexual relations outside of marriage. Of course, she will argue that in general, same-sex marriage is not allowed by law. There are at least three states where it *is* allowed by law, so why hasn't she and her lover gone there to marry?

The point is that just because some might argue that same-sex marriages can be just as good as heterosexual marriages, this does not negate God's will that homosexual unions are an anathema. However, this is what is becoming the normal fabric of our society today. Homosexuality is being foisted upon us from every corner. "*Will and Grace*" is a show where one man gives no outward impression that he is gay, while another man on the same show is flamboyantly gay. The "*Roseanne*" show had a same-sex romantic kiss between Roseanne Barr and another actress. On the same show, Martin Mull's character was gay.

It is almost impossible to see a movie or TV show today which does not include a gay character. The character is presented as normal, in the sense that you would not notice anything externally which would indicate he or she is gay. The idea of course is that the more characters like this are foisted upon society, the more normal and acceptable that lifestyle will become.

Dallas believes otherwise, insisting that homosexuality is a doorway to open pedophilia, and spends some time in his book highlighting that fact. The idea that 10% of the population is gay is also scrutinized by Dallas. This "fact" goes back to Alfred Kinsey's Sexual Behavior in the Human Male. The actual number is closer to 2.3% as reported in *USA Today* (April 15, 1993). Of that number, only 1.1% indicated that they were only homosexual (not bisexual). But this does not matter to the gay community, because they can and do shout much louder than these studies. Many of these groups can be and are patently obnoxious, pushing their agenda in your face whether you like it or not.

There are a number of things beside those already mentioned that the Gay community does not want you to focus on. The fact that many within the Gay community are simply after sexual liaisons is brought out in both Dallas' book as well as Dr. Ronnie W. Floyd's book, *The Gay Agenda*. Many homosexuals have hundreds, if not thousands, of sexual partners *each year*. Joe Dallas himself stated as much. He also indicated that even though many within the Gay community consider themselves to be "in relationship" with someone, it does not stop them from having sexual encounters with others many times over. The definition of "monogamy" does not apply to most within the Gay community.

We are all aware of the Gay communities within San Francisco or New York City, but how many of us are aware of what actually goes on in these communities? Of course, the behavior found rampant is often downplayed by leaders within the Gay movement who attribute it to a very small minority of extremist homosexuals. Is this true? Not if research means anything. There are many sites on the 'Net (sadly) that highlight a good amount of this type of behavior. If you want to know what Sodom and Gomorrah was like, all you need to do is visit one of these sites. The particular one that I am going to highlight is frank and extremely graphic. I am warning you that if you are easily offended, please do *NOT* go there. The individual who owns the site is not gay himself. He is a journalist who covers all types of events in the Bay Area, from gay events to environmental events to others. What he attempts to do (and he does it very well, in my opinion) is to show what the mainstream media will *not* show (or discuss). Obviously, the pictures he includes on his site could not be shown in any mainstream publication (again, you are warned), but the owner of the site also shows how the media (like the *Chronicle*, for instance) deliberately crops pictures of events in such a way that gives the public a completely different perspective from what is actually taking place at the event itself. His site can be viewed here: *www.zombietime.com*. (Please be warned that the site has graphic material unsuitable for children, adults who vomit easily, or merely those offended by seeing how depraved our "civilization" has now become!).

In another book I have just received, *Grave Influence*, the author - Brannon Howse - indicates that the church has lost the culture war. I could not agree more. He states that the only thing left is to fight to keep the church from being lost as well. We see that the last bastion for the Gay movement is the conservative or fundamental church. If they cannot win us over, they will shut us down or resort to name-calling, hopefully embarrassing us into silence.

The truth is that salvation is for *all* people. Does homosexuality keep people from Jesus? No, no more than any sinful activity keeps people from Him. What *does* keep homosexuals and all other people from Him is their abject refusal to see Jesus for who He is and for what He has accomplished on humanity's behalf. Does a person need to *promise* to stop being a homosexual before they receive salvation? No. They can and should come to Jesus just as they are; however, they can also expect a huge change in their life because of coming to Him, which also means the eradication of their homosexual tendencies.

The individuals who wrongly believe that being a practicing homosexual is compatible with being a Christian unfortunately *do* have it wrong. I remember reading an article a number of years ago about a prostitute at one of the legal bordellos in Nevada. The interviewer asked her if she enjoyed her job or not. Her response (my paraphrase) was that she believed God had given her a gift to make people happy, and she believed that it was being paid to have sex with men that made them most happy. Um...okay. This is like listening to a boxer who has just knocked the snot out of his opponent. After the fight he is handed a microphone and some of the first words out of his mouth are, "*I want to thank God for giving me this gift!*" Uh...yeah, I'm sorry, but I don't see *pummeling* as a gift of the Holy Spirit.

People today are making all types of excuses for their aberrant behavior. Rather than take God at His Word, it's much easier to *change* His Word to suit them so that they can continue to live their life the way they want to live it. I'm sorry, but this is not the definition of being a Christian. It is giving up your own will for that of another, and in this case, it is God. We adopt His will for our life so that He is glorified. He is not glorified through our sexuality, but He is glorified when we do things by the rules He has given us.

29

War in the Middle East Soon?

(Blogged: 04/15/2010)

Recently Joel Rosenberg announced: "*Russia has just announced that it intends to allow the Iranian nuclear reactor facility located in Bushehr (near the Persian Gulf) to go live in August.*"[54] As Rosenberg points out, this puts Israel in a critical position of having to do what Menachem Begin did in 1981 as a preemptive strike against Saddam Hussein's nuclear reactor in Iraq.

Ezekiel 38 tells of the Gog-Magog War. Some conservative biblical scholars believe this war will occur prior to the Tribulation, while others believe it will not take place until well after the Tribulation

---

[54] http://www.bible-prophecy-today.com/

begins. The first few verses of the chapter indicate an interesting phenomenon, though.

"Son of man, set thy face against Gog, the land of Magog, the chief prince of Meshech and Tubal, and prophesy against him, And say, Thus saith the Lord GOD; Behold, I am against thee, O Gog, the chief prince of Meshech and Tubal: And I will turn thee back, and put hooks into thy jaws, and I will bring thee forth, and all thine army, horses and horse-men, all of them clothed with all sorts of armour, even a great company with bucklers and shields, all of them handling swords: Persia, Ethi-opia, and Libya with them; all of them with shield and helmet: Gomer, and all his bands; the house of Togarmah of the north quarters, and all his bands: and many people with thee," (Ezekiel 38:2-7; emphasis added).

From the above text, we gather that the Lord is referring to the individual who leads this military invasion, whom He calls "Gog." We know this is not a name of a person, but a rank ("chief prince of Me-shach"). We also understand Him to be saying that He (the Lord) is the One who will cause Gog to turn against Israel ("I will turn thee back, and put hooks into thy jaws, and I will bring thee forth").

Let's consider the situation in the Middle East right now. Iran despe-rately wants nuclear bomb capabilities, so they are lying to the world about their nuclear reactor being built for peaceful purposes. They have also made their position against Israel widely known. Iran would like Israel gone - off the map - out of the area. Part of the world believes that sanctions against Iran are what is necessary and even President Obama has indicated this, yet as things in Iran con-tinue to move forward, national leaders are strangely quiet about these sanctions. It's almost as if they have said outwardly that sanc-tions should be implemented to appease people who firmly believe this should be done, but as it turns out have only mouthed the words with no intention of actually following through.

So Iran continues their course of action. Once their nuclear reactor goes online, is there a question as to what they will do with a nuclear bomb? It would appear as though Israel has always been in their sights. Having a bomb is what they want and getting rid of Israel is also what they want, so if we put two and two together we have little trouble seeing into the future.

But now we have Russia and their stated position. It turns out that they are siding with Iran, which is not unexpected. Since the United States is obviously against Israel and seems to be in favor of only Arab nations in the Middle East, Russia certainly has nothing to fear from the U.S. and Dmitry Anatolyevich Medvedev (along with his mentor, Putin) is quite aware of that.

So let's say that Israel, realizing that the time set for Iran to "light" up its nuclear reactor (this August) is right around the corner, must decide on a course of action. Does Netanyahu ignore Iran's nuclear capabilities from August onward, in spite of all the anti-Semitic rhetoric that has issued from Ahmadinejad's mouth, or does he consider a preemptive strike on Iran's nuclear reactor, mirroring Begins' strike against Saddam?

Let's say that Israel, realizing the risk of ignoring the nuclear threat is too great, sends jets in to destroy the nearly completed reactor before it goes on line. Is that it? Once destroyed, does everything calm down? Is it over, with Israel winning a decisive victory? I cannot see into the future, nor do I have a crystal ball, but considering the fact that Russia is now in the picture and siding with Iran, we may have a problem.

If Israel makes a preemptive strike against Iran and successfully destroys their nuclear reactor, overruling their ability to make their own nuclear weapons, it may well be that Russia will take offense at that and use it as a reason to come against Israel, saying that what Israel has done amounts to an act of war. IF this is the case, then it could very well be that we will see the makings of Ezekiel 38 come to pass.

Update: As of August 20, 2010, rumors of war in the Middle East over Iran's plans to put their nuclear power plant online, with the help of Russia, persist. This seems doubtful on Israel's part, because it may be that they have waited too long for the rest of the world to act with sanctions against Iran.

Iran continues their claim that the nuclear reactor will be used only for peaceful purposes. Of course, the rest of the world knows that is not true, but ignores it.

If Israel attacks Iran, it would likely be heard 'round the world and result in global disapproval of Israel's actions. By the time you read this, who knows what will have taken place?

30

Are Ex-Christians Really "Ex"?

(Blogged: 04/20/2010)

I wrote a book a while ago dealing with the subject (among other things) of people who referred to themselves as "Ex-Christians." When you talk with these folks, they will tell you directly that they *were* Christians, beyond doubt. There is no question about that, and they take umbrage at people who attempt to tell them that, based on their own testimony, they could not have been an authentic Christian.

Having done quite a bit of research on the subject (which went into my book) I found that by and large, the individuals who "*knew*" that

they were, without equivocation, Christians had two types of defini-
tions for what it meant (to them) to be a Christian.

1. *Believing the story of Jesus, or*
2. *Doing all the things that Christians do*

The first definition is an interesting one because it is extremely am-
biguous, yet it obviously means something to *them*. Natural questions arise, such as what part of the 'story' of Jesus did they believe,
or *which* story of Jesus, or something else altogether?

The second definition is also interesting. When you talk to those who
claim to be "ex-Christians," they will tell you what they used to do:

- *prayed*
- *read the Bible*
- *went to church*
- *sang hymns*
- *gave money or tithed*
- *spoke in tongues*
- *healed people*
- *memorized Scripture*
- *preached*
- *studied the Bible*
- *went to Bible college*
- *went to seminary*
- *fasted*
- *did penance*
- *visited the sick*
- *cared for the elderly*
- *evangelized*
- *street preached*
- *passed out gospel tracts*
- *taught Sunday School*

- *were baptized*
- *went up front after the service to pray for salvation*
- *prayed the sinner's prayer*

You can probably add your own - especially if you consider yourself to be an ex-Christian. The problem with that list is that none of it defines Christianity. A close look at Scripture indicates that Satan can cause people to do those same things. Beyond that, everything on the list is a type of *work*. If we compare any one of those (or all of those) to Scripture, there is nothing on that list that truly defines what it means to become a Christian as found in the Bible - not one thing.

If we only consider John 3, we read of Jesus' conversation with one of the Pharisees, who happened to be intensely interested in Jesus and what He had to say. He was still afraid of what the other Pharisees would say, though, so he met with Jesus at night, under cover of darkness. Sounds like Watergate.

In the course of the conversation, Jesus unequivocally explains what it means to receive salvation. Let's look at the text, shall we?

Nicodemus comes to Jesus and says, "*Rabbi, we know that thou art a teacher come from God: for no man can do these miracles that thou doest, except God be with him,*" (John 3:2).

Notice Jesus' reply to him. "*Verily, verily, I say unto thee, Except a man be born again, he cannot see the kingdom of God,*" (John 3:3). I find that fascinating. Nicodemus comes to Jesus and compliments Him. He does not ask Jesus a question. It appears as though Nicodemus was making his introductory comments and telling Jesus he knew that God was with Him (Jesus).

Nicodemus gets a bit more than he bargained for, because Jesus cut right to the chase and explained to Nicodemus that if he wanted to see God's Kingdom, he would need to be *born again*. Nicodemus takes Jesus' words literally (when He obviously meant them figuratively), thinking that Jesus meant that Nicodemus would have to be *physically* born a second time. "*How can a man be born when he is old? can he enter the second time into his mother's womb, and be born?*" (John 3:4)

Obviously, Nicodemus is confused, and fortunately for him Jesus clarifies by stating, "*Verily, verily, I say unto thee, Except a man be born of water and of the Spirit, he cannot enter into the kingdom of God. That which is born of the flesh is flesh; and that which is born of the Spirit is spirit,*" (John 3:5-6).

Here Jesus is telling Nicodemus straight up that in order to enter into the Kingdom of God, a person must be born once *physically* (water, in the amniotic sac) and then a second time *spiritually*. So right away we understand that Jesus is telling Nicodemus that becoming a Christian requires a *new* or *second* birth. Nowhere in the text does Jesus tell Nicodemus that he must *do* things like those in the previous bulleted list. He did not say that Nicodemus had to pray, read the Bible, preach, give money, or anything else. He simply told him that he had to be *born again*. This was not even something Nicodemus could do all by himself! It was something he could only ask for, and the Holy Spirit would accomplish.

Therefore, the big question is how one becomes *born again*. This is a good and an obviously important question. The answer means the difference between eternal *life* and eternal *separation* from God. Everyone needs to know the correct answer, no guesswork.

In order to determine the answer, we need to move a few verses down. There Jesus says, "*And as Moses lifted up the serpent in the wilderness, even so must the Son of man be lifted up: That whosoever believeth in him should not perish, but have eternal life,*" (John 3:14-15).

What could Jesus possibly be referring to here? The incident He is referring to with Moses is found in Numbers 21. Here we see yet another time when the Israelites became discouraged and com-plained against God. Apparently, God just did not come up to the high standards of the Israelites.

Therefore, "*the LORD sent fiery serpents among the people, and they bit the people; and much people of Israel died. Therefore the people came to Moses, and said, We have sinned, for we have spoken against the LORD, and against thee; pray unto the LORD, that he take away the serpents from us. And Moses prayed for the people,*" (Numbers 21:6-7).

Because the people realized they had sinned, the Lord provided Mos-es with the solution. "*And the LORD said unto Moses, Make thee a fiery serpent, and set it upon a pole: and it shall come to pass, that every one that is bitten, when he looketh upon it, shall live. And Moses made a serpent of brass, and put it upon a pole, and it came to pass, that if a serpent had bitten any man, when he beheld the serpent of brass, he lived,*" (Numbers 21:8-9).

Moses is told to place a brass snake on the top of a pole. Any Israelite bitten by a poisonous snake would be saved by looking at the pole with the brass snake on top of it, which was tall enough to be seen from any position in the camp.

Now, the thing to remember here is that it took *faith* to believe that simply by looking at the brass snake, a bitten Israelite would be saved. That is all it took, just to look at the brass snake. Of course, it took faith to believe that looking at the snake would make a differ-ence - and it did, because those bitten who looked at the brass snake did not die.

Jesus used this event in the Old Testament to testify of Himself. In fact, by referring to it Jesus was indicating that He believed it to have occurred. Just as the brass snake would be lifted up on the pole, so would Jesus be lifted up on the cross. Anyone who looked to Him in faith would be saved. In other words, by trusting in Jesus as THE antidote for our sin problem, salvation would be granted.

Believing in Jesus and His substitutionary atonement qualifies a person for salvation. We read in Genesis 15 that Abraham believed God and it was counted to him as righteousness. This means taking God at His Word, and it involves much more than simple *intellectual assent*. It is a deep conviction that God's Word is reliable, that His death on our behalf is the only thing that saves us.

Now, about that bulleted list - praying, preaching, teaching, giving, etc., - it all happens *after* salvation, from the heart. Doing what is on that list to earn salvation means absolutely nothing. In fact, it means less than nothing. The only thing that grants us salvation is our faith in Jesus' atonement on our behalf.

I have yet to meet an ex-Christian who gives me the proper definition of what it means to be a Christian. The most interesting part of the whole equation is that I have had a number of them tell me that though they *know* they *were* actual Christians, they *now* know that God does not exist. Never let it be said that people who call themselves "ex-Christians" are logical.

The problem is that you cannot have it both ways. Either God exists or He does not. He cannot exist when a person *thinks* they are a Christian but then cease to exist when they become convinced that they are no longer a Christian. How can that even remotely be possible? It does not even make sense, and it evinces a lack of understanding about being a true Christian.

It is only possible if being a Christian means following a *prescribed way of life*, just for the sake of following that way of life. For instance, someone who practiced yoga because they believed it to be beneficial, only to decide later on that they received absolutely no benefit from it, is in a completely different position from one who attests to be an authentic Christian at one point and becomes an atheist the next. If being a Christian actually involves a spiritual transaction (new birth), then obviously they could not have been an authentic Christian at one point, only to find out that it is now NOT true and that the God they thought they worshiped does not, nor ever did, exist. It either was true or it was never true. No one can have it both ways.

So the ex-Christians who firmly believe that they WERE Christians but are no LONGER Christians are kidding themselves. They were NEVER authentic Christians, and they need to be willing to admit it instead of continuing this illogical game of 'God existed when I WAS a Christian, but now He not only does NOT exist, but never did' dishonesty. That is not only completely illogical, but the fact that ex-Christians actually have the temerity to think people are stupid enough to buy it simply because they say it is as ridiculous as their position.

What are "ex-Christians," then? They are people who at one point in time firmly believed that they were Christians based on the things they did. However, it is clear from the Bible that people cannot lose salvation. The eternal security that belongs to the authentic believer is way too hard to miss in Scripture. Romans 8 starts out with the fact that once a person truly becomes saved, all condemnation is forever removed. There is no chance that the authentic Christian will ever be condemned at any point. Chapter eight of Romans ends with the fact that there is never going to be any separation. Authentic believers will never be separated from Christ - never.

People who call themselves "ex-Christians" are very much like the "tares" that Jesus describes in the Parable of the Wheat and the Tares (cf. Matthew 13). It's quite a simple, but profound, parable. Christ is explaining clearly about the characteristics of His Church. A man owned a field and planted good seed (wheat) in that field. While he slept, his enemy went to that man's field and sowed bad seed (tares).

No one realized what had occurred until the seed began to sprout. At that point, the servants began to notice something wrong and went to the owner of the field to ask what they should do about it. The reality here is that the workers are obviously the angels who gather people at the harvest. The seeds represent the authentic believers and the 'fakers' or the 'wannabes'; people who looked similar to wheat but were NOT wheat at all. In the parable, the owner of the field tells the workers that they should do nothing about the tares until the crop was ready for the harvest. The owner of the field was concerned about the possibility of ANY of the wheat being accidentally uprooted with the tares. Waiting until the harvest would eliminate that possibility because it would be much easier to see the wheat from the tares.

This is the visible Church today, folks. It has always been filled with wheat AND tares, and it continues to this day. The very first part of Matthew 13 explains the parable of the sowing of the seed and where it landed. The only surface that it landed on in which it actually took root was the good soil. On all the other surfaces, while it may have *looked* like it was taking root, it never did. What this means is that in this world, there are all types of people who believe that (and may even look like) they are Christians. They DO the things Christians do and they can SAY the things Christians can say, but the reality is that all that matters is what is in their hearts, not what is seen on the outside.

Against my better judgment, I recently posted on a site in which the main person attested to the fact that she believed herself to have been a Christian. I read through her blog and my heart went out to her for the amount of confusion, fear, and suffering she had gone through. She stated that she had been a fundamentalist, and was now happily not. I posted a few words and was met with remonstration from her; how I had missed the point, etc. I did my best to clarify why I had posted, but it seemed to make little difference. In fact, the more I posted, the more ludicrous the responses to my posts became, with one person accusing me of being there for the sole purpose of proselytizing, saying that my motives were completely transparent.

Here is the reality; if these people were in fact Christians, and had somehow managed to walk away (which I do not believe is possible), they have actually lost ALL chances to be redeemed according to the Bible. Hebrews speaks of the fact that those who have tasted the Holy Spirit and wind up walking away are condemned, because what they are then doing IF they want to come back to Christianity (if that was possible) is crucifying Christ all over again.

The actual text states, "*For it is impossible for those who were once enlightened, and have tasted of the heavenly gift, and were made partakers of the Holy Ghost, And have tasted the good word of God, and the powers of the world to come, If they shall fall away, to renew them again unto repentance; seeing they crucify to themselves the Son of God afresh, and put him to an open shame,*" (Hebrews 6:4-6). A close look at the text does NOT say that the individuals WERE Christians. It says they "tasted the good word of God" and had a sense of what it means to be a Christian. In other words, their eyes were open somewhat to the truth. Did they embrace it? Not all of it. They began to move toward it, but balked when things got tough. There was never any real conversion experience. This would have been like the thief on the cross realizing who Jesus was, but instead of asking to be remembered when Jesus came into His Kingdom instead continued to ridicule Him. He saw the truth but ultimately rejected it.

The people described by the writer to the Hebrews are beyond redemption. Trying to persuade this type of person to "give Christianity a second shot" is summarily worthless. They are no more interested in giving Christianity a second shot than poking their eyes out. Unfortunately, folks like this believe that they know it all when it comes to Christianity, simply because they believe they were in fact authentic believers when they were not. My preference for evangelism is face to face, not on forums where the only thing that is truly transparent is the fact that the Internet encourages people to hide not only their real identities, but their real motives for why they are on a particular forum. It is a huge waste of time to proselytize on any forum, because people are normally there to merely argue and debate. They think winning the debate is proof that they are right in their position. It may simply be that they are the better debater.

Since deciding to no longer post on that forum, I have received a bunch of other posts by people who I'm assuming have posted after me, taking me to task for this or that. Without reading them, I sent them to my trash. What is the point, since they are so convinced that I am there to proselytize? Another book I wrote - *Apologetics Never Saved Anyone* - is my response to those shenanigans and games. I did notice that prior to my original post, no one had posted anything after February 2010. Since my initial post there has been a good deal of activity, so maybe they should thank me for becoming the focused enemy, which allowed them to band together and attack. :) At least it gave them something to do for a few days. In a day or two when they realize I have no interest in debating and/or arguing with them, they'll go back to patting each other on the back and high-fiving one another, and then all will go quiet until the next person unknowingly walks into the same situation.

Ex-Christians - all of them - may believe themselves to have been authentic believers, but the tragedy is that there never was an authentic, spiritual new birth regardless of what they like to think. Everything they did was external, which is exactly WHY they struggled as much as they did and were able to walk away. It was never in them to begin with, and whether they like hearing it or not, that is the truth of the Scripture. Of course, they deny the veracity of Scripture, denying even that God exists. Yet, they cling to the label "ex-Christian" as if it is a badge of honor or a rite of passage. They unfortunately have no clue, but they think they have and they can point to their life filled with what they believe to be scars from being a Christian.

Authentic believers will persevere, and we do so because Jesus Christ is the Author and Perfecter of our faith (Hebrews 12:1-2). He ensures that we persevere. In short, being a genuine Christian means being in relationship with Jesus Christ. It is not following rules or regulations, thinking that this is how a person becomes a Christian. At its root, being a genuine Christian STARTS with a new birth, and everything stems from that.

People will stand before Jesus and be judged. Some of the saddest words in the Bible are those that Jesus speaks to those who THOUGHT they were Christians, but were not: *"Depart from me, I never knew you,"* (cf. Matthew 7). That's the key; not what we physically do, but WHO we spiritually KNOW.

— 31 —

Unique I.D. Number Up and Coming

(Blogged: 04/26/2010)

I am amazed at how many people either do not see what is happening throughout the world, or find a way to explain it away. Many are so convinced that there is no need to worry about any upcoming Tribulation, a "mark of the beast," or anything even close to that.

To hear some tell it, the Tribulation already occurred, and the Antichrist was Nero (or some other Roman Emperor). The only way to make those connections is to stretch the biblical text to fit them, and that can only be done through the erroneously-filled interpretive process known as allegory.

In their attempts to prove that prophecy has pretty much all taken place already (with the exception of the last two chapters of Revelation), they have to be wearing blinders! This is the only way they can continue walking through this world, whistling while they walk, oblivious to the tremendous amount of change that is occurring even as you read this blog.

We are all familiar with the "mark of the beast" phrase and those who are Bible-oriented know that it comes from the book of Revelation:

"And he causes all, the small and the great, and the rich and the poor, and the free men and the slaves, to be given a mark on their right hand or on their forehead, and he provides that no one will be able to buy or to sell, except the one who has the mark, either the name of the beast or the number of his name. Here is wisdom. Let him who has understanding calculate the number of the beast, for the number is that of a man; and his number is six hundred and sixty-six," (Revelation 13:16-18).

So what? Who cares, right? Well, frankly, YOU should care because it is already happening in India right now. It should not surprise anyone that it would happen in a godless place such as India. Having worshiped false gods for centuries, the amount of superstition, false beliefs, and anti-God viewpoints makes the possibility of this occurring in India simply makes sense. It could have begun in any nation that has the same type of superstitious, godless belief system.

Of course, the fascinating thing is that the Unique Identification Number (UIN) is based on biometrics, which means the number that is assigned to each person is not only unique, but literally becomes part of the person. Consider this quote from www.worlduin.com:

"The permanent identifiers will be place of birth, date of birth and name of parents. A gazette notification will soon be issued to set up a national UID authority under the Planning Commission. The head-quarters for the mammoth project will be in Delhi with offices in all states and Union Territories. Every Indian will soon be numbered. The government has prepared the ground for what could be the world's biggest project to provide unique identification (UID) numbers to citi-zens. A new body will give all Indians UID-based smart cards with their personal details embedded in them. Even infants will have tag num-bers and will get smart cards in due course."[55]

This system is designed to issue a specific number to each of the 1.2 billion individuals in India to be issued over the next five years, with a total of 600 million issued in that length of time.

The worldwide economy, along with a tremendous increase in identi-ty theft, is the catalyst for this system. In times like these, it should be obvious that a secure way to guard a person's identity and the fi-nancial facts associated with that individual becomes extremely im-portant. Because of that, people are not only willing to adopt this system, but seem to clamor for it. Government is certainly willing to comply.

At first, of course, the system will not be mandatory, but will be is-sued based on need and demand. The problem, though, is that once any system is in place, the potential for abuse (or mandate for that system by a government wishing to become too involved in people's lives) is automatically in place.

We are seeing a type of special numbering system being created for each individual in India. How long will it be before other govern-ments attempt to create a similar system for the populace of their nation? Though introduced as a completely voluntary approach to

---

[55] http://www.worlduin.com/ (emphasis added)

guaranteeing security of identities and financial information, it could easily become a mandated program in which no one would be able to buy or sell anything without first having a type of biometric-based number, digitally connected to the individual's body.

"Once the UID number is assigned, [those in charge] will forward the resident a letter which contains his/her registered demographic and biometric details and a tear away portion with the UID number, name, photograph, and a 2D barcode of the fingerprint minutiae. Residents can also update their [own personal] information with UIDAI. The UID number is a lifetime number, but the biometric information contained in the central database will have to be regularly updated. Children may have to update their biometric information every five years, while adults do so their information every 10 years."[56]

Too many people are walking around either seemingly oblivious or deliberately ignoring the signs of the times. Things are happening throughout the world. War seems to be on the verge of happening daily in the Mideast, a unique numerical code is coming to the fore in India, and the religion of Islam is being downgraded from a producer of terrorists and a religion of hate, to a religion of peace. The army, which just rescinded its invitation to Franklin Graham for his comments about Islam, states they are inclusive and will not stand for comments like those from Graham.

The problem, of course, is that Islam treats women in Muslim countries as far less than human. Consider also that by far, terrorists are often created through the tenets of Islam. They could care less about anyone who gets hurt or killed because of their belief-system.

The army has it wrong. Not long ago, the military in the United States was taken by surprise by a Muslim who went jihad on innocent soldiers. He was one of the ranks, but was obviously not really part of

---

[56] http://worlduin.homestead.com/NEWS_CURRENT.html

the U.S. military team. That's okay, though, because far be it for anyone to say anything bad about Islam, regardless of its truth.

The idea that the military is "inclusive" is ridiculous. Islamic jihadists or terrorists can use their religion to destroy lives at will; they can gun down or stab to death cartoonists or filmmakers whom they believe have offended their god, Allah. They believe that it is their job to defend Allah against any insults that are spoken, written, or drawn in any part of the world.

Of course, this only makes me wonder why Allah himself does not take matters into his own hands. If he is Allah, he would certainly have the power, wouldn't he? Yet not only does he not do anything, but he expects his own followers to murder people for any perceived offense. This is the type of religion that the Army is protecting, and on American soil.

President Obama has not only done nothing to contain this type of bias against Christianity and those who are not Islamic, but has done everything he can to promote Islam as a religion of peace, when in point of fact, it is not. Anyone who has actually read the Qur'an and can understand the words in context knows that Islam is not a religion of peace. It is fully anti-Semitic and dead set against those who they believe are infidels - those who are not Islamic.

This world is moving quickly, specifically, and definitely toward a one-world government, complete with a one-world religion. It will ultimately be ruled by one man who will have his way for seven years, the last week of Daniel's prophecy in Daniel 9:24-27.

Whether it is the continued jihad threat from Islam, the coming UIN, or something else entirely, it seems truly obvious that a world system is in place and growing that will allow the coming Antichrist to use these things for his purposes. It is happening and he will use these things to his evil advantage.

As for those people who seem blissfully unaware of what is happening, I often wonder just how much it will take for them to begin to question their own belief system. If war broke out in the Middle East tomorrow, and a company of invaders comprised of five nations attempted to take over Israel, and God stopped their invasion without Israel having to raise a finger, would they be convinced then? If not, then it is clear that they are blind because of a delusion that God sends. They will have continually and consciously rejected God's truth for so long, that He finally - in sending a delusion - allows them to wallow in their own belief system.

Don't let it happen to you. It's all coming to a head. It may take another year, five years, or even ten years, but it is coming. You have been warned by too many people, and if you continue to choose not to believe, you do so at your own peril.

32

James Cameron's AVATAR

(Blogged: 04/27/2010)

I finally watched the movie, AVATAR, from the mind of James Cameron. I was hesitant because I figured that it would be 162 minutes of Cameron's New Age preaching. After seeing a longer trailer than the one shown prior to the movie's release, I began to see the storyline and thought it might be interesting.

Ultimately, AVATAR is a movie of the white man pushing out the natives when America was being settled by European settlers. Of course, Cameron's story takes place in the future and on the planet Pandora, where the peaceful people called the Navi are settled.

The Navi are tall, bluish people who have this idyllic world in which strange animals exist, trees and plants glow and there is a specific harmony among all creatures, for the most part.

The movie begins with the "white" settlers from planet Earth moving in to take over aspects of Pandora for a particular ore that exists on that planet. It brings more than top dollar when brought back to Earth, so this outer space endeavor needs to happen because of the corporate greed here on Earth.

Of course, the military is involved and - as usual - seen as the bad guy. Cameron does a good deal of preaching in this story that he wrote. However, all he did was create characters and use the same white man settler against the Native Americans, simply moving the story to the far flung future on a paradise called Pandora. Starting from that point, the story probably wrote itself.

Some of the things were fairly interesting. The military personnel, working with scientists, were able to create these beings that resembled the Navi, down to their height and color. The human counterpart would get into a machine, go into some type of suspended animation, and literally live inside that particular AVATAR that was made for him or her. Once inside their AVATAR, they could enter Pandora as one of the Navi and hopefully be accepted by them.

This was the plan anyway, and for the most part, it worked. That is, until our main character's moral fiber took over. He then realized that the military did not care about anything except getting the mission done. It did not matter how many innocent Navi were hurt or killed and it also did not matter how destructive they were to Pandora. The only thing that mattered was getting it done and getting back for dinner.

Toward the latter half of the movie, the New Age teachings come to the fore big time. Here, we are introduced to the Navi version of Mother Earth, who connects to all creation on Pandora and speaks to and through them. This harmony, once broken by the invading forces, is fought for by Pandora's Mother Earth herself. Can you guess what happens?

What I find fascinating is people like James Cameron. They seem to want nothing more (or less) than a Marxist Socialism in this world, because they mistakenly believe that original sin and the fallen nature of humanity is a myth. If it were a myth, then all would be well if the wealth was equally distributed among all citizens.

The funny thing, though, is that it is a fact that when Socialism has its way, the rich get richer and the middle class is completely eliminated, leaving only the poor - all of whom are on the same level. Who controls things then? The rich, of course.

Cameron is certainly rich by my standards. His bleeding heart New Agism seems to have nothing but disdain for the white settler who pushed out the natives centuries ago. What would Cameron like us to do, give it all back? If so, where would he be now? He has made his fortune because of the freedom that capitalism allows. If this country were Socialist, where would he be?

This seems to be the same thing that Kevin Costner "preached" in his "Dances with Wolves" movie. We never hear in these movies how bad Native Americans were to one another. It's always how bad the settlers were to the Native American.

I'm not trying to soft-soap it or ignore the realities, because the situation that did exist when settlers came over was abominable in many respects. However, not all settlers were involved in it and it is not as if all Native Americans were free from prejudices and had never gone to war with other tribes.

All of this serves to point out that all people are fallen. For all the preaching this and other movies do, the Native Americans were not perfect. They knew what war paint was, and they had weapons (not just to use against animals either). Beyond this, while on the positive side of things they only took what they needed from the land and animal kingdom, their worship of nature was nothing more than idolatry.

This theme runs through the movie AVATAR. As stated, it is nothing more than the new settler pitted against the settled, with tragic consequences. I read in one report that many people were suffering from a type of depression after seeing AVATAR. Who knows how true that was, as it could have very easily been nothing but PR. The camera work, the digital work - all of it was certainly striking in the movie. From an actor's perspective, I would have hated acting in the scenes that were "on" Pandora, simply because they were shot on a sound stage, with blue and green screens, with actors wearing motion capture suits. Give me an onstage play any day!

Characters in the movie are strong, sometimes to a fault. There were some which were difficult to accept. Michelle Rodriguez, who was shuttled off "LOST" shortly after her DUI on Oahu (coincidence?) and later "came out," touting her lesbian lifestyle, plays a hardened copter pilot. Though tough as nails, she has a soft heart when the military moves in and starts blowing up the landscape and people of Pandora. It is just difficult to take her seriously as a tough person. Give anyone a gun and they seem tough (although we know it's really the gun doing the talking), but take the gun away and you're left with a person who comes across as someone who wants to be seen as tough, but just doesn't quite make it.

All this aside, if it is possible to watch AVATAR as simply a fantasy movie, then that is the way to see it. I wonder, though, how many of us can watch a movie like AVATAR and be able to completely ignore all the New Age references? Once you realize what is going on, you are pulled out of the movie because that "4th wall" is gone.

All in all, AVATAR did not leave me depressed, as if I really wanted to be there. It is an interesting movie, but with its overemphasis on New Age and its attempts to show the white settler and the military in the worst possible light, the message of the movie is all too obvious. I've known for a while that Cameron has no love loss with Christianity. It was not that long ago that he found an ossuary in which he claimed were the remains of Jesus of the Bible. This, claimed Cameron, also proved that Jesus had been married and had children. Rather than retract anything later on, he simply buried it and does not discuss it any longer.

AVATAR is a movie that took a great deal of money to make, what with all the special effects and digital compositing. The disc jewel case insert boasts that "...James Cameron's AVATAR [is] the greatest adventure of all time." I would strongly disagree with that assessment. There have been other movies that are far greater in scope and adventure than this one; the Lord of the Rings trilogy, for one.

AVATAR is a decent movie for what it's worth, but as stated, the obvious references inserted into the film by Cameron become annoying. Since I don't worship Mother Earth and I'm not a New Ager, then you can hopefully see why this became an annoyance to me.

Wonder what Cameron's next movie will be - a "re-imagining" of Jesus Christ?

33

Mark of the Beast?

(Blogged: 04/30/2010)

"And that no man might buy or sell, save he that had the mark, or the name of the beast, or the number of his name," Revelation 13:17

I t's funny how often we are told by Reformed, Covenant, or Preterist theologians that all of Revelation has occurred except the last few chapters. They insist that the Antichrist was either Nero or some other Roman Emperor of the past.

However, what is interesting is that in their zeal to allegorize Scripture, they miss points that are obviously to be taken literally. For instance, the mark of the beast and the fact that he (the Antichrist) will cause everyone to have it, and that without it no person will be able to buy or sell, seems to be a real factor in the End Times events.

Consider that in India a national biometric I.D. system is being set in place in which all people MUST have a number. Their unique number will be imbedded just under their skin. In essence, this makes the number part of them. This is being done to eliminate the problem of identity theft, and it is also being done so that people's I.D.s will always be with them.

Because of the problems with illegal immigration in the United States - as well as other countries - our Congress is moving to do what they can to shore up those problems. They are also seriously considering starting our own version of the biometric numbering system.

"[They are] focusing on three areas: [to] tighten security along the nation's northern and southern borders; register illegal immigrants with the federal government and set them on a path to citizenship if they pay fines, learn English and stay out of criminal trouble; and crack down on employers who hire illegal workers.

"[Congress'] proposal will require the government to secure the border first before we adjust the status of a single person here illegally — just what many of our colleagues are saying on the other side of the aisle," said Schumer, who insisted the border security proposals he is advancing are tougher than those considered during Bush's tenure.

"[The proposal] also highlighted a [plan] to implement a nationwide worker-verification program, which would require every worker to carry a national identification card with biometric information within six years.

"That proposal has already drawn fire from the American Civil Liberties Union (ACLU), but Schumer said it is essential to stem the tide of illegal workers.

"'Our proposal recognizes that no matter what we do on the border, we'll only succeed in dramatically reducing future illegal immigration

by creating an employment verification system that holds employers accountable for knowingly hiring illegal workers,' he said."[57]

The article goes onto say that it is really impossible to stop every car, truck or van entering into the United States to search for illegal aliens. A better system (biometric numbering) would allegedly solve this problem because of the worker verification system built into it.

While I am NOT saying that this new system IS the mark of the beast spoken of in Revelation, I AM saying that a system such as this could EASILY be manipulated by the Antichrist to be a mandatory system in which EVERYONE will need to take such a mark. It will be the government's way of keeping tabs on everyone.

Now please note that they are referring to a type of card for the United States, not necessarily a number that is somehow embedded into a person's skin. This is also included in India's system.

The problem is that they will likely discover - duh - that simply issuing a CARD to people does not solve the problem of identity theft. This will be the reason that they say they must move to a system in which the person's unique number is somehow embedded under their skin. If the number is attached to each person in this way, identity theft could become a thing of the past. I'm sure hackers will find a way around it, but that may take a great deal of doing. Even so, if a law were passed that made it impossible to buy or sell anything without that unique identification number, people would obviously need it. In essence, it would become illegal to attempt to make a purchase without having that number.

There really would be no reason that a law like this would be made unless the institution making the law simply wants to keep tabs on its citizens. In the case of the Antichrist, he will make the law to ensure that only those who are loyal to him take that mark.

---

[57] http://www.wnd.com/

Again, I am NOT saying that this upcoming system presently being instituted in India (or even the one they are talking about here in the United States) IS the system that the Antichrist will utilize for his benefit and to advance his power.

All I am saying is that it is certainly not far-fetched to think that such a system like the biometric numbering could wind up being used for such purposes. It is also very possible that this biometric system is simply a precursor to the system that the Antichrist uses for his own purposes.

One question that we need to consider is, when in history has a system such as this ever been utilized, with the type of technology that is being discussed today? Never. There has never been this type of numbering system that is being brought to bear on the people of India. There has never been a biometric numbering system that the United States Congress is considering for citizens here.

While people may point to other systems, the ones being discussed and implemented today are by far much greater in advanced technology and potential for harm than any system previous to it.

In spite of this, Reformed, Covenant, and Preterist theologians will continue to deny what is logically apparent. They will continue to point to the past and say that the Antichrist, along with the Tribulation, has already been here.

If more countries are going to begin adopting this type of worker verification system, how difficult would it be for a one-world ruler to use that system to weed out the "unfaithful," those who are not sold out to him? It could easily happen.

Those who do not believe in the upcoming Antichrist or the coming mark of the beast will simply cast this off as fantasy and go on with their lives. The principles involved in this new biometric numbering system are too much like that described in the book of Revelation to be coincidental.

If the system whereby the Antichrist can make everyone take the mark is on its way to us in the guise of worker verification, then maybe other things in the Bible are not so improbable either. In fact, I believe a number of things are pointing directly to the upcoming Tribulation:

- there are various earthquakes happening all over the world in unprecedented destructive waves
- the current administration has placed the United States firmly on the road to Socialism
- things have been heating up in the Middle East for quite some time and they are simply getting worse since President Obama became president
- this is the first time since Israel became a nation that demands are being made to them that they stop all construction before anyone will be willing to enter into peace talks with them
- Iran has arrived as a nation that has nuclear capabilities
- Syria, Iran, Iraq and other nations have all expressed their hatred of Israel
- Russia has begun openly supporting Iran's nuclear capabilities and has sold them arms
- Islam is becoming a dominant religion throughout the world, and it seems that leaders of many nations are bending over backwards to placate Muslims so that they are not offended (the problem, of course, is that they are merely playing into the hands of Muslim extremists)
- Christianity is slowly being silenced here in the United States and other free countries like Great Britain
- Christians are actually being thrown in jail for "offending" Muslims by providing their opinion about Muhammad

- Islam will not stop until Sharia law becomes THE law of the world

The plain fact of the matter is that this world is moving toward another holocaust. In this day and age, people are still being executed in places like Iran for having the audacity to protest their government. Recently, many young men were strung up on the end of cranes until they were dead because they dared to speak out against Sharia law.

It should also be understood that Islam awaits its final Mahdi, or Imam, the individual they believe will usher in world peace through enforcement of Sharia law. This individual is understood to be the Antichrist, according to Christians who take the Bible literally.

So it is not simply Christians who are speaking of an end times situation in which one individual will rise to the top of the heap to rule the entire world. Islam believes it as well.

We also need to remember the nation of Israel. Orthodox Jews are still waiting for their Messiah. Since their forefathers rejected the actual Messiah - Jesus Christ - roughly 2,000 years ago, they believe that their Messiah is yet to appear.

Is it any wonder that this coming individual - the man believed to be the Antichrist by Christians, the man believed to be the last Imam by Islam - will be seen as the Jewish Messiah?

He will make a covenant with Israel for one week (7 years; see Daniel 9:27), and will break it in the middle of the week after just 3 1/2 years. He will initially be seen as a Superman who brings peace to the Middle East after everyone else has tried and failed.

May God open your eyes to what is coming, headed by one man; the world's final ruler, before Jesus Christ returns to take possession of what is rightfully His.

34

Today's Atheist: Modern Day Pharisee
(Blogged: 05/01/2010)

The title of this particular blog may seem strange because atheists generally claim no religious affiliation. However, when we take the time to really look at things, there are more similarities between atheists and Pharisees than not, especially for those atheists who like to refer to themselves as "ex-Christians."

The Desire for Accolades
The Pharisees (along with the Sadducees) were two groups of religious men. Interestingly enough, though the Sadducees and the Pharisees both sat on the Sanhedrin (the governing religious board of

Jesus' day for all matters related to Judaism), it was the Sadducees who actually did not believe in any form of life after death. Of course, this simply proves that they were on this religious board for their own satisfaction and feelings of self-worth.

The Pharisees - interpreters of the Mosaic Law that arose during the time between the testaments - were of course known for their legalism, as well as their inability to comprehend basic Scriptural truth. They were devout legalists and they loved the accolades of the commoners, who bowed or moved out of their way as the mighty Pharisee walked through the market place.

Ancient Gangsters?
Think of the scene in the first Godfather movie where a very young Robert De Niro hurries across the rooftops of "Little Italy" in order to be at a certain apartment before the renter arrived home. That renter was in fact marching slowly through the streets, enjoying the praises of the common people as they all enjoyed the Italian parade. As he strode along in his white suit, white hat, and cape, he took out a crisp piece of paper money and, while everyone was watching, attached it to the statue of the Madonna, to the delightful oohs and ahs of the crowd.

Of course, the people of Little Italy hated him because they feared him. He was nothing but a gangster in a dry cleaned white suit, stealing from the hardworking business owners in the neighborhood. His white suit gave the impression that he was "pure." Looks, of course, are deceiving. What matters to most people is how a person comes across, not who they really are inside. The opposite is true with God.

Knowledge without Insight
For all their religious knowledge, the Pharisees had little to no real insight into Scripture. They had the same exact same Scriptures that Jesus, Paul and others studied, yet they were completely unable to

discern the truth of the Scriptures at all - especially where it related to Jesus, as much of it does.

Anyone who has read the Bible, or even just the four gospels - Matthew, Mark, Luke, and John - is aware of the types of problems the Pharisees, the Sadducees, the Scribes, and the religious lawyers constantly tried to create for Jesus. They always wanted to trap Him in their asinine and superficial arguments, yet were never successful. All this did was increase their ire and desire to kill Him.

Atheism Then...
The reason that the Pharisees and the others gave Jesus such a hard time had to do with the fact that they refused to believe that Jesus was actually God the Son. They were actually religious atheists, meaning they failed to believe the truth about religion, choosing instead to believe their own inventions about religion. They rejected truth, replacing it with self-created fantasies.

Their lack of belief, along with their abject failure to understand biblical truth, created a situation in which they directed their anger at Jesus, because He consistently pointed out their inadequacies and failures. He did so for two reasons:

- the Pharisees constantly confronted Jesus about what He taught or what He did, and
- Jesus needed to counteract their false teaching, which people accepted because they did not know any better themselves

By far, the biggest problem the Pharisees had was that they were unbelievers when it came to Jesus. What created this unbelief? Their erroneous interpretation of Scripture and their high view of themselves. They had placed themselves in a position of authority, yet they did not use the Scriptures as their authority. They used traditional teaching and their own opinions. In essence, far from viewing

Scripture as the highest authority, like today's atheists they had become their own highest authority.

In reality, the Pharisees were religious teachers who had an air of authority which the people outwardly respected (primarily because of the position of the Pharisees in the community). They wore their religious garb, presented themselves as "know-it-alls," and enjoyed their high position in the community. Ultimately, they were wolves in sheep's clothing because they had absolutely no interest in the average Jew, whom they were supposed to lead and teach.

The Pharisees had three problems:

- unbelief
- a high view of themselves
- turning people away from actual salvation

So how are atheists of today like the Pharisees?

Today's Atheist
First, they are obviously unbelievers as far as religion is concerned. They are not unbelievers in every area, and they are not without faith, but with respect to religion - and especially Christianity - atheists are complete unbelievers in any religion that has anything to do with a personal deity.

Proving God Does Not Exist
Let's be honest and direct here. Atheists cannot prove that God does not exist. When you ask them to prove it, they will immediately retort that you cannot prove a negative. This is simply a smokescreen because they will tell you point blank that God does not exist. In essence then, if they are so positive that God does *not* exist, they must have a way of proving it to themselves. If they have proven it to themselves, then why are they unable to prove it to everyone?

The Religion of Atheism

The reality is this: atheism is a religion, which utilizes faith in order to exist. Since atheists cannot prove the LACK of existence of a personal deity, they are then left with a group of beliefs and tenets based on their own thinking and reasoning, which they are unable to prove. Yet they pretend that what they believe is a done deal, an incontrovertible set of facts.

Atheist Rejoinders

Atheists use sarcasm, castigation, denigrating remarks, rhetorical questions and rejoinders to redirect instead of answer direct questions. When they do appear to answer questions directly, it is normally filled with philosophical jargon that the average person couldn't care less about, but since it can have the tendency to sound intelligent, it must be true. Throwing in words like "paradigm shift" and other philosophical jargon is done to throw their opponents off balance. It is nothing more than cannon fodder.

I'm an "Ex" Something or Other

Within atheism, a group boasting that they are "ex" something or others ratchet atheism to the next level. Whether they are ex-Christians, ex-fundamentalists, ex-pastors, or something else entirely (but still related to religion), they believe they have not only proven that they have debunked Christianity but have gone beyond it to bring a new reality to atheism.

Panhandlers in Atheism

When you read books by John W. Loftus, Joe Holman, Dan Barker or others, the level of intelligence is severely lacking. I do not say that out of meanness. I say that because it is difficult to read their books without laughing. There is nothing there that promotes their own set of beliefs that they have debunked Christianity. How could there be, since nearly everything is based on either their opinion or someone else's? This is especially obvious when these "retired" pastors/evangelists start to exegete Scripture, which is simply the process of interpreting it. They are woefully (and even painfully) in the dark about the Bible and what it says to us.

Of course, the saddest part is that they firmly believe they are correct, so when someone comes along critiquing their inability to interpret the Bible, they simply label that critique as having "no substance." This is as far as they go, refusing to offer a detailed rebuttal, because they are actually unable to do so. When they do stoop to respond to you, they are usually very quick to shift gears and redirect. Such is the thinking of arrogant atheists who believe that the only people who must prove anything are Christians.

The Atheist's New Definition of Christianity

The further tragedy related to the new atheist and their claim they are post-Christians, or ex-Christians, has to do with their definition of Christianity. They firmly believe that at one point they *were* Christians. They point to all that they did, all that they believed and all that they taught, which they think made them a Christian. Unfortunately, the stupidity of this is lost on other atheists and many who also call themselves Christian, who wind up tripping over one another to see who can high-five the fastest.

What IS a True Christian?

The truth of the matter is that there is only ONE way to be a Christian (how could there possibly be more than one?), and it requires faith (confidence, deep conviction, or trust) in who Jesus claimed to be and what He claimed to accomplish for humanity. Becoming a Christian does not happen by saying a "sinner's prayer," or by raising your hand in church, or even by walking down the aisle during an "altar call." I don't see any of those in the Bible at all. Do you?

Being a Christian involves a spiritual element above all things. It is a spiritual transaction, which Jesus referred to as being "born again" or being "born from above." It is not "I am a Christian because I felt warm all over," or "I prayed the sinner's prayer, therefore I am a Christian."

Christian One Day, Atheist the Next?

You cannot BE a Christian one day, and then at some future point, NOT be a Christian! That is biblically impossible (and I am very aware of the way people twist Scripture in their attempts to show that people can lose salvation). You cannot lose salvation. This denigrates God's immutable and all-powerful strength. I realize that people argue about this, yet the Bible seems to be clear on the subject when taken in its entirety.

The problem with today's atheist is that they are actually very religious. They are religious about their atheism.

- They use faith
- They believe certain things
- They believe what they cannot prove (that God does not exist)

The atheist of today is no different from the Pharisee of Jesus' day. Both are unbelievers. Both reject Jesus as God. Both see no value in the substitutionary atonement. Neither group sees beyond themselves as their final authority.

As much as atheists would like to be free of religious structure, it is clear that atheism is as religious as the next religion. They are religious about their beliefs, all the while denying that religion has a place in society.

When ONE atheist is able to PROVE beyond doubt that God does **not** exist, I'll listen. Until then, their religion of faith is no different from mine, except that they are on the wrong side of it.

35

Obama, Israel, and Arabs...Oh My!

(Blogged: 05/03/2010)

There have been a couple of interesting developments related to the Middle East. First, apparently President Obama is laying the full blame of the stalled peace talks on Israel. It has become exceedingly clear that President Obama is fully siding with Arab nations over and against Israel.

He believes that Israel is stalling the peace process and, if nothing happens soon, will convene an international summit in the hopes of promoting a Palestinian State.

It really has taken President Obama little time to express his dissatisfaction toward Israel, as well as his full approval for a Palestinian State as a solution to the ongoing problem in the Middle East. One of the more interesting things that Obama has focused on is Israel's apparent nuclear capabilities, while totally ignoring the fact that Iran has been moving to the point of having the same capabilities. This does not seem to concern Obama at all, and why should it, since he is so overtly in favor of the Palestinians over Jews?

History has PROVEN beyond doubt that regardless of what Israel gives up or concedes, it is NEVER enough for the Arab nations that surround her. Recently *Israel Today* reported, "*Israeli Prime Minister Benjamin Netanyahu implemented the 10-month freeze at the behest of Washington in order to test the Palestinians' readiness to return to the negotiating table. When it was first announced last November, US officials praised Netanyahu for taking 'unprecedented' steps for peace. Now that it is clear the Palestinians are not going to respond in kind, the Obama administration appears to be blaming Netanyahu for not having done enough.*"

It is unfortunately becoming way too clear that President Obama is more of a puppet for the Arab nations than anything else. What is to be expected when the highest ranking leader of the free world goes around said world bowing to other dignitaries? What is THAT about?

Shortly after the election, Michelle Obama commented that this was the first time she had been proud to be an American (my paraphrase). Frankly, I'm embarrassed to be one, and it has nothing to do with the color of Obama's skin. It has everything to do with the way he is handling foreign affairs, AND the way he belittles things like the Tea Party, AND the way he completely ignores the constant call to prove he is a natural born citizen of the United States.

Coupled with this, it has just been announced that the Vatican has signed an agreement with Arab League to promote peace in the Middle East. So now Roman Catholicism is siding with Islam? How does that work? It works because since the days of Augustine, the Roman Catholic Church has viewed prophecy related to the End Times allegorically, and because of that interpretation, anti-Semitism became rampant the world over. Though the Reformation occurred, which attempted to end the RCC's interpretation of salvation by faith plus works and to eradicate the use of indulgences, what followed was simply a breaking away from the RCC by Luther, Calvin and others.

In spite of this, though, Luther continued with the RCC's eschatological views, and toward the end of his life he became predominantly anti-Semitic. Hitler read Luther's works and credited him with some of his ideas for the Third Reich in at least one of his speeches.

So, it is really no surprise that RCC sides with Islam. It is really the RCC continuing to do what they have always done, which is to come out against the Jews. What does the RCC honestly think will occur here? Islam has power, backed by their reserves of oil, and they have tenacity against the odds.

Many within Islam delight in the opportunity to die as a suicide bomber so that they will be guaranteed salvation (they believe). Other than this, their salvation (and how long they spend in a purgatory-like setting after this life) is anybody's guess.

This, brings us to the failed bombing attempt in NYC's Times Square. Originally, it was downplayed as merely stemming from one crazed individual. No terrorism connection. Now, however, the international scope of this near-tragic event is coming to light.

Frankly, I'm surprised it has taken this long to happen. I in NO way want it to happen, by any stretch!! I'm simply surprised that we have not seen this type of activity occurring in the United States as it routinely occurs in other parts of the world. Since 9/11, security has made it extremely difficult for a terrorist to use a plane, so the natural solution is for the terrorist to search for other means of creating death and mayhem. To their twisted way of thinking, a car bomb in a very busy place makes sense.

The damage to life and limb that would have occurred had this SUV bomb actually gone off is too scary to consider. However, we need to consider it because it is likely that we will see more and more of it as time goes on.

Fethullan Gulen is considered to be one of the most dangerous terrorists alive, and yet he resides not in the wilds of southern Turkey where he is from – but the mountains of Northeastern Pennsylvania! Below is an article of interest.

"From his fortress headquarters, located on 28 acres at 1857 Mt. Eaton Road in Saylorsburg, Pennsylvania, Gulen plots the overthrow of secular governments and oversees the spread of education jihad throughout Asia, Europe, and the United States.

"Gulen is surrounded by an army of over 100 Turkish Islamists, who guard him and tend to his needs. The army is comprised of armed militants who wear suits and ties and do not look like traditional Islamists in cloaks and turbans.

"They follow their hocaefendi's (master lord's) orders and even refrain from marrying until age 50 per his instructions. When they do marry, their spouses are expected to dress in the Islamic manner, as dictated by Gulen himself.

"The Saylorsburg property consists of a massive chalet surrounded by numerous out buildings, including recreational centers, dormitories, and cabins for visiting foreign dignitaries, a helicopter pad, and firing ranges.

"Neighbors complain of the incessant sounds of gunfire – including the rat-tat-tat of fully automatic weapons – coming from the compound and the low flying helicopter that circles the area in search of all intruders.

"The FBI was called to the scene, the neighbors say, but no action has been taken to end the illegal activity."[58]

How does this happen on American soil? How is it the FBI can go to this man's fortress in Pennsylvania and do NOTHING? What we are seeing in the United States is exactly what is being stated in *Muslim Mafia* and *Grave Influence*, two books that every American (who LOVES America) should read! We are being taken over from the inside and it will only get worse.

In the book of Revelation, we read of martyrs who die by beheading (cf. Revelation 20). Does anyone care that the method of execution favored by Islam is beheading? We have seen that repeatedly with Saddam Hussein's regime, where heads rolled like donuts on a conveyor belt.

Not long ago, during a brief time when people in Iran protested the results of a "free" election in which Ahmadinejad's appointment was questioned, people were rounded up and sentenced to death by hanging. One after another, they were attached to the end of cranes and hung until dead. Certainly not as quick as beheading, but less messy.

I am amazed at how many people in America seem not to notice what is taking place in our country. They seem totally unaware of the fact that Islam is serious when it says it will one day rule the world through Sharia Law!

---

[58] http://www.wnd.com/

Some have described Sharia Law as nothing more than *mob rule.* There are a multitude of pictures and videos on the 'Net of punishment under Sharia Law; hangings, beatings and even a video of a stoning that took place recently! Be warned, if you are easily offended or have a weak gag reflex, do not search for them.

I am amazed, but not fearful. I know that God is fully in control of all that is happening. However, my response to what is happening is to understand that even though God is fully in control and allows what transpires in this world, evil is still evil. Wrong is still wrong.

I am getting to the point where I am growing just a bit frustrated, not because I do not see God doing anything, but because I do not how much longer things will continue to go on like this until it becomes clearly seen that He IS in control.

The way things are coming to a head is remarkable. If I were not seeing it with my own eyes it would be difficult to believe, but it is like the Bible is unfolding as I write this, and as we live.

Now is the day of salvation. Today is the day. Putting off what will make a difference between heaven and hell is not a good choice. God is working out His purposes, and while this may not appear to be the case all we have to do is open the Bible and read it for ourselves.

Start with the book of Daniel. It is all there. Ultimately, God gains the glory, as He will bring about His plans and purposes. I pray that you have entered into a relationship with Him. I pray that you have begun to trust that He is who He says He is, and that He has done what He has come to do for YOUR salvation.

Roughly 2,000 years ago, Jesus Christ died on the cross, shedding His innocent blood for YOU and me. To trust in that fact makes the difference between eternal life and eternal death. It is YOUR choice. God has provided the way, but He will not force you to choose Him in order to save yourself.

36

Christians: How to Get Arrested!
(Blogged: 05/04/2010)

There has always been a certain amount of freedom of speech throughout most of the free world, especially in a democratic society. Obviously, there is a limit to what can be stated in public. Things that are meant to deliberately cause harm to people like shouting "Fire!" in a crowded area when there is actually no fire is against the law.

For quite some time, Gay groups have been pushing their own agenda in which the Gay lifestyle becomes increasingly viewed as normal. If it becomes understood as normal, then laws could be passed that would prohibit people from condemning the lifestyle. Recently, Al Mohler wrote a blog he titled "*It's Getting Dangerous Out There - A Preacher is Arrested in Britain.*"

Mohler states, "*We have seen this coming for some time now. The public space has been closing, especially when it comes to Christian speech — and especially when that speech is about homosexuality.*

"*Now, a Christian preacher has been arrested in Britain for the crime of saying in public that homosexuality is a sin. This arrest is more than a news event — it is a signal of things to come and an announcement of a new public reality. Even if all charges are dropped against this preacher, the signal is sent and the message is clear. The act of Christian preaching is now a potential criminal offense.*"

Based on this, it is clear that both Jesus and Paul would be arrested today for their temerity in referencing Sodom and Gomorrah and being even more explicit in Romans. The most ironic part is that if I say something like "Prostitution is wrong," nothing happens. There is no law broken, no moral code set aside, and no one is offended. Even prostitutes themselves who might disagree with that statement understand why it is perceived as being wrong.

Mohler continued, "*Street preaching has a long and well-recognized history in Great Britain. Indeed, preachers of every sort are hardly alone in continuing Britain's tradition of public rhetoric, seen quintessentially at 'Speakers' Corner' in London's famed Hyde Park. Dale McAlpine of Wokington in Cumbria has been preaching on the streets for years. The 42-year-old preacher, a Baptist, was arrested after telling a passerby that homosexuality is a sin.*"

Of course, to say that homosexuality is a sin is based upon the biblical text, both from the Old and New Testament. The Bible also teaches that lust is a sin, as well as stealing, murdering, and a host of other crimes, because these things break His laws. Brian McLaren seems to believe that the only good Christian is a silent one (if that particular Christian agrees with God that homosexuality is, in fact, sinful activity). We have already highlighted McLaren's book in a previous blog, so there is no reason to delve into it again. I bring it out again here simply to point to the fact that there are individuals like McLaren within the Emergent Church who do not agree that homosexuality is wrong, and they vilify those Christians who do.

"He was arrested under Britain's 'Public Order Act,' which, the paper reports, 'has been used to arrest religious people in a number of similar cases.' The law allows the arrest and prosecution of anyone who, with intent to harass or cause harm, uses 'threatening, abusive or insulting words or behaviour.'

"In this case, the simple act of stating in public that homosexuality is a sin was enough to get this preacher arrested. He is not the first. The Telegraph also reported that Harry Hammond, a lay preacher, was convicted in 2002 for holding a sign that read 'Stop Homosexuality. Stop Lesbianism. Jesus is Lord' as he preached in Bournemouth, near Southampton.

"The arrest of Dale McAlpine is attracting some degree of international media attention, but the case represents far more than a media spectacle. This arrest is a clear sign that the logic of 'hate speech' laws and similar rules and campus codes runs into direct collision with religious liberty and the freedom of religious speech."

In essence, *"Dale McAlpine was arrested for saying that homosexuality is a sin and for doing so 'in a voice loud enough to be heard by others.'"*

This is absurd, but it is also the way societies of the world are moving. Years ago, we were consistently told over and over by the bleeding heart liberals and socialists that you couldn't legislate morality. Apparently, some of these same people believe that outlawing certain statements that they believe should not be stated in public (which is the same as legislating morality) is perfectly fine.

So Dave McAlpine was actually arrested for stating something that the Bible teaches. What's next, are murderers or rapists or burglars now going to push for legislation that will outlaw people from saying that those things are wrong as well?

The strangest thing is that even though this is happening in Great Britain (and it's not the first time), there is an increasing presence of Muslims in that nation as well. Are homosexuals prepared to take them on with their Sharia Law? Are they not aware that Sharia Law forbids homosexuality and is punishable by execution? If not, they had better get their act together and figure it out, because Muslims are making their way into publicly held office and into Parliament. If the homosexuals of today actually believe this cannot be true, all they need to do is search the 'Net and they will find that even recently in Iran, homosexuals have been put to death by hanging solely because they are homosexual. If homosexuals actually believe that by outlawing certain comments from being made in public that will put an end to what they believe is "harassment" of homosexuals, they really need to think again.

We are all aware of Muslims who have a "jihadist" mentality, and by that I mean that they have no problem killing people whom they believe have offended their god; the Dutch filmmaker a few years ago who was killed in the street, the recent threats against the creators of South Park, the also recent bomb scare in NYC Times Square by a guy that neighbors describe as a "family man" and "quiet."

Muslims who believe they have a right to kill based on their own religious beliefs and value system do not care about laws that would attempt to prohibit their public comments regarding what is right or what is wrong. They go far beyond simply saying something is wrong. They put their beliefs into action and take the lives of those whom they call "infidels."

Homosexuality is sin, according to Scripture. If homosexuals are offended with that then they need to take it up with God, who decreed that it is wrong, instead of attempting to pass legislation as they've done in Great Britain, with which they hope to keep people from literally sharing their faith with those who are lost.

— 37 —

Media: Soft on Muslims
(Blogged: 05/06/2010)

I 've noticed this for quite some time: when the media is referencing Muslims or Islam, they often tend to tread very lightly. Why? It's simple. They know that out there somewhere are Muslims with that jihadist mentality like Faisal Shahzad, who has absolutely no qualms about killing "infidels." Anyone who speaks ill of Muhammad or Allah is considered an "infidel" and someone who is liable to be executed for their rudeness.

Did you read that? If someone speaks ill of Muhammad or Allah, it is perfectly fine for any Muslim to kill them. It is permissible under Islamic Law (Sharia Law). In a video related to Shahzad, an unnamed individual is quoted as saying:

"Terrorists come from religions that preach hate - that is easy to say. When a religion says our way is the only way, everyone else is going to hell - it becomes easier for a terrorist to kill non-believers since they are going to hell anyway. His god doesn't like them, so what's the harm in killing them? These people are innocent men, women & children - but hey my god is going to roast these same innocents, isn't he? Isn't that what bible thumpers believe? What is the new earth? An earth where 5 billion innocents pay with their lives simply because they don't have the same beliefs as yours? Funny that, the man who kills innocents is evil but an entity that sends billions of innocents to hell is a 'god'?

"Beware of the follower who says he is just a solider of god - for when the king says kill, the soldier must do so - even if the victim is a woman, child or a baby! The soldier bears no responsibility. It is easy then for a conman to manipulate brain-washed soldiers like these & send them out to do 'god's' work. I am not condoning what this nutcase has done - simply saying that terrorists usually come from King Religions - Religions that make the follower a subject/slave/servant at the service of his lord. Beware of those religions that ask you to kneel to god, Fear god, beg for his mercy. People who do that lose their freedom, becoming slaves of this master who promises salvation. The fact that he is sending billions of innocents to hell doesn't matter. Then a terrorist is born."

What has just been stated above is interesting to say the least. Obviously, the individual is referencing the Christian religion. But notice also how this person attempts to draw a comparison between what Shahzad did and what it is believed that Christians do? He stated, "*Funny that, the man who kills innocents is evil but an entity that sends billions of innocents to hell is a 'god'?*"

The person speaking is attempting to say that this "god" is more evil than Shahzad or anyone who acts as he does, taking innocent lives. The point, though, is that IF God ALLOWS (not SENDS) people to end up in hell solely because of decisions THEY made - that is not evil at all. If God has provided the means whereby people can AVOID hell but they refuse to take Him up on it, then how is God to blame for that?

On the contrary, people like Shahzad are culpable for their own crimes (or attempted crime in this case). In essence, Shahzad is acting like a god by deciding who lives and who does not, but without the omnipotence that makes God who He is as God.

Nonetheless, the problem of how the media deals with and treats Muslims and Christians is apparent. Dr. Michael Youssef pointed out in an article recently that the reason the media treats Muslims with kid gloves has to do with one word: *cowardice*.

Youssef explains, "*Fear of Islamic swift retribution and retaliation has kept the secular media in the West hiding in their proverbial foxholes. Ever since the Danish cartoonist Kurt Westergaard ignited a worldwide firestorm with his depiction of the Islamic prophet Muhammad with a bomb in his turban, members of the western media have been falling over themselves to praise Islamic ideologies.*"

In short, the media FEARS what members of Islam's "religion of peace" will do, so they avoid going head to head with them. They avoid fanning the flames where Islam is concerned because they are afraid of what will happen. This is not journalism, but as Youssef states, is cowardice. He also states the following:

"*Attacking Christians as a matter of course for causing every ill in society -- from the economic crash to every form of bigotry -- has become not only fashionable but desirable. You need only to read the BBC's website on any given day and you will find countless examples of con-*

demnation of Christians around the globe. For instance, take the case of a government registrar who refused to deny her Christian conviction by performing a marriage ceremony for same-sex couples. In contrast, you will find only praise for the courage of Muslims who fulfilled their religious duty by going to the Hajj while braving the threat of Swine Flu.

"It is safer to pick on Christians. After all, the essence of their faith is love, forgiveness, and peacemaking. They would never respond in similar fashion to their Muslim counterparts. "

This is unfortunately true. While there ARE extremist Christians (and we have mentioned that before in this blog) that take it upon themselves to kill a doctor who performs abortions or attempt to destroy an abortion clinic, by and large most Christians would never even consider doing what many Muslims do on a daily basis. The Christian does not believe that taking up arms (or a knife) and literally killing someone who offends the God of the Bible is what that God would have us do. If that were the case there would be FEW people left in this world, since it is extremely common to hear someone take either God's Name in vain or God the Son's Name in vain. It is common place in societies throughout the world.

What would happen, though, if the god of the Muslim world became a swear word? Can you imagine it? It would become a full-time, round the clock job killing all the infidels who used their god's name in vain! As Youssef states, it is easier to pick on Christians - extremely so. You think I'm exaggerating? Youssef's article goes on to point out a brief conversation with a Muslim: "*Back in 1981 when I met someone conveniently labeled (in the West) as a 'militant Muslim,' his complaint to me was that 'Christians are cowards.' When I inquired as to his reasons he simply said, 'the name of Jesus is used as a swear word in the movies and on TV.' When I asked for his advice for Christians, he replied: 'They should kill every actor and producer who would blaspheme their Jesus.'*"

These actors and producers are not Christians, by and large. If they ARE Christians and they can use Jesus' Name in vain because it is "in the script," shame on them! So this Muslim (and I'm sure many more) believe that people should be killed for using Jesus' Name in vain. I don't. I would rather leave it in God's hands. Yet it is precisely because I think like this that I am branded a coward by at least some Muslims. What I do is not cowardice. It is being obedient to the God I worship.

It is obvious the media knows how Christians will respond to any given situation. It is easy to hold Christians up to ridicule because they speak out against sin of all types, including homosexuality, or because they stand by their convictions of not officiating at same-sex weddings. The media can play that up big time because they not only know that multitudes will agree with them, but Christians themselves will do nothing except continue to turn the other cheek. God says vengeance is His and He will repay. He does not tell me that I must avenge myself, or that other Christians must do that. He will take care of it. My job as a Christian is to spread the good news: salvation from Jesus Christ, which ALLOWS people to completely bypass hell.

When the media is dealing with jihadist Muslims they tread very lightly because they do not want to be marked for death themselves. This is the way it was during much of the Roman Empire, when Christians were blamed for many things, and especially during the reign of Nero, when even though he set the fire to burn Rome, to deflect problems he pointed to the Christians. They were unmercifully set upon, tortured and killed for something that they did not do. Had Nero pointed to Muslims (which of course did not exist at that time, but for the sake of argument, let's say they did), they would have fought back.

What people fail to realize is that it is God who is the only One who has the right to avenge anything. Only He is perfect, righteous, just and holy. We are nowhere near it. We are fallen creatures, who have invited sin into God's perfect Creation. We all deserve nothing less than hell, but because of God's perfect love He has provided a way in which we might not only avoid hell but live with Him in eternity.

To read the rest of Dr. Youssef's article, see it here:
http://www.onenewsnow.com/Perspectives/Default.aspx?id=998384

Fear is a powerful fact of life. Whether it is the fear of acts of terrorism or fear of incurring the wrath of Islamic investors, both can be easily exercised with impunity.

38

Jesus Cartoon at Comedy Central

(Blogged: 05/06/2010)

Y ou may have read this as well, but it is being reported that the folks at Comedy Central are tossing around the idea of creating a cartoon based on the (modern) life of Jesus Christ. Wow, why didn't they think of this sooner?!

"Titled 'JC,' the series depicts Christ as a 'regular guy' who moves to New York to 'escape his father's enormous shadow.' His father is depicted as an apathetic man who would rather play video games than listen to his son talk about his new life.

222

"Comedy Central has pushed the envelope in the past: The long-running 'South Park' features Christ as a regular character.

"The network says 'JC' is on its development slate, steps away from the pilot stage and eventual airing. Many television series in development never make it to air."

I see. So this might make a good show? Why, because it mocks Jesus Christ and Christians like me? Also because Viacom (parent company of Comedy Central) has no fear of receiving death threats, since they would only be ridiculing the Founder of Christianity and not mocking Allah or Muhammad, the founder of Islam?

In reality, isn't the idea of a sacrilegious cartoon about Jesus Christ running to New York City to get away from His Father kind of boring? I mean, what will happen? How will they move the series along without it losing steam? The only way, of course, is to become more sacrilegious with each individual show.

Sure, both Viacom and Comedy Central will get protests and threats of boycotts by Christian groups - who will be lambasted by the liberal media for standing up for something they believe in - if they go ahead with the project.

Wouldn't it be far better to do a cartoon on the life of Muhammad? They can have him relocate to Jerusalem. There, he could muster the troops to keep all Jews and Christians away from the Temple Mount. It would be a laugh riot, with Muslims led by Muhammad tossing matzo balls and dead fish at any non-Muslim trying to reach the top of the Mount.

Then, of course, one episode might incorporate the fact that on the Sabbath orthodox Jews are unable to do anything as they are pelted with smoked bacon from high atop Antonio's Fortress. The hapless orthodox Jew would be unable to defend themselves AND unable to run away, since either might constitute "work."

No? Not good, huh? Oh, I see. Yeah, there might be - no, make that would be - death threats, and some jihadists would likely carry out those threats. That would not work. Hmmm, what to do?

I guess Comedy Central is right. It is far better to poke fun at a group which simply remains within the confines of the law (protesting, boycotting) and turns the other cheek. Certainly, the Christian God does not need to be protected or avenged for what people do or say about Him. As mentioned previously, if that were the case there would be few people left on this earth alive, since the majority only speak about Jesus Christ and God in the course of swearing. That's as close as they will ever get to praying.

It's interesting, is it not? Out of ALL the religions in the world and all the religious figures associated with those religions, only the Names of Jesus Christ and God (the Father) are used as epithets and expletives.

Yeah, it's far better for Viacom and Comedy Central to stick with a cartoon about the Founder of Christianity. I mean, Christians are a bunch of judgmental, no-good whiners who really should not have a voice at all in America, right? This in spite of the fact that we pay taxes, work hard to support our families and are generally law-abiding people (with few exceptions).

Better to keep from offending those whose religious ideals rest on the Five Pillars of Islam and avoid problems with them and their god. Christians? Who cares.

Care to complain? You won't find contact information at Comedy Central, so it's best to go straight to the top with Viacom. You can send an email of complaint here:

http://www.viacom.com/Contact/Pages/default.aspx

Oh, and you atheists, you'll want to be sure to send an email of congratulations to Comedy Central for having the guts to push the envelope even further than "South Park" has done.

Update: August 15, 2010 - As of the date of this book, the show was still in development, and being protested by a number of Christian groups.

39

Arizona Boycott and the End Times
(Blogged: 05/14/2010)

Within the past few weeks, AZ Governor Jan Brewer signed into law what already existed at the Federal level. In other words, the Federal Law already ESTABLISHED the guidelines and procedures for illegal immigration. What Brewer gave authorities in the state of AZ the right to do is to put the law into effect in her state - at the local level, in other words.

Since the law passed, Democrat Darryl Steinberg of California was one of the first ones to come out to condemn it and call for a boycott. Also shortly after this law was put into effect, President Obama announced that he was going to have the Federal Justice Department check into the legality of the law. We've heard nothing from Obama since, so I can only assume that someone informed him that the law already existed at the Federal level and Brewer simply signed into law in Arizona what already existed Federally. If that's the case, then it does not surprise me that President Obama has not followed up his first "foot-in-mouth" comment with an endorsement for Arizona's new law. Let's face it, when you are trying to move an entire country toward Socialism, it does not look good for you to approve of laws that curtail illegal immigration.

In one of Paul's letters to Timothy, he notes, "*But realize this, that in the last days difficult times will come. For men will be lovers of self, lovers of money, boastful, arrogant, revilers, disobedient to parents, ungrateful, unholy, unloving, irreconcilable, malicious gossips, without self-control, brutal, haters of good, treacherous, reckless, conceited, lovers of pleasure rather than lovers of God, holding to a form of godliness, although they have denied its power...*" (2 Timothy 3:1-5). Whether you agree that we are in the last days or not really does not matter. All one has to do is look around and understand that people are not getting better at all. If it were possible, it actually appears as though people are de-evolving.

In actuality, people are turning into brutes with no sense of right or wrong. There are photos on the Internet of people carrying placards clearly using inciting language and death threats in attempts to force the Governor of Arizona to do what they wants done. Many of these people are demanding free healthcare as if it is their inherent right to have it. The temerity of some to state that America owes them is unbelievable.

Such is the danger of entitlements, otherwise known as free programs. People actually get to a point of believing that they are in fact entitled to have free food, housing, and healthcare. They obviously do not consider the fact that those programs are paid for by taxpayers. If they do recognize it, they couldn't care less, preferring to find some reason to believe that they are truly entitled to it. It's always difficult to know how people come to determine that they are entitled to these programs, especially if they are illegal immigrants. As far as the law is concerned, I'm not sure how illegal immigrants have rights in the United States. If I smuggled myself illegally into France, Japan or any number of other countries, I cannot imagine that I would somehow be able to force that country to provide me with food stamps, or healthcare, or to have every legal document converted into English so that I could understand it, without having to immerse myself in that country's culture. It is patently ridiculous, yet here in America we have who have no problem making incendiary statements as they protest the alleged unfairness of Arizona's law.

We have many individuals who are calling for boycotts of Arizona, one in particular who is a legislature in the state of Arizona. He is calling on everyone to boycott his state. Question. How does that help the small businesses? How does that help Arizona's economy? Of course, someone will say that this is the purpose of a boycott, to force people through economic means to change something that others consider to be unfavorable. I understand how boycotts work. The problem, though, is that Arizona has done nothing illegal, since the law is already on the books at the Federal level.

But let's look at illegalities. There are people who promise to kill all Arizona police officers as some have done in their protests. Is that protected under free speech? They threaten to kill people until they get what they want. This is not a boycott. It is blackmail, and blackmail is a crime. I would imagine threatening police officers is also a crime. If it isn't, it should be. I have to wonder how many people who spend their time protesting actually have jobs and are actually here illegally. We'll probably never know.

This is the huge difference between people today and generations ago during and following the Great Depression. Years ago when millions were out of work and the government began trying to do something about it, the men were unwilling to take a handout. There was no welfare, no credit cards (as if they would have been any good at that point anyway), no unemployment benefits and no healthcare. Those men were too proud to take a handout. They insisted that they work for any money that the government issued to them. This meant any menial job that could be found or created; painting park benches, picking up trash, or whatever. They needed to feel good about themselves by actually doing something in return for the money from the government.

This is not the case today. People will not work for something they believe they should freely receive. They are actually too arrogant to believe that they should have to work when they can just stand there with their hands out. Of course, the result of that is that people often do not appreciate what they get free. That's the type of mindset that entitlement programs create.

Even with homeless people, the situation has become absurd. Homeless people deliberately head to California's capitol solely because of the fact that there are excellent benefits through organizations like Loaves & Fishes. They have showers, food, lockers and everything else. I'm not saying that those things should NOT be available. I just think it's interesting that homeless people from other states move to California's capitol because there is better free "stuff."

Homeless people are becoming stranger. More of them have wild-eyed expressions and you really don't know if they are crazy, possessed or just paranoid. No longer do they ask for a quarter or "extra change." They now ask for "a buck or two." If you don't have anything extra, they may get angry, flip you off, or just stare at you. It can be unnerving to say the least.

What I'm NOT saying is that people should not be given a hand from the government. What I AM saying is that the "hand" should not be turned into a generational inheritance, where it starts with one person in the family and then gets passed on down the ranks for generations. That is not why these government programs were started. Unfortunately, it is what they have become.

Poor people have nothing to give, so giving is up to the Middle Class. Rich people DO have something to give, but they give paltry sums compared to their wealth. Brad Pitt gave $10,000 to one of the propositions he supported in the last election. Everyone cheered. Whoopee. How many MILLIONS of dollars does he HAVE? Ten thousand dollars is like pocket change to you and me. So even when the rich give something, it only appears to be large because we immediately compare it to what we do NOT have.

This is why - in a Socialist state - the rich will get richer and the Middle Class will disappear. The rich give out of their excess. The Middle Class do not. We do not know what "excess" really means. When we give, it normally hurts. Not so with the rich. When Socialism really kicks in in America, the rich will STILL only give out of their excess, and what the Middle Class HAS will be taken away from them so that everyone is POOR at the same level. Nice.

So Paul wrote to Timothy about the way people will become. Are they like that now? Absolutely. They love themselves more than anything. They talk trash, they are rude and contemptuous toward anyone they care to be, and they walk around with this huge chip on their shoulders, believing that the world owes them everything and if it doesn't pay up, it'll be sorry. Their favorite word begins with "F" and it can generally be used as a noun, an adjective, an adverb and anything in between due to its versatility. People use it because they think it makes them sound tough. Actually, it makes them sound asinine because it obviously shows a limited vocabulary, which they attempt to make up for it with the "F" word and anger.

These people's consciences have been seared. They have absolutely no sense of God's definition of right and wrong - none whatsoever. Since their main concern is themselves, then it is clear that they will find some way to justify their beliefs and demands in their own favor and ignore or denigrate yours.

The fact that people like the ones already referred to can act the way they act and say the things they say is unconscionable. The fact that they can do it here in America where their freedom of speech is supposedly protected is something of which the irony is lost on them.

People in the United States are getting tired of illegal aliens coming here to live off our system, all the while complaining because they feel they are not getting enough. When I hear things like "this could be a violation of people's civil rights" (in reference to the newly passed law in AZ), my first question is "How is it illegal aliens HAVE any civil rights in the United States? They are here illegally." Yes, they should not be harmed or taken advantage of, but their presence does not mean they get to live off our system.

Not to be outdone, though, the president of Mexico came out on TV and lambasted the United States for its inhumane immigration laws. If there was ever a case of a hypocrite speaking the language he is most comfortable with, this was certainly it. The previous president of Mexico said the same thing about the U.S. All we have to do is look at the immigration laws in Mexico to determine whether or not they are humane.

Here are some of Mexico's FAIR and HUMANE immigration laws:

1. If you migrate to this county, you must speak the native language.
2. You have to be a professional or an investor. No unskilled workers allowed.

3. There will be no special bilingual programs in the schools, no special ballots for elections, and all government business will be conducted in our language.
4. Foreigners will NOT have the right to vote no matter how long they are here.
5. Foreigners will NEVER be able to hold political office.
6. Foreigners will not be a burden to the taxpayers. No welfare, no food stamps, no health care or other government assistance programs.
7. Foreigners can invest in this country, but it must be an amount equal to 40,000 times the daily minimum wage.
8. If foreigners do come and want to buy land that will be okay, BUT options will be restricted. You are not allowed waterfront property. That is reserved for citizens naturally born into this country.
9. Foreigners may not protest; no demonstrations, no waving a foreign flag, no political organizing, no badmouthing our president or his policies. If you do you will be sent home.
10. If you do come to this country illegally, you will be hunted down and sent straight to jail.

In fact, Amnesty International has filed complaints regarding Mexico's "humane" immigration laws.

"From the Associated Press: 'Central American migrants are frequently pulled off trains, kidnapped en masse, held at gang hideouts and forced to call relatives in the U.S. to pay off the kidnappers. Such kidnappings affect thousands of migrants each year in Mexico, the [Amnesty International] report says. Many are beaten, raped or killed in the process. One of the main issues, Amnesty says, is that migrants fear they will be deported if they complain to Mexican authorities about abuses'.

"Many are beaten, raped or killed in the process."

"Amnesty International called the abuse of migrants in Mexico a major human rights crisis Wednesday, and accused some officials of turning a blind eye or even participating in the kidnapping, rape and murder of migrants."

So, to Mexican President Felipe De Jesus CALDERON Hinojosa, Arizona Congressman Raul Grijalva and others who believe that the Arizona immigration law is racist and therefore should be annulled, I say two things:

1) Fix your own immigration problems in Mexico before coming down on the United States.
2) If Mexico treated their own citizens properly, by providing jobs, education and more, would Mexican illegals NEED to come to the United States?

It is easy to condemn the United States when we attempt to tighten the border situation or make it difficult for illegal aliens to remain in this country. We are actually helping Mexico out quite a bit because it takes the pressure off of Mexico and their UNWILLINGESS to help their own citizens. The United States is providing illegals with what they cannot get in their own country. It makes sense that El Presidente would condemn us, because the more illegals there are who stay in Mexico, the greater their problem economically.

The United States cannot continue to support millions of illegal aliens who arrive in this country without proper papers. Meanwhile, some of the states bordering Mexico report that ranchers are being killed by illegals. Why? Because the ranchers deign to rid their land of the large cache of illegal drugs that illegal aliens (drug cartels) are storing on their lands in order to move it further into the United States.

If the Federal Government were doing its job, the patrol at the border would be far more effective. Illegals would have a much more difficult time coming into this country and remaining here.

Instead, the Federal Government, having passed immigration laws, either refuses to enforce them or simply does not want to do so. Either way, this country has a huge problem now because of the financial crisis that has been created by millions of people who are here from Mexico and get free schooling, free medical, and free whatever else they can get.

Those who DO work usually get paid cash and do not have taxes taken out of their pay. They go back to Mexico with thousands of U.S. dollars in their pocket to make a better life for their family. Who can blame them, since Mexico's government is unwilling to provide decent jobs for them? The problem, though, is that they arrive here and wind up only taking, thumbing their nose at the United States all the while.

I am dumbfounded that so many people in the United States are seemingly unaware of the fact that illegal aliens are here ILLEGALLY. Since this is the case, the very fact that they have gone AROUND the law should not put them in the position of receiving free services. Yet some legislators insist that illegal aliens should be given driver's licenses! Why? They seem to be getting along fine without them - or insurance.

No one wants to see people go without. But it is incumbent upon the nation to which these people are legal citizens to provide for their own, and not force them (by doing nothing) to enter another country illegally to stay alive. As long as the President of Mexico (and anyone else) believes that by attempting to shore up the holes in our immigration laws we are doing something immoral, they only need to ask themselves why these people NEED to come here from the start. They also need to turn their attention to their own immigration laws, which leave a great deal to be desired, especially in the area of civil rights and inhumane treatment of foreigners.

Greece is going bankrupt. They can no longer afford entitlement programs. Trying to change them has simply created huge problems in addition to money problems for Greece. Other nations are already lined up behind Greece; how far behind them is the United States?

The world is a tenuous place, where tensions run high and are running higher as we progress toward the edge. When I look around this world, I see a great many people with attitudes that are so "me" oriented that it is impossible for them to see anything else but themselves. Take the time to search and view photos and videos of people protesting Arizona. They are obviously healthy enough to be out carrying placards announcing mayhem and death if their demands are not met. Are they too healthy to work, or are there just no jobs available? According to President Obama, the economy is doing well, and while things still need to improve, he is confident. If that's the case, then these individuals should be out working, or at least going to school or college to improve their chances for gainful employment. Can't pay for college? No problem, because there are plenty of financial programs to help the downtrodden.

I'm afraid that we here in America will not wake up until it is too late. We just keep thinking things are fine and will only get better; what we're experiencing now is just a bump in the road. Sorry, that's not what is happening. What is happening is that this country is moving toward Socialism right alongside the rest of the world. One day, out of necessity, there will likely be a one-world government. We're already hearing about it in the code phrase "new world order" or the need for a major "paradigm shift" in reference to the political landscape.

I think we can probably all agree that this world is getting smaller, and that is due to technology. We have more people than this poor old earth can handle and in spite of the fact that 150,000 die daily, more are born every day. As noted yesterday, we are experiencing earthquakes, volcanoes, tornadoes, floods, crop loss and the like such as we have not seen in centuries.

So Gov. Jan Brewer signs into law what the Federal government should have already been enforcing. Because of it, she is panned, protested and vilified. I believe she is a very brave woman. If you would like to sign her petition of support, please do so by following this link:

http://www.janbrewer.com/

40

Kryon: Does He Speak the Truth?

(Blogged: 05/17/2010)

I f you cruise the Internet looking for things spiritual, it is not long before you find yourself on pages that deal with beings like:

- *Archangel Michael*
- *Raphael*
- *Gabriel*
- *Seth*
- *Kryon*
- *and others*

Many within Christendom are familiar with the names Michael the Archangel and Gabriel. What about the others, Seth and Kryon? Ask just about any New Ager and they'll tell you about those two beings. The same New Agers will also give you their opinion about Michael and Gabriel, though their opinion will not necessarily match the biblical records.

Rev. Daniel Neusom is one person who claims to channel Archangel Michael, as he refers to him. In the Bible, Michael the Archangel does not speak much at all. In fact, about the only time you'll read Michael saying anything is when Jude quotes something he says to Satan during the dispute over Moses' body.

However, apparently Michael has a lot to say through people like Neusom. In one video on the 'Net, Michael speaks about the fact that God wants us to be free and fulfilled...on the earth. He says that repeatedly, in various ways, and then finally gets to the heart of his message, which is that God is LOVE...only. According to this Michael, God is not judgmental, not harsh, does nothing unloving at all, and is certainly not worried about justice or holiness. God is love...and that's it. Michael describes God has someone who does not withhold, does not chastise and does not harm.

Frankly, it is not difficult at all to see why people would eat this up. By dialing into this viewpoint, one is literally held captive by Michael's understanding of the meaning of love. After all, why would Archangel Michael lie to anyone here on earth? Through Rev. Neusom, Michael encourages us to get rid of the ancient religion - but not all of it. He wants us to keep the part about "God is love" and get rid of the rest.

So who is Archangel Michael? Well, if you ask the people who tune into these videos and buy the books, he is the very Michael that the Bible speaks of, who is here on earth to bring hope to the masses. Is there another option? Of course there is, and for the Christian it is not difficult to see behind the veneer and understand that this Michael is simply some demon disguised as Michael in order to spread the lies and agenda of his boss, Satan.

I know what you're thinking if you're not an authentic Christian. You're likely thinking that saying demons are behind something like this is just too easy and too predictable of what a Christian would say. Even so, that reason does not necessarily negate that possibility of it being a fact.

What I find fascinating about all of these beings who channel their message through some hapless human being (who believes they have stumbled onto some secret door to a higher plane) is that their messages are generally the same. They are all about love, how the human beings of this planet are imprisoned by their own bodies, and how their souls yearn to be free. Fortunately for us, they are here to tell us that, and they also attempt to show us how to walk through that door which leads to the higher plane.

Ultimately, when Seth states "reality is what you make it" (or something similar), or Michael tells us that God is love and only love, or some other entity intones that we must learn to put our prejudices born of ancient religious thought behind us, we are being force-fed the doctrines of demons. People argue about the veracity of the Bible all the time. Yet many of these same people have little to no difficulty in hearing and accepting as true the gobbledy-gook that comes out of the mouth of some human being like Jane Roberts, Ruth Montgomery, or the aforementioned Rev. Neusom. This is tragic, if you stop to consider the fact that none of these beings bother to take the time to prove anything. They simply ramble on and on about the plausibility of our inner soul searching for the door to that eternal plane, which unfortunately, due to the darkness of our own thinking, keeps us bound within the chains of our corrupt desires, blah, blah, blah. Sound familiar?

However, every once in a while some entity comes along who has more to talk about than simply the subject of love. After all, that gets old quickly if you stop to think about it, except to those individuals who are so softhearted that they find it very appealing to embrace that emotional side on a moment-by-moment basis.

So out of the mix comes someone like Kryon. Kryon is described by some as God, who is separate from the earth plane or from Mother Earth. Others describe Kryon as a higher intelligence, here to teach humanity the way of love and peace, not just love.

I have to say that this Kryon tends to go out on a limb when speaking of peace. By that I mean that he is willing to speak in more specifics than many of the other entities who simply speak of freedom, fulfillment, and love. Through the person of Lee Carroll, Kryon has spoken to members of the United Nations in the past. In fact, since 1995, "*Kryon was invited to come to New York and channel for the Society of Enlightenment and Transformation (S.E.A.T) ... a member of the United Nations Staff Recreation Council.*"[59]

That's an interesting thing when you stop to consider it. Here is a man, who is said to be the channel for Kryon to speak to humanity, having been invited to the UN and essentially given an audience.

I won't bore you with all the vernacular and verbiage (it's incredible how some of these entities can ramble on and on! You would think higher intelligence would mean an economy of speech, but...nope), but I did find a very interesting tidbit about the Middle East situation, which I thought I'd quote here. You can decide what you think about it.

Now remember, these demons lie. That is their native language; however, this does not mean that everything they say is a lie. It means that they easily mix truth with lies so that it becomes difficult

---

[59] http://kryon.com/k_un.html

for the uninitiated to determine when they are lying and when they are telling the truth.

I have found that quite often, these demons actually relay truth but they wrap it in a package of lies. I've discussed this in one of my previous books and it is fascinating to me to see how much truth they will mix with their lies. People who are already deceived have no problem at all swallowing everything they say, hook, line, and sinker.

In 2009, when Kryon shared his wisdom with the folks at the UN, he spoke of the Middle East problem and what he believed might very well be the solution. Oh, that's another thing they do. They will also caution their listeners about taking their words and statements as FACTS. While they are speaking them, they are facts; however, the responsibility is always on human beings. We make or break the deal, and by presenting it this way they are never seen as liars. If it doesn't come to pass, oh well, it's because there weren't enough humans who believed it or some such nonsense.

Anyway, check out part of Kryon's message in 2009 as he speaks through Lee Carroll:

"It brings me now to the prophecy I've been giving for some time. For it remains strong [the potentials have not changed]. One of the most unusual things that you ever, ever could imagine may happen, and it involves Iran. I will say it again to you as I've said three other times to three other groups. Now I will state it in these halls of the United Nations. Iran may hold the key to the most stable, most profitable, most influential nation in the Middle East. And if this potential is fulfilled, it will be the young people of Iran who will create 'The Great Iranian Revolution'."

Are you starting to see something? Here's more:

"The last thing you're going to see or imagine you would ever see has a strong potential to happen. The potentials are that Iran will actually

invest in the peace of Jerusalem and that their influences and their
funding will begin to have great influence for a solution in Israel - not
just a solution between Israel and those called the Palestinians, but a
greater one that creates solutions with the Islamic states around
them."

Huh? What? Did Kryon just say that there is a great possibility that
Iran itself will be the major promoter of peace in the Middle East?
These statements were made back in November of 2009, which of
course was not that long ago. Last November, Ahmadinejad was
every bit the anti-Semite that he is now. Yet Kryon is telling these
people at the UN that over time, a new generation of Iranians will
rise up and approach the entire problem of the Middle East in a completely different manner.

Kryon has even more to tell us. "*You will see the countries around*
Iran join with Iran, even former enemies. Borders will be relaxed. Even-
tually, it will affect Pakistan and Afghanistan, who won't want to be
left out of the new Middle Eastern union. India will also be involved in a
way that embraces Pakistan in trade like never before. Those who fea-
ture old energy thinking will have no place to hide, for peace will be the
way of it. A brand new idea will emerge that says, 'If we can stop the
traditions of hate now, and teach our children to hope, eventually there
will a group of nations who will only remember what the tensions used
to be, from reading their history books.' It's a quantum generation that
is coming, one who can think ahead, way past their own lives... past
their parents' teaching of old hatred and old ways. This, indeed, is part
of the new rift that will develop between parent and child for the next
50 years in the Middle East."

He also told the people listening that "*This is what we see and it is*
within the lifetime of many here. It may go slower, depending on what
you do. It may go faster, depending on what you do." No prophecy can
be given by these entities without the general disclaimer at the end,
which absolves them of any responsibility. Almighty God - Everlast-

ing Father - Jesus Christ, King of Kings - on the other hand, has specific times and dates and none of His prophecies are dependent upon humanity at all. His will and purposes come to fruition at the EXACT moment He foreordained that they would.

Can we bank on what Kryon tells us? No, we cannot. However, I believe that within all of these statements, there is truth. They see the truth and use it for their own agenda. The young woman in Acts who became the carnival barker for Paul and his companions spoke the truth. What the demon said through the woman was absolutely true: *"These men are the servants of the most high God, which shew unto us the way of salvation."* (Acts 16:17b). The problem was that Paul did not like the idea that a servant of Satan was actually barking out that truth.

So between this and numerous other statements in the New Testament, we know that demons tell the truth. Sometimes, it's what they do NOT say that makes them a liar because of the impression their words give.

So here is Kryon revealing what he says will come to pass in the Middle East. Ultimately, he states that it will be the people in the Middle East that solve the problem of the Middle East! Interesting, isn't it?

Those listening had no clue that this may in fact be the absolute truth. However, Kryon neglected to go into the many details related to that peace and the fact that any brokerage of peace in the Middle East will actually be handled and overseen by Antichrist. Why bother with the details?

What I find even more fascinating than anything Kryon said is the fact that he has actually spoken to groups within the UN; and not just once, but seven times! How does THAT happen? It happens in a world where people want to believe that they are their own god, and that the all-powerful, all-knowing God of the Bible does not really exist at all. That's how it happens.

We will undoubtedly hear much more from entities like Kryon and Archangel Michael, as well as others. In fact, it seems that as time progresses we can expect channeling to become much more readily accepted, until it likely becomes a type of normative way of living. It will in essence become like another news source, from the other worlds to our world.

I am not saying that we should stop what we're doing and start paying attention to the messages of these entities that channel their speeches through human beings. What I AM saying is that we should recognize the fact that these entities are DOING that, and with greater frequency. Moreover, there are more and more people tuning into their messages, wholeheartedly believing and embracing them.

This is where the world is heading, and the difficulty is in keeping this out of the church. Many churches - via the Emergent Church - have been overtaken by it in some form or another. Christians need to be vigilant and, of course, not give heed to these seducing spirits. We must not only NOT be taken in by them, but we must do all that we can to help others understand that the messages they are hearing may have some truth. However, the source of those messages has absolutely no interest in our welfare. They wish to deceive in order to overcome.

We must warn, whether they listen or not.

— 41 —

Grave Influences

(Blogged: 05/18/2010)

The opening sentences of this book are interesting. *"We've lost the culture war. I wish I could tell you otherwise and go happily along with the many Christians who still think we can recapture America, return to our moral and spiritual roots, and revitalize our wayward institutions. But I can't, and someone needs to tell you – loudly and clearly. My job is not to be optimistic or pessimistic but to be realistic."*

And with those words, Brannon Howse is off and running in his book titled *Grave Influences*. Once you start reading, it is difficult to stop reading because each enthralling chapter takes you to the next one and they all connect in one way or another.

Grave Influences is a small hardback book, measuring 6.25" x 4.5" x 1". It contains 23 chapters spread out over 368 pages. The subtitle of Howse's book is "21 Radicals and Their Worldviews that Rule America from the Grave." Each of the 23 chapters is part of a specific section, one of five (though the TOC inadvertently lists them as Part 1, 2, 2, 3, 5):

- Part 1 – Things Are Worse Than You Thought
- Part 2 – Brought to You By the Occult and Pagan Spirituality
- Part 3 – Compliments of the Apostate Church
- Part 4 – Courtesy of the Educational Establishment
- Part 5 – And Now from the Government-Corporate Complex

Howse begins by pointing out that attempting to reclaim the culture is futile. It has already been lost. What needs to be done is to focus on reclaiming the church. Unless you've been living in a cave, or simply refuse to accept things as they are, you have no doubt seen a downturn in the way of the church. Of course, we are talking about the visible church, not the invisible church. The visible church – comprised of authentic believers (wheat) and authentic unbelievers posing as Christians (tares) – is on a crash course to hell.

The one thing that can cause a slowdown in giving up ground to the enemy is to understand how the enemy has worked since the 1880s in this country. What has been interesting is to see all of these people thrown together in one book, their secrets lying naked before us. It is somewhat easy to consider Alice Bailey or any of the other radicals by themselves. Though we understand Bailey's impact in the area of occult teachings, it is only when we see Bailey in connection with the 20 other radicals that Howse highlights that we begin to fully appreciate (and not in a good sense) just how massively complex the effort has been by Satan to bring about his kingdom on earth.

When these 21 radicals are taken together, the full scale of Satan's scheme is clearly seen and graphically understood. In fact, finishing Howse's book is a bit breathtaking because of the realization of just how organized the assault has been on society.

Grave Influences brings to the fore the reality that we are now facing and how we arrived at this point. It is impossible to come away from this book without comprehending that the effort has always been to create a one-world government with a one-world religion right next to it. Ever since God confused languages and cultures during the time of the Tower of Babel, Satan has continuously worked to bring all of humanity together in an effort to not only recreate the Tower, but do so on a far grander scale.

Over the past ten to twenty years, English has become the global language. Yes, people still speak their own language, and in Europe they often speak more than one. Yet nation after nation has undertaken to learn English. Apart from the third world tribes that literally live in prehistoric conditions in 2010, is there a nation whose citizens do not speak English? It is not that people could not or did not communicate before this, but because English has become a dominant global language, it has made the process of communicating that much easier.

Over the past forty years or so, technology has made it possible to communicate through the air, wirelessly. I still remember the first cell phone I bought my wife. It looked like an actual (old fashioned) phone with a cord that connected to a "bag" that was where the battery was stored. It was larger than her shoulder purse! Yet at the time it was impressive. Now, of course, cell phones have gotten much smaller and far more powerful than any predecessor has been.

In the 1970s, I recall the first personal computers (PCs), which were DOS-based and had black screens, white letters and no bells or whistles. There was no such thing as the Internet because Al Gore had not yet "invented" it. Jump ahead to today and we see that everything has gotten smaller and faster, and what would we actually do without the Internet? We can literally see a news story halfway around the world on our phones or computers in less time than it takes a newspaper to report on it. I'm frankly surprised that newspapers are still around.

So we see that our world has changed, and it has changed drastically. There is no going back, and as we look to the future we can see that we are picking up speed as we go. Satan knows that his time is limited. The Creation has just about had it, groaning under the weight of the curse from the fall.

Once we understand the background of our society and the technology that has enabled us to make such quantum jumps, it becomes far easier to gain an awareness of where the 21 radicals fit into the picture and how they have helped move things along.

Communitarianism

What is striking is some of the verbiage that Howse introduces to the reader. "Communitarianism" is a light version of Communism. *"[Communitarianism] opposes both authoritarianism and individualism, and promotes instead a social organization that is governed by policies designed by civil society to limit individual freedom as required for the benefit of the community."*[60]

Does this recall for you President Obama's comment to Joe the Plumber during his campaign for election where he essentially stated that he wanted to spread the wealth around? The tragic thing, of course, is that in any system like this the rich get richer and the middle class evaporates into oblivion, so that only two classes remain: the rich and the poor. Of course, everyone is poor on the same scale.

---

[60] Brannon Howse Grave Influences (Worldview Weekend Publishing; 2009), 29

There always has to be someone to rule over the poor, and that is the job of the rich.

Howse lists six main worldviews which govern societies throughout the globe and even societies within societies:

- Biblical Christianity
- Secular Humanism
- Cosmic Humanism (New Age)
- Islam
- Postmodernism
- Marxism/Leninism

Of the six listed, only one as we know contains truth because it is built on truth: Biblical Christianity. The others are all lies of the enemy, yet how many of the world's citizens have readily bought into these lies? Most have.

Howse also indicates that when a nation *"has rejected the God of the Bible [the] people begin to worship creation rather than the Creator God."*[61] Paul speaks of this, of course, in Romans 1. People who insist on dismissing the God of Creation eventually get their wish and wind up worshiping anything that is not God. Howse continues by stating that *"By destroying the influence of Biblical Christianity within a culture, globalists remove their main obstacle to socialism, radical environmentalism, active euthanasia through socialized medicine, compulsory abortion, the end of parental authority, the elimination of an armed populace, private property, homosexuality (homosexuals are favored because they do not reproduce and add to world population), and the indoctrination of our children with their worldview."*[62] Take a moment to go back and read that quote. It is mindboggling in its scope, and it is happening in society the world over.

---

[61] Brannon Howse Grave Influences (Worldview Weekend Publishing; 2009), 35
[62] Brannon Howse Grave Influences (Worldview Weekend Publishing; 2009), 36

Of course, one of the huge pushes has been and continues to be population control. This is neatly tied into environmentalism. People should save the earth by using less, even if that means that some alive today suffer and die. The goal is to have food, plants, and animals for the next generation. This of course makes no sense, because we are literally being told that it is fine for people living now to die through starvation or something else in order that future generations will have food available to them. It is nonsense. Yet because it has an air of selflessness, people adopt it greedily. Go figure.

There is also a growing trend to blame Christianity for all the world's ills. Just Christianity alone. Not even Judaism takes the blame as does Christianity, though Jews do not escape the world's wrath.

Howse believes (and I agree) that as America has increasingly turned her back on Israel, God has increasingly turned His back on America. This is roundly denied by many within Reformed, Covenant and Preterist circles, yet it appears to be biblical fact. As we continue to deny rights to Israel, we are asking for God's judgment. The two go hand in hand and judgment is unavoidable. It is interesting that the Old Testament is filled with example after example of just how God judged nations who rejected or triumphed over Israel. While He certainly used some of these nations to overthrow Israel (as a form of judgment on Israel for their waywardness), the nations that attacked Israel were culpable for their actions and were eventually "rewarded" for the same.

Over the past fifteen to twenty years, we have seen each administration pull back from Israel a bit more, making it easier for her enemies to gain more of a foothold in Israel. We now have an administration that has not only thrown Israel under the bus but denies doing it, believing that by doing so the world will be convinced that President Obama is actually in support of Israel. Granted, much of the world believes, with the Arab nations, that Israel should not be there in the Middle East, and certainly not as a sovereign nation. Those of us who support Israel (on the grounds that that Land is GOD'S Land, and Jerusalem is HIS center of the world) know that the problem lies deep within anti-Semitism. Who is the greatest foe of the Jew? Satan - and this is certainly the demeanor he has brought to the fore in virtually all nations and people. He hates the Jews because salvation comes from them in Jesus. They are the people he has no patience for, and though he hates all of God's Creation, he hates the Jew the most.

Because of President Obama's policies, what are we seeing now? We are seeing a President whose support for Iran and other Arab countries seemingly knows no bounds. If he could get away with it, he would undoubtedly force Israel to give up at least half of Jerusalem along with all of the West Bank, which includes the Mountains of Israel. He knows he cannot do that, so he bides his time, playing the game of politics.

He is the first president who has come out and stated that Iran should be allowed to have nuclear capabilities. By doing so, he throws Israel's safety to the wind, proving that not only does he care less about their safety, but is in full support of Iran's desire to destroy Israel. The game that President Ahmadinejad and President Obama play, as if they really do not like one another, is merely a game of politics and nothing more.

Howse makes another great point when he states, "*Sadly, as America goes under, Christians who were committed only to the reconstruction of America or building a Christian America will retreat from the culture. This is not how Christians should respond. If indeed God is judging America (and I believe He is), and if His judgment is going to greatly increase (and I believe it will), then we need to use His judgment as an opportunity to preach the Gospel to the unsaved.*"[63] Frankly, I could not agree more. Whenever God sends judgment in Scripture, there is

---

[63] Brannon Howse Grave Influences (Worldview Weekend Publishing; 2009), 55

always opportunity to spread the salvation message because it is during times of judgment that people begin to look up.

For too long Christians have been attempting to modify America, trying desperately to get her back to the days of old when right was right and wrong was wrong. Those days are gone forever. We cannot and should not be waging a culture war. We desperately need to be about the Lord's business, and His business is not in saving nations, but saving lives of the lost.

Alice Bailey

Howse begins highlighting the radicals that have made this country what it is (under God's watchful eye). He begins with Alice Bailey and her publishing company, Lucifer Publishing Company, which eventually became Lucis Trust.

Most of us are undoubtedly familiar with Bailey and her occult connection. She wrote 24 books, but it's actually more accurate to say she wrote down what she was told, as in a form of dictation. Maybe she was allowed to put things in her own words, but whether that is the case or not, the medium she said she gained this information from – the Tibetan – guided her into filling thousands of pages of text. Of course, we understand that the Tibetan is none other than some demonic entity whose job it was to prevail on Bailey so that she would come to believe that the "truth" she was being given would begin a new age. A new age it has created, but to what end?

Reading some of Bailey's words is not too different from reading books by individuals who believe in Pleiadians or other alien entities. Bailey saw these beings as Ascended Masters, but today's New Agers see them as aliens from much higher and more advanced civilizations. It doesn't matter really, because Christians understand them to be powers, principalities and spiritual beings opposed to God who exist in the spiritual realm. It has always boggled my mind that people will take the word of these beings for granted, yet have tremendous difficulty believing that God exists and that He could have written a book. These beings offer virtually no proof for anything they say, yet because they bestow extraordinary feelings of love, self-worth and freedom upon human beings, then what they say must be true without question.

It is also interesting the way Howse provides the contrast and comparison between what he calls "The Public Face of Bailey's Private God." People like Bailey act exactly like their god, Satan. He is the master deceiver, presenting himself as an angel of light, yet he is the epitome of wickedness. This is what he passes onto his followers: the ability to deceive through an angelic front.

In truth, Bailey has been a strong foundation with which Satan has begun building his kingdom by toppling God's standard of morality in favor of his own. This was really the first stone in the entire edifice of Satan's new Tower of Babel, and it has been upon this stone that the phrase "new world order" is intoned. It is fairly commonplace to hear that phrase used throughout the world. As Howse points out, it does not matter if the people using the phrase are politicians, educators, religious leaders, or corporate CEOs. What matters is that the mindset of the world is being directed to that one playing field where a supposed order, which will emerge from the chaos, will bring in the utopia everyone has dreamed of since it was first lost in the Garden of Eden.

Everything from the time since Bailey has been leading to a one-world government and one-world religion. Of course, unbeknownst to most, this government will ultimately be headed up by Satan's own son, the Antichrist, and the religion will come to be understood to mean worshiping him as god. Satan will have his dominance for a time at least in this earthly sphere, as he does in the realm of the air now.

Howse points out that Bailey supported the UN, and it is not surprising that the UN adopted her outlook, mentality, and beliefs. Over the long haul since the time of Bailey, three essential worldviews have merged:

- Evolutionary humanism
- Hindu pantheism
- Occultism

Who does not see these individual strands at work in societies throughout the globe? Together, they create an attitude that devalues human beings and elevates a strong global government. They are pushed for the good of all, instead of the rights of the individual.

Helen Schucman

Schucman's work *A Course in Miracles* was resurrected, or at least brought to the fore, by none other than Oprah Winfrey and Marianne Williamson. For the longest time, any author who appeared on Oprah's show and wound up being endorsed by Oprah increased book sales by 100 fold or more. *Course* is a New Age tech book, presenting point after point of what it means to know God, what it means to be God, and what it means to live as God.

Oprah Winfrey literally came out of nowhere. I remember seeing her in the movie, "The Color Purple." Then all of a sudden, she's a talk show host - and not a particularly great one either. Somehow, she became popular seemingly overnight. Personally, I believe her near-instant popularity derived from the fact that she adopted and embraced numerous forms of New Age thought and spirituality. The demon gods were pleased and gave her wealth, admiration, and loads of success. It is just uncanny when one person gains that much from nothing. We have at least two other examples of that as well, in the author of the Harry Potter series as well as another author, who wrote the Twilight series. Both of these series deal in aspects of the new age and occult. Both of the authors came out of nowhere, complete unknowns. Yet today they are rich, famous, and their books have become either TV series or movies or both. How does that happen? It happens when people give themselves over to the demons who present themselves as Ascended Masters or something else.

Howse points out that for Oprah specifically, she entered into the New Age realm after rejecting her Baptist roots. Howse points out: *"she rejected the doctrine of her Baptist church because she didn't like it when her pastor claimed God is a jealous God. The notion of divine jealousy offended her, and 'that's when the search for something more than doctrine started to stir within me'."*[64]

It is incredible how often I hear church people rejecting out of hand some doctrine or truth in the Bible because they do not like it. In cases such as this, that individual is setting themselves up as their own authority, and ultimately as their own god. Their rejection of some Scriptural truth is normally predicated upon the fact that they simply do not understand it, nor can they see that truth from God's perspective, which is the only perspective worth anything. In essence, then, people like Oprah are not only guilty of calling God a liar, but are contributing to the fact that they have encouraged multitudes of others to do the same thing!

Julius Wellhausen

Next on the list is Julius Wellhausen, who is known for his "higher criticism" of the Bible, which led to his rejection of the fact that Genesis, Exodus, Leviticus, and Deuteronomy were written by Moses. He points out differences in verbiage, vernacular and other things to make his case. It was jumped on by other critics who were itching to find some way to castigate biblical truth. This rationalization created by Wellhausen and adopted by others in Germany's society became the reason why the Bible and Christianity in Europe began to change into something it is not.

---

[64] Brannon Howse Grave Influences (Worldview Weekend Publishing; 2009), 79

All of this led to a type of humanism, in which the Bible was brought low (as was the God the Bible purported to point to) and man was elevated to a supreme status. It was this humanism that led to the success of Adolph Hitler and other dictators like Mussolini.

Kierkegaard and Nietzsche

Søren Kierkegaard and Friedrich Nietzsche are well known names within religious and philosophical circles. Kierkegaard, known for his existentialist outlook (after rejecting Christianity), believed there was no absolute morality. The idea is actually nothing new, since we know that it was scoffed at by Pontius Pilate ("What is truth?") in response to Jesus' point about truth. Nietzsche is not only known for declaring that God had died (God is dead), which of course presupposes that He existed in the first place, but he came to hate Christianity so much that he referred to himself as the "Antichrist."

With Kierkegaard and Nietzsche the stage was set for apostasy, which we see thriving around us today. Howse makes the logical connection between the beginnings of this apostasy with the two men just referenced and the Emergent Church of today. In point of fact, there is little difference, if any.

If truth is subjective, as Kierkegaard believed, then anything goes. There is no standard by which everything is judged in this world. It is all up for grabs. It is clear to see this all around us and even within parts of the visible church. If there is no true moral standard, then obviously the Bible should not be considered *the* standard, but possibly only *a* standard. It is left up to the interpretation of each person to decide for themself.

One of the biggest pushes within the Emergent Church, aside from de-emphasizing the inerrancy of Scripture, is a socializing of the gospel. All one has to do is read through just one of Brian McLaren's books and it becomes very clear what his views are on the subject.

McLaren, together with others like Tony Campolo, preaches a different gospel, that Paul would say is no gospel at all.

They believe that the gospel comes alive when it is seen in the lives of professing Christians who are concerned about society (though it does not have to be seen in Christians for a person to BE a Christian, according to Tony Campolo). Do people have enough to eat? Do they have places to live and/or sleep? Do they have jobs? In other words, the emphasis should be on improving the conditions of society, rather than presenting truth that will help a person gain eternal life. While authentic Christians obviously need to be doing what they can to help the poor of society, the idea that people need salvation should never be ignored or relegated to some back room somewhere, only to be brought out as a last resort.

In truth, the forces which have been at work behind these individuals have worked hard and diligently to create a society in which everything is literally turned upside down. Instead of valuing human beings because we are made in God's image, humans are seen as valueless. It is the entirety of society which has value, not the individuals that make up that society. Because of this, abortion on demand, murdering the elderly and infirm (called nicely enough *euthanasia*, or "youth-in-asia"), and even going so far as to place animals above human beings as some cultures have done, like India often becomes common practice. Starvation is rampant there, but it is forbidden to eat a cow because it could be a relative who has simply been reincarnated as a bovine.

This trend is absolutely absurd, but such is the way things go when Satan is allowed to turn God's Creation upside down with himself at the top and the pinnacle of God's Creation (man) on the bottom.

Educational Establishment

As far as the educational establishment goes, there are some well-known names there too. John Dewey, the Frankfurt School, Betty

Friedan, William James, Alfred Kinsey, and others dot the educational landscape. What astounded me was the connection of almost every one of these individuals with Socialism or Communism.

Dewey was heavily involved in the influence of the American educational system. Perhaps the most astounding piece of information Howse reveals is the peculiar interests of Edward R. Murrow!

In fact, what I frequently heard myself saying as I read Howse's book was, "No way!" or something similar. In truth, there appears to be very little difference between the Republican and Democratic parties. While some Republicans are truly conservative, the GOP itself is very one-world oriented, as is the Democratic party. Both have been pushing American society toward the believed utopia of the one-world government through Socialism.

What has always amazed me is that though Socialism has never worked anywhere in the world, people continue to talk it up, believing that it is the only real way to go so that people are treated fairly. One church-going individual told me that he firmly believed Jesus was a Socialist, and he pointed to the early church in Acts. Here, they sold what they had and gave it to the body so that everyone in the local body could benefit. This has nothing to do with the concept of Socialism and everything to do with the love authentic Christians are to have for one another.

The reason neither Socialism nor Communism works is that people are what we are; fallen, corrupt human beings, incapable of living altruistically.

If/when the United States becomes a Socialist nation, three things will happen:

- The poor will get poorer
- The rich will get richer
- The middle class will evaporate

The rich folks will never have a problem in either Communism or Socialism because they rise above it. The people who are not wealthy are the ones who are grouped together to live off the hand of the government. What rich person would not want a Socialist or Communist agenda, as long as their riches stayed where they are - in their wallets?

Does anyone honestly believe that if this country becomes Socialistic that people like the Kennedys, or the Bushes, or even President Obama are going to be the first to step up to the line and spread their wealth around? This is not what Obama meant when he stated that during his campaign. What he meant was that he wanted to take from the middle and upper middle class and spread what they get out to the poor, thereby putting people on an even playing field. Even when the rich go bankrupt, it isn't long before they can climb right back on top. William Randolph Hearst did this by borrowing one million dollars from his mistress. In short order, he was back where he had been before he lost all of his money. No such thing exists for the poor and middle class.

Benjamin Bloom

Benjamin Bloom is another individual Howse highlights, and anyone who has ever taught in the public schools knows of "Bloom's Taxonomy." According to Howse, what Bloom and others did through standardized testing - why it was started and how it is used even to today - is not what we are told.

I have to shake my head in disbelief because I spent ten years in the public schools teaching grades four through six. The standardized tests were ridiculous at that point in time, and the process of using Whole Language to teach reading and writing was even more ridiculous. I could see using Whole Language to teach spoken language because it is a very fast way to pick up language, much like being immersed in the language. However, Whole Language has absolutely no capacity to teach kids writing, reading, or spelling. It's just not part of the system. Is it any wonder we have young adults today who cannot read, analyze, write, or spell?

Karl Marx

Marx, like other Socialists and Communists, believed many things very strongly, including the idea that there is nothing higher than man. A quick look at the Emergent Church and its beliefs brings out that fact even there. The Emergent Church has made Christianity man-centered, and what the Emergent Church has done for Christianity, Karl Marx and others have done for corporate America.

Most may be familiar with the ten facets of Communism, but how many of us are aware of the 45 goals of Communism? I was not, and Howse brings those out. It is also unbelievably shocking to realize how much our own government has adopted nearly all of these goals!

You see, according to Howse, the goal of people like Marx, John Maynard Keynes, Sigmund Freud, Margaret Sanger and others has been to infiltrate America and destroy it from within. In fact, everyone mentioned in Howse' book has had a hand in that, whether they were/are actively aware of it or not.

The tragic truth is that the way this has been done to the United States would have required the constant vigilance of sentries placed in every area of society in order to notice and then flesh out the perpetrators. This was not done and for good reason. It would have been impossible.

Satan has undertaken (under God's watchful eye) to overthrow America, because of the fact that this country was founded on Christian principles and because of our long history of support for Israel. However, instead of coming at us in a true frontal assault that would have been noticed, he did the more intelligent thing and placed people in various roles throughout America's society. Taken togeth-

er, as each person began carving out their niche, endeavoring to eradicate this or that belief - which by itself may not have seemed like or
amounted to much - the amount of energy that the devil has spent
overthrowing America from within is nearly unbelievable. If not for
the fact that the Bible warns us what life will be like in the end times,
it would be very difficult to believe.

Yet this is what has occurred, and most of it right under our noses.
Might does not always make right. Sometimes, insidiousness is the
best way to go, and if we look back through the pages of history, with
the help of Howse's book, we come away with much more than a
glimpse of what has transpired. What we see today are the results of
Satan's diabolical web that he has spent untold amounts of time
spinning.

By the time Alice Bailey came onto the scene, Satan was able to work
faster and smarter, and things picked up speed from there. Don't get
me wrong, I'm not high-fiving Satan by any means. I am simply saying that he has been allowed (the operative word here) by God to do
what he can do to bring prophetic truth to fruition.

What we are seeing today is the result of it. Though the culture of
America is indeed lost, Howse indicates that not all is lost. In fact, as
far as God is concerned, nothing is lost. Instead of hiding in a closet
or underground shelter somewhere, Christians should be up and out
witnessing for God, in order that the lost individuals that will turn to
Him for salvation will do so in a timely manner.

I cannot imagine living during the time of the apostles. What they
and authentic believers of that day went through was horrific. Yet,
God saved lost members of humankind. Though the world was falling apart, God was at work, bringing multitudes to Him for eternal
life.

Our world is falling apart. Creation is more than groaning. In many ways, with the recent rash of earthquakes and volcanoes, it appears to be vomiting. We have a president who is the most Socialistic of them all and seems not to care one iota what anyone thinks of him. Not only is he callous, but he is narcissistic to a level that surprises many.

If we focused on what is happening in this world we would likely live in constant dread. However, we do not have to do this, because the authentic Christian knows that God has already gained the victory.

Christians must endeavor to use the times to kick it up a notch or two when it comes to evangelizing the lost. We can no longer sit on our soft, comfortable sofas, believing that someone else will do it. Time is short and we are moving ahead at such speed that one can only wonder how things can remain attached to this world.

God does not want us in fear. He wants to us to understand what is happening around us so that we will take the Great Commission much more seriously. Brannon Howse's book is a must-read for every authentic believer. It takes the reader through the process by which this country (and eventually the world) has been overrun by demonic activity in the areas of the occult, the apostate church, education, and corporations. *Grave Influences* is a telling book that unveils how the enemy of our souls has worked in this nation's history.

As Howse says, this can be the Christians' finest hour. I concur, so let's get to it!

42

And They Say Christians Are Intolerant!

(Blogged: 05/21/2010)

C hristianity constantly gets a bad rap for being "intolerant."
This is in spite of the fact that this country was founded on
Christian principles and many of our founding fathers were
Christians or deists. The reality is that what is happening not only in
this country but throughout the world is an intolerance exercised
toward Christians and Christianity.

If you are a "Christian" who believes that Christianity is good for you
but may not be the way for someone else, you are exempt from this

growing intolerance. Of course, you are probably exempt from salvation as well, since you disagree with Jesus Himself on that score.

Here in America, it has become fashionable (thanks largely to the Obama Administration) to view even fanatical Muslims as downtrodden and misunderstood. Countries throughout the world are rolling out the red carpets for Muslims. They believe that if they befriend Muslims, terrorists will look elsewhere for targets. This is false and it will be seen as so eventually, but for now people live with false hope that jihadist Muslims (terrorists) will ease up on their fanaticism and stop killing people who leave THEM alone. It won't happen. It simply proves that people who do this know nothing of the Qur'an or Islam. They do not realize that the Qur'an refers to non-Muslims as infidels. Infidels should be killed according to jihadist Muslims.

I just received an emailed news bulletin from *Prophecine.com* in which we read firsthand what Muslims think of non-Muslims:

"Iraq (MNN) — Muslim extremists are warning Christians in Iraq to leave the country immediately or risk violent death. The threat mentions believers in Baghdad and Mosul--already troubled areas."

Voice of the Martyrs reports that an Iraqi bishop received a letter from the General Secretariat of the Islam Supporters warning Christians in Baghdad and other areas to "*leave the country of Muslims (Iraq) for good and immediately in the form of mass transmigration.*" It continues: "*You can follow Pope Benedict XVI and his followers who have disfigured humanity and Islam...There's no more room for you, infidels, among the Iraqi Muslims. Our swords shall be placed upon your necks and the necks of your followers and other Christians residing in Mosul.*"

Jerry Dykstra of Open Doors USA confirms the hostility against followers of Christ. "*Christians are just being further marginalized, as we've heard the reports of random violence. It comes down to this: Christians there are being targeted because of their faith in Jesus Christ."*

Sunni Muslim insurgents have frequently targeted members of Iraq's Christian minority. Iraq's current government is Shiite-led. As a result, Christians have found that they are in the crossfire. Many thousands have already fled to neighboring countries.

Christians make up roughly 3.3 percent of Iraq's people. It's estimated that the remnant church is well below the 500,000 believers who were in Iraq before the Iraq war.

Still, Christians in Iraq remain strong in their faith. Dykstra says, *"the Gospel is going forward, and people are coming to Christ. People have to meet more in secret, but the good thing is that when they meet in secret, they're praising the Lord and lifting up their needs."*

Pray for ministry opportunities for churches and Christian relief organizations working in Iraq.

Teams have to work carefully. Dykstra says even though the church is isolated, *"Fortunately, Open Doors has put programs in place in literacy training and praying with them that will help Christians."*

Iraq is 17th on the Open Doors World Watch List of top 50 countries known for their persecution of Christians.

I do not see an ounce of tolerance in that news bulletin, do you? What I see are jihadist Muslims who are threatening to execute (by beheading) non-Muslims who remain in their country. Iraq believes in Sharia Law and as it applies to infidels, it is fine to kill them. Allah approves of it.

I have said this before, but last year throughout the world over 150,000 Christians were martyred for their faith, and it looks like things are just starting to heat up, too.

Here in America, we do not kill Muslims. They are welcome, as long as they do not break the laws of the land. In fact, anyone who can legally enter this country is welcome, with the same proviso. In Iraq, it is very possible to be killed just for being a Christian.

In Great Britain, people have recently been arrested for "offending" Muslims and their beliefs by stating Allah is not god. When considering the last days, the coming Tribulation and the atmosphere during that time, it becomes clear that a type of Sharia Law will become the law of the world, at least for a time. Under the leadership of Antichrist, anyone who does not worship him will be executed.

When a Christian repeats what Jesus says in John 14:6 about Him being the way, the truth and the life and that no one comes to the Father except through Him, that Christian is accused of being intolerant and offensive. However, what if there IS only one way and it IS through Jesus Christ? In that case, the Christian is repeating *truth*, which means that *truth* becomes offensive and intolerant.

Kids are raised to believe that it's only sticks and stones that can inflict real pain, and they should ignore it when being called names or when they come across someone who is intolerant in word. Yet in the adult world, this is not the case. Tell people today that homosexuality is wrong and you could possibly go to jail (it's already happened in Great Britain). Tell people that Jesus Christ is the only way to receive salvation and be accused of being intolerant. If you happen to be a Christian living in Iraq, then you'd also be prepared to give up your life too.

Let's face it, the only hate crime that is legal anymore is one that bashes Christians. We can be called hatemongers, intolerant, and more. We can be despised because of our audacity in believing that we have the truth and no one else does. It is coming to a time when authentic Christians will be killed for their faith. Does that seem right? Does that seem equitable?

It's certainly one way to separate the sheep from the goats, the professing Christians from the authentic. We excuse Iraq on the grounds that they are living in the dark ages. We expect countries like Iraq to come against Christians. Will our president come out and condemn such actions? He likely will not because he is too busy courting Muslim countries, joining societies and associations that condemn Israel, and in general doing whatever he cares to do to promote his own Muslim agenda.

Intolerance against Christians is fast becoming the norm from all groups. We do nothing except repeat what is taught in the Bible. Muslims do the same, and many of them - jihadists - take it to the extreme by killing innocent people in the name of Allah. Authentic Christians do not do that. We preach the gospel. We do what we can to feed the hungry and clothe the naked.

If I believe I have salvation through Jesus Christ and that it is the only way TO salvation, how could I not share this with others? But in doing so, I am now classified as intolerant or worse.

I came across this comment on another blog recently and it fits here perfectly: *"When covering the different civil wars and conflicts between nations, if the news agencies identified the religions or political ideologies of each side, it would quickly become clear that almost all of them are between Muslims and someone else. And in almost all of them, Muslims instigated the conflict but consider themselves merely "defending" Islam."*[65]

---

[65] http://www.citizenwarrior.com/2007/11/muslims-are-still-going-on-slave-raids.html

And for those who say that there is no coming Tribulation and no Antichrist, I say wake up! Wake up! For more information on dhimmitude, go here: http://www.citizenwarrior.com/2007/10/dhimma.html

43

Israel Is Always Wrong

(Blogged: 06/02/2010)

It doesn't matter what Israel does, she is always wrong, according to the vast majority of people in the world. Take this recent issue over the flotilla situation off the shores of Gaza. We are all pretty much aware of the situation: Israeli commandos rappelled down onto the deck of the ship headed for Gaza because Israel was concerned that among the contents of the humanitarian aid were weapons that would go directly to Hamas.

It is interesting to note a couple of things. First, Israel had previously offered that the ship could be unloaded at an Israeli dock and Israel guaranteed safe passage of all humanitarian aid to Gaza. It was roundly refused. Second, in spite of the fact that the Israeli commandos came onboard the ship with PAINTBALL guns and pistols, it is obvious that the "humanitarians" onboard picked up anything they could find - short iron pipes or poles, knives, batons, etc. Some even managed to take away a pistol from one of the commandos. During the event, a total of 9 people were killed.

Aaron Kline noted, "*Prior to its violent confrontation with Israeli commandos, the commander of the six-ship pro-Palestinian flotilla announced participants were planning to use 'resistance' and declared the ship's activists wanted to die as "martyrs" more than they wanted to reach the Gaza Strip, according to Hamas television.*"

Read more at: www.bible-prophecy-today.com/#ixzz0pjxa9DyS.

It is clear that Hamas has and will try anything to smuggle weapons into Gaza. Many of their tunnels have been uncovered in which they actually dug under parts of Israel to get their weapons in the hands of their comrades in Gaza. Netanyahu stated recently, "*Hamas continues to arm. Iran continues to send weapons to Gaza. Iran's rockets are intended to hit Israeli communities, not just in the vicinity of Gaza, but in Tel Aviv and Jerusalem. It is our right according to International law to prevent arms smuggling to Gaza and that is why the naval blockade was put in place. The flotilla intended to break the blockade, not to bring in emergency supplies which we allow to reach Gaza.*"[66]

All of this means nothing to people who stand against Israel. It is obvious that they are fully deluded into thinking that Israel is actually the problem in the Middle East, when it is clear (for anyone who knows the actual history of that region) that not only is Israel surrounded by Islamic and Muslim nations, but all of them would prefer to see Israel eradicated off the Middle Eastern map! The terrifying truth is that if Israel allowed ANY ship to get through their blockade,

---

[66] http://www.jpost.com/Home/Article.aspx?id=177286

more weapons would wind up in the hands of Hamas. It is that simple, yet the world continues to deny it.

Israel has promised that it will continue with the blockade and I think that is the only rational way to go. How the world can hypocritically thumb their collective noses at Israel as if many of these countries bordering Israel do not harbor terrorist regimes is unconscionable. However, this is the way things are going because in this day and age it seems that no one can think analytically anymore.

I read this morning that even the press was behaving like idiots and asking asinine questions. Of course, that is not a real eye-opener since they seem to major in idiocy, however, when the press actually begins to think that this ship moving toward Gaza was in fact humanitarian and ONLY humanitarian, they are guilty of being naive at best and absolute morons at worse. I don't think anyone denies that the ship contained items that were absolutely for humanitarian purposes. Only the shallow and mindless believe that humanitarian items were the ONLY items on that ship, no weapons of any kind or anything that would give Hamas the edge over Israel.

The world turns a blind eye and a deaf ear to the fact that in SPITE of everything that Israel has done over the past forty years or so, rockets continue to be launched INTO Israel from outside forces and many of them are from the Gaza strip. For Israel simply to shut their eyes and throw up their hands at a ship sailing toward Gaza would be the height of naiveté. Israel has every right to protect themselves, and more power to them for doing it.

Unlike the United States, where we have a president who buddies up to the hypocrite from Mexico (where illegal immigration laws are FAR more harsh than anything in the United States), bows to every other world leader as if he is subservient, and who seems intent on chipping away at the freedoms citizens in this country have enjoyed since this nation's founding, Israel's government wants to protect its citizens. Israel is a small country, yet the world's eyes are constantly focused on that corner of the world. We are quickly and consistently moving toward a major showdown, and who knows what the triggering point will actually be?

Israel deserves praise for their position against all odds. The world needs to drop its anti-Semitic stance and endeavor to start treating Israel as the sovereign nation that she is in 2010. In spite of the odds, she became a nation in 1948. Over denouncements and vitriol, she has continued to exist even way past the Six-Day War. There is SOMETHING - or is it SOMEONE? - who keeps Israel alive and kicking. Any other country would have gone down the drain long ago.

One day, a number of nations will decide that Israel has been around long enough. They will band together to eliminate Israel's presence. They will move on her, endeavoring to rid the Middle East of Israel and the Jewish presence. However, they will be dealt with by God Himself. What people continually forget is that Israel is GOD'S Land and Jerusalem is GOD'S holy city. It is no more a bargaining chip for peace than Ahmadinejad is not anti-Semitic.

The world needs not only to stop standing against Israel, but needs to start supporting her. While the protests continue in the streets here in America, with people bemoaning the fact that U.S. tax dollars are helping Israel and the protesting taxpayers are sick of it, MY tax dollars are paying for millions of abortions every year and I am sick of THAT!

The truth of the matter is that as hard as the world tries, they will NOT be able to get rid of Israel. It is the thorn in the flesh that will not go away.

"This is the word of the LORD concerning Israel. The LORD, who stretches out the heavens, who lays the foundation of the earth, and who forms the spirit of man within him, declares: 'I am going to make

Jerusalem a cup that sends all the surrounding peoples reeling. Judah will be besieged as well as Jerusalem. On that day, when all the nations of the earth are gathered against her, I will make Jerusalem an im-movable rock for all the nations. All who try to move it will injure themselves. On that day I will strike every horse with panic and its rid-er with madness,' declares the LORD. 'I will keep a watchful eye over the house of Judah, but I will blind all the horses of the nations. Then the leaders of Judah will say in their hearts, 'The people of Jerusalem are strong, because the LORD Almighty is their God'." Zechariah 12:1-5

Whether the world likes it or not, Israel is fully under God's control. One day, the Jews of that land will realize who has been their protection for these many generations and those of the Remnant will be saved. All who have come against Israel will suffer the consequences of touching the apple of God's eye. Better clear a path, because when that day happens the Lord will take vengeance for all who have wronged Israel. He will do this not because of the Jewish people, but because of His own honor.

44

Mosque at Ground Zero? Really?

(Blogged: 06/07/2010)

Things are beginning to heat up against the idea of a mosque being built at Ground Zero. While many Muslims like the idea, Imam Feisal Abdul Rauf, the chief sponsor of the Cordoba House mosque project in the shadow of Ground Zero, insists that the $150 million mosque is meant to heal the wounds of 9/11. He stated, *"We've approached the community because we want this to be an example of how we are cooperating with the members of the community."*[67]

---

[67] http://www.israelnationalnews.com/News/News.aspx/137919

Most people are not buying the flimsy reasoning. Pamela Geller, executive director of Stop the Islamization of America, said, "*Building a mosque just several blocks away from Ground Zero is an insult and an affront to every single person that was killed on 9/11, to their families, to the first responders and every concerned American who cherishes liberty, democracy and freedom.*"[68]

Other people also spoke about the mosque and related events in the world. James Lafferty of the Virginia Anti-Sharia Task Force, who traveled to New York to speak at the rally, declared, "*3000 pairs of eyes are looking down at us today...These evil, cowardly bastards who took the lives of those proud Americans on 9/11 will be remembered forever and this mosque which represents the triumph of Islamic fanaticism will not be built if we have anything to say. Lafferty received thunderous applause when he said, 'The good people of the USA must also stand in solid unity with the Israel Defense Forces who are waging a war against Hamas terrorism as was evidenced several days ago when they intercepted a Turkish based flotilla of ships whose aim it was to break the Israeli blockade of Gaza. It is the IDF who is on the front lines in the battle against Islamic radicalism and we must support them'.*"[69]

Still other speakers garnered enthusiastic applause and shouts of agreement from the audience. "*Dr. Babu Suseelan, a Hindu human rights activist told the crowd, 'We Hindus and Sikhs have a story to tell. Islamists killed 80 million of us since 700 AD and they continue to kill us. They destroyed 3000 glorious temples and built mosques over them. In the last 60 years, Islamists in Pakistan wiped out infidel Hindu and Sikh populations. At one time we represented 25 percent of the population and now we are less that 1 percent.*

---

[68] http://www.israelnationalnews.com/News/News.aspx/137919
[69] Ibid

"Know this: The 9/11 mosque is not a symbol of understanding. It is a symbol of conquest. Imam Rauf is a master of Taqiyya, which is the use of deception to forward the agenda of Islam. What Faisal Shahzad failed to accomplish in Times Square on May 1st with overt jihad, Imam Rauf will succeed with stealth jihad'."[70]

While some Muslims are busily involved in terrorist activities throughout the world, others are attempting to overthrow governments from within, and the attempt to build a mosque is a case in point. The idea that building a mosque at Ground Zero would somehow heal the wounds caused by 9/11 is the height of lunacy. Expecting people to believe it is ridiculous in and of itself. The mosque would only benefit Islam and the Muslims who would worship there. It would benefit no other group.

I do not hear or read about calls to build a synagogue or a church at Ground Zero. The area should be left as a memorial. If anything related to Islam should be included, it should be information that Islam often incites violent jihad by those Muslims within who believe they are doing Allah a huge favor by defending his name.

As far as I am aware, Islam is the only religion in which people believe it is perfectly acceptable to kill others if they somehow offend their god (Allah) or their prophet (Muhammad). On these grounds alone, it should be clear that Islam is not a religion of peace. It is a religion of intolerance and hatred in which those who disagree with Islam are often executed. All non-Muslims are considered infidels, worthy of death.

In fact, it is not uncommon to hear at least some Muslims describing Christians as "weak" because of how often people take the Lord's Name in vain; yet Christians to do react to that act by killing people.

---

[70] http://www.israelnationalnews.com/News/News.aspx/137919

The Bible says, "Vengeance is Mine, says the Lord. I will repay." We are content to let God take care of it, in His time and in His way.

The God of Christianity is more than capable of avenging Himself for any and all wrongdoing by people on this planet. He did not raise up authentic Christians to pick up the sword and lop heads off people who take His Name in vain, using it as an epithet. We are also not supposed to hijack and fly planes into Islamic buildings or Islamic nations.

The people of Islam will not stop (and have no intention of stopping) until the entire world is Islamic and governed by Sharia Law. Those who resist Islam will be eliminated; it is absolutely that simple. Is it any wonder that the book of Revelation speaks of all the martyrs who will lose their lives through beheading during the Tribulation?

There is no room for a mosque at Ground Zero. Frankly, I do not believe one more mosque should be built in the United States until Islam allows synagogues and churches to be built in Iran and other countries that are Islamic. Turn around is fair play.

When Muslims stop throwing rocks at Jews and Christians who are merely trying to visit the Temple Mount in Jerusalem, then we can sit down and discuss building more mosques in America. Until then, Muslim groups do not need any more tax dollars to build their mosques, run their organizations, and attempt to brainwash the people of the United States with their printed and spoken propaganda.

It is time that we put a halt to Islam's reach in this country, and take back what has been lost.

45

Become a Christian and Die

(Blogged: 06/09/2010)

The year is 2010. Around the world, the threat of Islamic terrorists continues. Recently, plans were discovered that reflected terrorist desire to disrupt the upcoming Soccer Games in Africa. Jihad is still very much alive and well.

Beyond this, Muslims in America want a mosque at Ground Zero because they say it will help "heal" the nation. In Kansas, a Muslim group is taking one city to court in order to have an area of the city cemetery earmarked only for Muslims.

President Obama has some interesting individuals helping him create policies for this nation. People like Pelosi and Reid are fully in Obama's corner, ready to give the man anything he wants. We will see how long they remain in office - all of them.

All of the above, while real and tragic, is not the worst of it.

Christians are routinely touted as being intolerant. This charge is leveled due to the fact that we have the audacity to believe and say that Jesus Christ is the only way to heaven. For some, that is discriminatory and even hateful language. Apparently, Christians are entitled to believe this, but some in the United States want to remove our freedom to say it in public. The way they are attempting to do this is to attempt to pass bills that include anti-hate and anti-discriminatory language thereby making it illegal to voice those types of opinions. The problem, of course, is that we say what we believe. We do not kill people if they take Jesus' Name in vain, nor do we threaten them with death.

Muslims, on the other hand, continually get their way through fear and intimidation. As far as they are concerned, insult Allah or Muhammad, and that is an invitation to be killed. Draw a picture of Muhammad (even a very nice, high quality illustration) and you have provided Jihadists with grounds to kill you.

The world does not know what to do about this. Because so many people in the world actually fear death, they do what they can to placate these murderers, fully believing that if you just give them what they want, they will go away in peace.

The people who believe this are not only naive, but they are morons. Muslim extremists have proven repeatedly that they will get what they want with force. They are not opposed to it. They present a very wide definition of what constitutes an offense worthy of death.

People like this have no qualms about killing those who are considered to be "infidels," and that is anyone who is NOT Muslim.

All of this is beginning to remind me of the Inquisitions, as well as certain emperors of Rome who not only allowed Christianity, but often persecuted those who were not Christians.

The point of this? It is simply to say that if you are a Christian in certain parts of Africa, it could mean your death, especially if you became one from being a Muslim.

An Afghan parliamentary secretary has called for the public execution of Christian converts from the parliament floor, according to International Christian Concern.

On Tuesday, the Associated Free Press reported that Abdul Sattar Khawasi, deputy secretary of the Afghan lower house in parliament, called for the execution of Christian converts from Islam.

Speaking in regards to a video broadcast by the Afghan television network "Noorin TV" showing footage of Christian men being baptized and praying in Farsi, Khawasi said, "*Those Afghans that appeared in this video film should be executed in public. The house should order the attorney general and the NDS (intelligence agency) to arrest these Afghans and execute them.*"

An ICC spokesperson told ASSIST News Service that the broadcast triggered a protest by hundreds of Kabul University students on Monday, who shouted death threats and demanded the expulsion of Christian foreigners accused of proselytizing.

As a result, the operations of Norwegian Church Aid (NCA) and US-based Church World Service (CWS) have been suspended over allegations of proselytizing.

The ICC spokesperson said the Afghan government was currently undertaking an intensive investigation into the matter.

"According to Afghan law, proselytizing is illegal and conversion from Islam is punishable by death," the spokesperson said.

ICC sources within Afghanistan have reported that many national Christians are in hiding, fearful of execution. Under government pressure during investigations, some Afghans have reportedly revealed names and locations of Christian converts.

Aidan Clay, ICC Regional Manager for the Middle East, said, *"It is absolutely appalling that the execution of Christians would be promoted on the floor of the Afghan parliament.*

"Khawasi's statement sounded a whole lot like the tyrannical manifesto of the Taliban not that of a US ally. American lives are being lost fighting terrorism and defending freedom in Afghanistan - yet Christians are being oppressed within Afghan borders.

"This comes after billions of US dollars have been invested in the war effort, and millions more have been given in aid. The US government must intervene to protect the religious freedoms and human rights of all Afghans. The US is not a mere outside bystander - but, is closely intertwined within Afghan policy."

Clay added, "Intervention is not a choice, but a responsibility, as Afghan policies reflect the US government's ability and commitment to secure a stable government in Afghanistan."

Interesting, isn't it, that it is fine to be a Christian or a Muslim in the United States. It is fine for Muslims to come here and build their mosques. However, it is NOT fine for a Muslim to change his faith to Christianity and live in certain parts of the world. In that case, it could very well mean that person's death.

This is the type of person that the United States is allowing into this country. People like this have only one mindset, which in and of itself is not necessarily bad. However, they are prepared to do whatever they need to do to foist their mindset on the public.

Sharia Law is that which closely follows traditional and orthodox Muslim ways. The punishments for infractions are swift and often end in torture or death. This is the system that radical Muslims want to foist on the entire world. By doing nothing, the world is saying, "Fine, Sharia Law is okay with us!"

Well, it's not okay with me. This country was founded by right-wing extremists who above all things wanted the citizens of America to be free from the tyranny of other countries. Islam wants to push the world back to the dark ages. Is that okay with you? If it is, you're either Muslim or just plain blind. I hope you wake up, and soon.

By not resisting radical Islam's push into this country, we are already admitting defeat. We need to turn the tide and we need to do it now.

46

Tortured in North Korea
(Blogged: 06/18/2010)

With much of the world focused on the Middle East and much of the United States focusing on Arizona, there are other very important issues throughout the world that are going virtually unnoticed.

We are all aware of the problems in the Middle East, and either you are for or against Israel's position. That's nothing new. In fact, we know that the situation will worsen before it gets better. Muslims in the United States are taking their cases to the cities that they have immigrated to in the hopes that these cities will sign a pledge or something similar that asks to open the way for ships to get into Gaza. No mention is made of Israel's own need to defend her interests. The only thing that matters to most is that humanitarian aid be allowed into Gaza. Many believe that Israel has no right to inspect the contents of these ships or block them from moving on to Gaza. Those opinions are foolishness, and if they really understood their history they might have a better grasp of the situation.

Too many throughout the world are under the false impression that the Protocols of the Wise of Zion are actually authentic documents. This is in spite of the fact that they have been shown to be nothing more than poorly plagiarized pieces of garbage, composed by an Anti-Semite after stealing from a parody that was written and did not even focus on or refer to Jews. You can't tell some people anything, though. If they came to embrace the truth they would have no reason to continue to hate Jews, so they prefer to believe a lie. It's very sad.

Here in the United States, Arizona has passed a law that simply puts teeth to the FEDERAL LAW that is already ON THE BOOKS. This does not matter to the average individual, though, because whenever the race card is played, you'd have to be an idiot not to change your tune. So now Los Angeles has passed a resolution that will completely bypass Arizona. No sense giving your money via business to a state that houses a bunch of racists, right?

I read in the paper that Sacramento, CA just yesterday did the same thing. I saw bits and pieces of the council meeting on the tube and there were plenty of people rallying behind the "racist" mentality. One guy even got so upset he couldn't get his words straight, saying "This is the skin of our color" instead of "This is the color of our skin." It doesn't matter though, because call someone a racist, and that's what they are...whether they really are one or not.

I received a general email from Ray Gano over at Prophezine.com today, and it was titled "*Islam's 12 Steps to Destroy Dar al-Harb (The*

Land of the Infidels)." Now, who would not stop to read that one? Listed among the twelve steps was the concept that Muslims will use the liberalism in America and turn it against America. The explanation was, "Currently being labeled a "racist" is a fate that is worse than death in most Western countries. When they oppress Muslims and seek to stem their tide, use their fear of that word against them. They will never be able to convincingly assert that discrimination against one group is bad (e.g. gays) while maintaining that discrimination against Muslims is good without appearing to be hypocritical and intellectually corrupt, thus they will lose the propaganda war. Recruit liberal academics and media outlets to assist in this campaign."

As far as Arizona goes, with the cities in America that are beginning to boycott Arizona, all I can say is that the people who will be hurt will be small businesses. I guess if enough cities boycott Arizona, then the governor may change her mind; at least that's what the hope is, yet the Federal Law remains, so in essence Arizona has done nothing illegal or wrong.

So what does all this have to do with North Korea? Both the situation in the Middle East and people's reaction to Arizona's law are problems. There is a much larger problem, though, that no one really cares about because you don't read about it in the news.

In North Korea, it is against the law to be a Christian. It is against the law to own or carry a Bible. The only churches that exist in North Korea are the ones that are state-sanctioned. This is done in order to pretend that people in North Korea have freedom, which of course they do not.

Chuck Missler recently stated, "*North Koreans are required to worship Kim as a god. He is to be the object of all their worship. Since the slightest questioning of authority or disrespect for Kim is considered unacceptable, true faith in a God or admiration of any government beyond*

Kim and his provision is intolerable. To admit that anyone or anything might be greater than the Dear Leader would weaken the power he wields over a tiny, densely-populated country almost devoid of natural resources."[71]

That is more than sad. What's even worse is that Christians are routinely arrested and subjected to beatings, torture, and even bio-chemical testing (to see what works and what doesn't, it is assumed), and then eventually killed.

Missler continued, "*Four hundred thousand to one million people may have died in North Korea's forced labor prisons since 1972. Untold numbers have been tortured and interrogated over suspicions of holding Christian beliefs or having associated with Christians. Yet Christian insider organizations report that, based on former prisoners' stories of torture and confessions, as many as one in four North Koreans may hold to some sort of Christian belief system."*[72]

In North Korea, Christians are hated. They are routinely discriminated against. They are tossed in jail, often without knowing why or being given an explanation. They are tortured and killed. This is because they are CHRISTIANS. And no one cares. The world is too busy caring about Gaza or the alleged racist law in Arizona.

So we will likely see more minorities come forward with terrible stories of how they were pulled over because they ran a red light or changed lanes without a blinker, cutting off other people, and that while they were pulled over, the Police had the mendacity to ask for proof of residency. How dare they! Don't they know that all Hispanics in Arizona are here legally?

---

[71] http://www.bible-prophecy-today.com/2010/06/still-tortured-in-north-ko-rea.html?utm_source=feedburner&utm_medium=email&utm_campaign=Feed%3A+BibleProphecyToday+%28Bible+Prophecy+Today%29#ixzz0r4xmawEW
[72] Ibid

By the way, do the folks who want nothing more than for any and every illegal to be able to walk into this country without fear of reprisal have any idea how many young girls are *raped* by other Mexicans as they try to make their way to the United States? Of course, that is our fault too. Let's not consider the fact that once again, Mexico's president would rather affix blame to someone else than deal with the actual problems within his own country.

The saddest part of this is twofold:

1. If Mexico was doing its job to take care of its own citizens, those citizens would not need to come here trying to earn a buck to provide for their own families back home
2. Mexico's president is a huge hypocrite for condemning the U.S., all the while having some of the strictest anti-immigration laws on the books

Because of the drug cartels that are busy killing one another, innocent people, and the police in Mexico, at least some of that carnage is spilling over into the United States. Ranchers along the border have been shot at and murdered.

I grant you that the majority of Mexicans who come running up here from their country are not criminals. However, they ARE here ILLEGALLY. Because of this, the economies of states like Arizona and California are being destroyed by the preponderance of illegal aliens entering these states.

The problem is that millions of illegals come to this country in the first place. Aside from that, though many are often caught and sent back to their country, they simply turn around and attempt to smuggle themselves into this country again. In North Korea, if you are a Christian, you are as good as dead. Tragic, but true.

So which problem is worse? If you have to think about it, then I feel sorry for you.

Here are some links you may wish to check out that deal with the problems in North Korea:

http://www.myspace.com/mindgasms

http://www.christianpost.com/article/20100425/north-korea-freedom-week-kicks-off/index.html

http://www.christianexaminer.com/Articles/Articles%20Feb10/Art_Feb10_17.html

47

Israel Stands Alone...

(Blogged: 06/18/2010)

It is clear from history (for anyone that can approach it with an unbiased viewpoint) that regardless of what Israel does, she is never correct. If she gives back land she rightfully won in the 1967 6-Day War in exchange for promised cease fires, the firing of rockets still continues as they are daily lobbed into Israel. The enemies simply move in closer, quickly taking up positions in the land that Israel gave back.

No other country that I am aware of in these modern times is forced to give land back to nations that attacked another nation. Yet Israel is given one ultimatum after another. In 1967, Israel was attacked by forces from Egypt, Jordan, and Syria. Again, Israel was ATTACKED. Other nations "donated" troops to the effort of eradicating Israel. Yes, I realize that in many ways the "official" war started because of Israel's preemptive attack; however now, as then, Israel finds herself in the same position. Should she wait until Iran decides to attack, or should she strike preemptively to minimize damage to civilians and others?

Had not the Arab nations that surrounded Israel in 1967 been assailing Israel both physically (with bombs, rockets, and mortar fire) as well as verbally (just as they are doing today), there would have been no need for Israel to retaliate. So, during the first few weeks of the 6 Day War Israel loses much ground, but in the following few weeks after that she gained back what she lost and took even more land. All is fair in love and war...unless the name of your country is "Israel."

Today we have despotic idiots like our friendly North Korean dictator Putin from Russia and President Ahmadinejad from Iran. President Mahmoud (Hamas) and others are all calling for Israel's destruction. So Israel has gone on the offensive, doing their level best to eliminate problems BEFORE they crop up. This is the case with the flotilla that was blocked from entering Gazan waters. The world knows the situation (or at least they think they do; and of course, to most, Israel is again to blame).

Israel has every RIGHT to protect herself. She has every right to be concerned about what goes in and what goes out of Gaza and other neighboring areas. Many times, Israel has been the victim of weaponry and arms being smuggled into various parts of Israel and beyond by the use of tunnels. These tunnels, often starting in Egypt, go far into Israel, completely underground. As Israel discovers these tunnels, they are destroyed. The enemy, however, moves quickly to create new ones.

With President Obama's ignorance and ability to lie with a straight face, it is absolutely clear to anyone who has eyes to see that in spite of the promises he made to Jewish groups here in the United States to defend Israel, he has done nothing of the sort. He has repeatedly treated Netanyahu with disdain, as if Netanyahu was nothing but a slave, hardly to be given the time of day. As a father chastises his wayward son, so has Obama treated Netanyahu in a disgusting display of unmasked hatred.

It is also clear that in spite of Obama's promise to protect and defend the United States Constitution, this appears to be the furthest thing from his mind. He is much more interested in making the world safe FOR Muslim Jihadists and Islamic Extremists who want nothing more than for Sharia Law to take effect throughout the world. Apparently, Obama believes he will be safe from the ire of Islam, yet many consider him to be an infidel in spite of his Muslim leanings.

With Obama and pretty much the rest of the world (with the possible exception of Canada) wishing nothing but ill will on Israel, Israel stands alone, trying to do what the world wants while attempting to keep her own borders and the people within them safe. Unfortunately, Israel is going to have to learn the hard way that she cannot do both. In this most recent situation, Netanyahu has opted to ease the blockade for ships entering Gazan waters. He has done so because he knows he has virtually no support in the world.

What Netanyahu needs to realize is that if he were to turn to God, He would be Israel's support. Israel does not need the United States or Canada or any other nation in this world. The fact that Israel became a state in 1948, has maintained that statehood in the face of unprecedented odds, and continues to exist today, says something about God's ability to keep Israel a sovereign nation. However, if the leaders of Israel would take the time to look at the book of Ezekiel, Isaiah and other books from the Bible, they would hopefully see that God saves Israel for one purpose: for the sake of His Name (Ezekiel 20:9).

Here are just a few verses where God without equivocation teaches that what He does for Israel, He does for the sake of His Name. He does it because He has promised to do so, and it is His reputation that is on the line.

- 1 Samuel 2:22
- 1 Kings 8:41
- 2 Chronicles 6:32
- Psalm 23:3
- Psalm 25:11
- Psalm 31:3
- Psalm 79:9
- Psalm 106:8
- Psalm 109:21
- Psalm 115:1
- Psalm 143:11
- Isaiah 45:4
- Isaiah 48:9-11
- Isaiah 66:5
- Jeremiah 14:7
- Jeremiah 14:21
- Ezekiel 20:14
- Ezekiel 20:22
- Ezekiel 20:44
- Ezekiel 36:22
- Daniel 9:19

The above verses represent some of the many times that God is called upon or states that He will save Israel or her people for the sake of His holy Name. Some theologians conveniently allegorize Israel into the Church and therefore state that God is speaking about the Church. This is garbage, because if things were kept in their context it is clear that God is referring to the actual nation of Israel, not the Church.

The leaders of Israel need to do a number of things:

- stop worrying about the world and who does or does not like them
- stop worrying about the Arab nations that seek to destroy her
- start getting right with God
- commit their ways to Him, so that He will be able to work in and through them for His purposes (though God will save Israel for the sake of His Name, He prefers that Israel come to Him on their own)
- do whatever they can to ensure the safety of their own country
- ignore the U.N. and the rest of the world's demands, just like Iran and other Muslim countries do

Israel should NOT have opted to lighten up on the flotilla's attempting to gain entry to Gaza. It is like leaving the door to the chicken coop open because the wolf says he is merely trying to bring the chickens food. Israel will come to regret her decision, because the world will not stop with this demand. The world will continue to chip away at Israel's borders and actions, little by little, until there is nothing left of Israel except what is on paper.

Israel has a right to protect herself. This is something she MUST do, in spite of what the world thinks. Does Israel actually believe that by caving into the demands of the world, she will somehow gain the world's respect? It will not happen, because most of the world HATES Israel and the Jews. Has Israel learned nothing from the Holocaust? I do not say that as a joke, or to condemn. I say that to remind Israel that since God created their nation, the world - led by Satan - has been out to destroy her. Every time Israel concedes, she is destroyed a little more.

I pray that Israel will wake up to the fact that she needs to do what is in HER best interests, and to heck with the rest of the world! This is exactly what many nations around the globe are doing anyway, so why is Israel the one made to look like a rogue nation?

To Prime Minister Benjamin Netanyahu, I implore you to consider ONLY what is good and right for Israel. Consider God and how His hand has been in your nation since the beginning. Commit your way to him and He will direct your path. Open yourself up to ALL of His Righteousness and you will be SAVED.

Please read Psalm 22, Mr. Netanyahu. Read it over and over and over again, until you see its truth and that truth becomes part of you.

48

Obama Sues Arizona

(Blogged: 06/18/2010)

You know, the more I consider this announcement from the Justice Department, the more I think that someone is attempting to start another Civil War here in the United States, or maybe race riots. Sure, that is strong language, but the reality is that since Obama has taken office, instead of defending the United States Constitution he seems intent on dismantling it.

Obama has gone around the world bowing to other leaders as if he is somehow subservient. He has opted to make Islamic Jihadists and extremists look better by removing certain phrasing from connection with them.

He has pushed through a hasty Obamacare medical package that could easily bankrupt this country, foisting Socialistic medicine on the masses. He has tossed Israel under the bus and has consistently come out in favor of Islam and Muslim countries in the Middle East, and now he has decided that though there are laws at the Federal level that have to do with illegal immigration, the Federal government should sue the state of Arizona!

"The move is a rare instance of the federal government forcefully intervening in a state's affairs, and it carries significant political risks. With immigration continuing to be a hot-button issue in political campaigns across the country, the Arizona law, which gives local police greater power to check the legal status of people they stop, has become a rallying point for the Tea Party and other conservative groups."[73]

Apparently, Clinton spilled the beans during her visit to Ecuador. Regarding the Arizona situation, Clinton stated, *"The Justice Department, under [Obama's] direction, will be bringing a lawsuit against the act."*[74]

Governor Brewer of Arizona does not strike me as an idiot. I find it difficult to believe she would have signed this "act" into law if it had been determined to be unconstitutional. In fact, does anyone really believe that Brewer did not have anyone check into the constitutionality of the law first?

But that does not seem to matter because the whole thing plays well in the "race card" arena. People get all up in arms, as if every Hispanic individual in Arizona will automatically be stopped by law enforcement officials because of the color of their skin. It is ridiculous.

With respect Clinton's comments, the article continued: *"A State Department spokesman, Philip J. Crowley, said Mrs. Clinton was respond-*

---

[73] http://www.msnbc.msn.com/id/37789246/ns/politics-the_new_york_times
[74] Ibid

ing to deep unhappiness over the law that has been expressed in Mexico and other Latin American countries."[75]

So? People from Mexico and other Latin American countries? What do they have to do with United States policy? The article continued to say, *"At home, polls show that a majority of Americans support the law, or at least the concept of states more rigorously enforcing immigration laws."*[76]

So I guess we are now making policy and laws based on what other countries think about us? When did that start?

In the meantime, President Obama has done precious little to quell the problems in this country. In fact, with the problem of the oil spill in the Gulf he has been a Johnny-come-lately, finally getting around to looking at the problem and then talking tough to the American people about "making BP pay." The posturing gets a bit asinine. His strings are starting to show...

I am beginning to believe that President Obama would like nothing less than civil war in the United States. The more turmoil that can be created, the more people will demand the Federal government to do something. When it comes to that point, people will willingly give up even more of their rights if the government will be able to bring peace within America's borders.

This is not as far-fetched as some might believe. Things are starting to add up, and it does not look good for this country of ours. We have a probable Muslim as a sitting president (he may in fact not even be eligible to be there), and now he wants the Republic of the United States to become a socialist regime. Wow, he's accomplished quite a bit in only a short time.

---

[75] http://www.msnbc.msn.com/id/37789246/ns/politics-the_new_york_times
[76] Ibid

49

Is Islam a Religion of Peace?

(Blogged: 07/01/2010)

I slam is three things: 1. a religion, 2. a political movement, and 3. a military movement.

I have absolutely no problem with the first one. I DO have a problem with the second and third ones for a very important reason. Because Islam is a political movement, proponents of it have been working very hard, often within the weaknesses of Democracy in the United States, to overcome America's system (or to take advantage of it) from within. Keith Ellison was elected to Congress in 2006. Though never making a big deal of being a Muslim while campaigning, after he was elected it became the core from which he worked as a Muslim member of Congress.

Beyond this, because Islam is a military movement, Muslims see absolutely no problem with killing "infidels" simply because they are infidels. To be clear, according to Islam, anyone who is not part of the Islamic religion is an infidel. Specifically, here are some interesting admonitions for Muslims from the Qur'an itself:

- Believers, take neither the Jews nor the Christians for your friends. (Sura 5:51)
- Infidels are those who declare: "God is the Christ, the son of Mary." (Sura 5:17)
- Infidels are those that say "God is one of three in a Trinity." (Sura 5:73)
- Make war on infidels who dwell around you. (Sura 9:123)

The above statements are directly from the Qur'an. While someone might argue that context is important, I would agree. I would also encourage the person who believes that these statements were ripped from their context within the Qur'an to look them up and see if that is true. Here are more:

- The infidels are your sworn enemies. (Sura 4:101)
- When you meet the infidel in the battlefield, strike off their heads. (Sura 47:4)
- Mohammed is Allah's apostle. Those who follow him are ruthless to the infidels. (Sura 48:29)
- Prophet, make war on the infidels. (Sura 66:9)
- Kill the disbelievers where we find them. (Sura 2:191)

It should be noted that the Qur'an is largely a book of sayings. There is no real context to it. It is one saying after another with no real context. Each individual saying is a belief that true Muslims hold dear. They believe them and work to bring them to fruition.

In his book *What Every American Needs to Know about the Qur'an* William J. Federer makes the following statements:

- Islam is the opposite of freedom. It means surrender, submission or subjugation. A Muslim is someone who has submitted. A "dhimmi" is a non-Muslim forced to submit.
- Mohammed divided the world into two parts: those who have submitted to the will of Allah and those yet to submit. He called these the House of Islam (dar al-Islam) and the House of War (dar al-harb).
- Whereas "world peace" to a westerner means peaceful coexistence, "world peace" to a Muslim means "world Islam," the world submitting to the will of Allah."[77]

For Americans who doubt this or who believe that this will never happen to the United States, consider the fact that our current president - Obama, for those who have not been keeping track - is more Muslim than anything else. He hopes to partner with Islamic nations and he has shown no interest in supporting Israel at all. In fact, if he could, he would completely do away with Israel in order to become a hero to Muslims around the globe.

Islam has no patience or room for anyone or anything that opposes them. Those who are not with Islam are automatically opposed to it. This is why Islamic Jihadists have no qualms about killing innocent people, whether they do it by blowing up buildings, become martyrs for Islam through suicide bombings, or some other way entirely. To Islam, there is no one outside of Islam who is truly innocent. Because they are not innocent, they deserve to die. This is a foregone conclusion.

Federer indicates that the world has two types of Muslims; 1) Moderates, and 2) Violent. The former believes that the world will at

---

[77] William J. Federer What Every American Needs to Know about the Qur'an (2008), 17

some future point completely submit to Allah. The latter believes that the world must submit now, and they feel privileged to be part of the solution by making it happen now. Many of the moderate Muslims become targeted by the violent Muslims for not being Muslin "enough." The moderates are content to allow the world to become Muslim in due course (if that is to happen), whereas the violent Muslims believe that it is the obligation of every Muslim to join in the reformation of the world in order that Islam (and therefore Sharia Law) would become worldwide in scope.

A few days ago, I was watching a video in which Pamela Geller (from Atlasshrugs.com) was on CNN discussing aspects of Islam as it relates to the desire of Muslims to build a mosque at Ground Zero, right near the World Trade Towers. Of course, these towers, in which over 3,000 people lost their lives through the cowardly acts of a few highly incensed Islamic Jihadists, were felled, and today there remains little of anything left except a large empty space.

The proponents of the mosque say that it will help heal the community, and they also point out that it was due to United States foreign policy that brought this situation on. What they do not point out is that historically, whenever Muhammad built a mosque, he always did so after he took over a new area or region. He would often destroy existing churches and/or synagogues and erect a mosque. This was a show of victory. When a mosque goes up in an existing region that previously was not Islamic, or did not have a mosque, it is due to one reason and one reason only: conquest.

The folks who support the idea of a mosque at Ground Zero have all the excuses and rationale ready to go. The trouble is that they are simply not being truthful at all. This is another thing that Islam allows. It enables a Muslim to say one thing to an infidel (remember our definition?), but what they say and what they intend or mean can be two different things. Geller was essentially called a liar, or at the very least, misinformed, not only by the news anchor, but by the

Imam who stood opposite her. Unfortunately, Geller was not given the last word either. While the media plays into the hands of Islam, little do they realize that they are being unknowingly subjugated.

This is also why peace will never work in the Middle East until Jesus Christ makes it happen. Muslims are forbidden to enter into an agreement with infidels. They are supposed to vanquish their foes, not work with them in compromise. The only time they should accept a truce is when they are weak. When they are strong, they should fight with no mercy at all. There should only be one winner in Islam and it is Islam. Any means can be used and appropriated for such gains, even lying, maiming, and killing.

When I was growing up I got into a few scraps, as most boys do. Whether right or wrong, it seems to be a rite of passage. At any rate, on one occasion I was involved in a fight in which I had bested my opponent in spite of the fact that he was bigger than I was at the time. He "gave up," so rather than continue to humiliate him, I got up to let him go. He then grabbed my leg and twisted it until I fell and then attempted to beat me. My anger kicked in and decided that less mercy this time would be the best route.

The problem was that he had twisted my leg, and I walked with a limp for a few weeks until it healed. He had given up, but really had not. He simply used it as a ruse to put himself in a better position, hoping to take advantage of me then. This is what the violent Muslim is taught to do. They want mercy when they are weak, but refuse to give it when they can overcome their perceived enemy.

This country has become the harbor for Islamic radicals and their ideals. They have quickly learned how to use the system to their advantage and they refuse to give in until they get what they want.

Too many people actually believe the saying that "Islam is a religion of peace." In one sense it is, but only as they mean it. Muslims believe that one day the entire world will be Islamic, with Sharia Law as the only law. When that happens, it WILL be a religion of peace, as far as they are concerned. No other religion will be allowed to exist. There will be no such thing as tolerance. Islam, by its very nature, is completely intolerant of any other religious system. So convinced are Muslims that Islam is the only truth that they are willing to foist it on those who do not agree. Refusal means execution. The last time something like that happened was during the burgeoning Roman Catholic Church's persecution of those who failed to become Christians. Convert or die, or "by this sign, conquer," was Constantine's mantra.

Will people wake up? Will freedom-loving Americans ever come to believe that Islamic law could take hold in the United States? It won't as long as the United States remains the United States. There is a day coming when the United States will completely shed its borders and take up its position with the rest of the world, proclaiming that the world needs one government, one religion, and one humanity. Sounds far-fetched, doesn't it? Sure does, but that does not mean it cannot or will not happen. They said the same thing about a man walking on the moon (it'll never happen!), or that there would never be a need for a computer to be in every household (IBM). Stranger things have happened.

I feel like I am talking to a wall half the time. If you become too animated against Islam, people think you're working yourself up into an unnecessary lather. The problem, though, is that I cannot help what I see, and neither can others who are also warning anyone who will listen (or not listen).

I am currently working on a new book, a commentary on the book of Revelation. While this is admittedly a tough book, it can be understood. I am writing it for the average person who may not have a great deal of biblical knowledge already. I am making it as easy to grasp as possible, given the complexities of Revelation. I guess studying Revelation all over again has brought certain concerns to the fore. Revelation is a book about the end of this age, prior to the new age of the Messiah.

Revelation is a book that highlights God's wrath from the opening of the first seal in Revelation 5 to the last bowl and beyond. We also see how the Antichrist makes his way to the top of the heap, how he reveals himself to the world, how he tricks Israel into signing a seven-year covenant, and how he eventually breaks that covenant in the middle of the seven years.

Revelation is a book that showcases God's absolute sovereignty, His wrath, His judgment, and His mercy. It is a book in which the enemies of God are confounded at every turn, yet that does not keep them from trying. Unfortunately, I believe that Islam will play a huge role in the coming Tribulation, because in order for the Antichrist to be a "hit" with the Jewish people AND Muslims, he will either have to be Muslim himself, or someone that Muslims can trust implicitly. If he is not Muslim, then Muslims will have to know up front that he has every intention of changing things up on the Jewish people and Israel halfway through the Tribulation. If he is not Muslim, I don't see how he could gain Muslims' trust any other way.

However, he does it; he will be someone who is extremely enigmatic, charming, extremely intelligent, and able to solve manifold problems in a single bound. He may even be able to stop bullets. He will be a man of miracles, and both Islam and Israel will claim him as the Messiah/Mahdi. He has huge shoes to fill, but he will fill them with ease.

Ultimately, he will break the covenant with Israel that he brokered (remember, a Muslim CAN lie if it serves their purposes) and will proclaim himself to be worthy of worship as the only god. The only people who will have a problem with that are Jews and Christians. Once the Jews head for the hills - after their eyes are opened to the fact that they were conned - Antichrist will turn his attention to Christians, because they will have refused to accept the mark.

It is coming, folks. It is coming, and we are closer than we can possibly imagine. I'm not a prophet, nor a seer. I am a Christian who believes the Bible. I believe that the Bible reveals nine specific birth pangs that will occur prior to the Tribulation. Three have already been fulfilled and at least one of the others appears to be so close that we can feel it. Tensions in the Middle East are at an all-time high, and there is a good chance that Israel will strike Iran preemptively to destroy their nuclear capabilities. If that happens, it may create a situation in which several nations get together and invade Israel with the intention of overtaking and destroying her. You can read about it in Ezekiel 38.

This world is a fascinating and scary place. Fascinating because we know that God is in charge, and scary because we know where everything is leading and we know what it looks like as we move toward that time.

Violent Muslims are inadvertently helping to prepare the way for the Antichrist. When he arrives, he will be heralded as the last savior of the world! No, that honor belongs to Jesus Christ who will come after this last false messiah enters the world's stage. I hope you're ready. I hope you have salvation in Jesus Christ. I hope your eyes will be opened to the truth.

While it IS too late to change the course of this world, it is NOT too late to determine your eternal future. My suggestion is that you look at Jesus and accept Him for who He says He was/is: Lord, God, Savior. He came and died for me and you. Too many people reject that truth because it is either inconvenient or unbelievable. If you're having trouble believing it, my only suggestion is that you go to God and ask Him to open your eyes to that truth.

The world is on a headlong path toward catastrophe, yet at the same time, not one of us knows when we will enter eternity. You could enter it long before the Antichrist shows up. In fact, it could be today, or tonight. What then?

When the Antichrist reveals himself to the world as savior, statesman, king, and all around swell guy, he will be heralded by billions as the one who will solve our problems. He will not solve any problems. He will begin to create problems for every person on the face of this earth.

When President Obama ran for office as president, there was this groundswell movement that lifted him up to the level of messiah. People (led by the media) called him "the one" or "the chosen." So intent were people to believe that this one man was THE answer to the problems facing the United States that many were willing to label him a god, or savior. He's not.

Think about how people will be swept up by the message and presence of the coming Antichrist. Unlike Obama, the Antichrist will likely appear as humble, self-deprecating, and flexible, while still maintaining his air of super intelligence. All that will give way to an evil hardness that comes only from his father, Satan.

Atheists love to say that God does not exist. They cannot prove it, but they continue to say it as if it has been proven. If they are wrong, they've made a huge mistake in judgment. The same can be said about the coming Antichrist. Most will embrace him, few will reject him.

This world needs God, not Allah. It does not need Muhammad, it needs Jesus Christ. This world, led by Islamic extremists, is headed toward a complete breakdown. Out of the ashes the one-world ruler will rise, promising to make all things right. The Antichrist - Islam's Mahdi - will ride in on a figurative white horse, promising peace but bringing destruction. He will be the consummate liar and Muslims will know it, will approve it, and will be glad for it.

50

More on the Ground Zero Mosque
(Blogged: 07/14/2010)

I t appears as though the "dialogue" between Muslims and non-Muslims continues to heat up (and rightly so) over whether an existing building near Ground Zero should be converted into an Islamic mosque. The religion of the Muslim is Islam. It would be one thing if Islam were only a religion. It is not. Islam is multi-pronged. In Robert Spencer's book *The Politically Incorrect Guide to Islam (and the Crusades)*, Spencer notes the following:

Muhammad was a Prophet of War. He essentially began his religion through raids, assassination and deceit. This is clear from the Battle of Badr alone. The truth of the matter is that it is impossible to negotiate with those of Islam. While they are free to make a covenant with infidels (those who are not Islamic), the very fact that they are entering into a covenant with an infidel allows them to break that covenant anytime they wish.

The Qur'an is a Book of War. Anyone who reads the Qur'an understands that at nearly every point, war with infidels is encouraged. Though it is often said by Muslims that Jihad is emotional, or spiritual, this is only said as a form of disinformation. In truth, Jihad is very physical, involving the killing of as many infidels (non-Muslims) as possible. The Qur'an does NOT teach tolerance of other religions, nor does it teach that believers can take up arms against an opponent only in self-defense. *"O Prophet! Strive hard against the unbelievers and the hypocrites, and be firm against them. Their abode is Hell, an evil refuge indeed," (Qur'an 9:73). Warfare is to be directed not only against infidels (primarily), but also against Muslims who are not as extreme in their beliefs as Jihadists. Throughout the Qur'an, Muslims are commanded to make war on Jews and Christians. Spencer points out, "Oft-quoted tolerant, peaceful Qur'anic verses have actually been canceled, according to Islamic theology."*[78]

The idea that Islam teaches tolerance and peace is a misnomer. Spencer states, *"The closest the Qur'an comes actually to counseling tolerance or peaceful coexistence is to counsel believers to leave the unbelievers...so that Allah can deal with them."*[79]

By the way, as a bit of an aside, the Qur'an is one thing, but the Hadith are another altogether. The Hadith are books upon books filled with stories of what Muhammad allegedly told his followers, when to do certain things and when not to, etc. When Muhammad allegedly quotes Allah in any of the Hadith, devout Muslims view those words just as important as those in the Qur'an. Much of the focus in the volumes of Hadith is war.

---

[78] Robert Spencer *The Politically Incorrect Guide to Islam* (Regnery Publishing), 19
[79] Ibid, 21

Unlike the teachings of Jesus, Muhammad endorses and taught to war against all unbelievers. Jesus on the other hand taught us to love our enemies and pray for those who use us for their evil ends.

Islam is a Religion of War. Muhammad was a man of war and this is the ideology he passed down to his followers through today. He taught that there is nothing better (or holier) than jihad warfare, and he was NOT talking about some inner struggle with one's self. Muhammad also taught his followers that all non-Muslims should be offered three things: 1) conversion to Islam, 2) subjugation by Islam, or 3) death.

Islam is a Religion of Intolerance. Islamists fully desire (and work toward) the day when Sharia Law will be THE law of the entire world. Sharia Law is often meted out brutally by mobs. Most of the time, the victims are given neither a hearing or trial. They are simply pronounced guilty and the mob decides what punishment to mete out. It is often death, either by stoning, or hanging. If someone steals, his hand should be cut off. If he lies, his tongue should be cut out or the front part off. This is the law that Muslims yearn to see spread across the world. They fight to make this law THE law area by area. The more Sharia Law becomes the law, the sooner the final Imam, or Mahdi will appear as Savior and Ruler of the earth.

Islam is a Religion of Oppression. Women are seen as less than. In fact, they are not much better than furniture. Muslims will say that the reason they want their women to wear Burkhas is to protect the women. That is garbage. It is because the men cannot control themselves and because women are seen as temptresses. If a man commits adultery with a woman, it is often the woman only who is put to death because she tempted the man and because he was weak, he gave in...against his will. Muslims beat their women (sometimes to death) for the smallest of infractions. Children are often treated better. If a woman is raped, she is not believed unless there are at least four witnesses to the crime, like THAT'S going to happen. Consider the fact that quite possibly all four "witnesses" were also her rapists. Are they going to confess? What about others who may have witnessed the rape, but were not part of it, nor did anything? Are they going to step forward?

Islam is a Religion of Crime. Under Islamic law, while stealing is against the law, as is lying, or even killing, it all boils down to the circumstances surrounding that particular "crime." The circumstances will determine whether an actual crime has been committed.

Islam is a Religion Based on Sexual Proclivities and Rewards. Muslim men look forward to entering into paradise and gaining access to...oh, seventy wives, all for their good pleasure. The only guarantee that a Muslim male WILL receive this as his reward is when they take the lives of infidels and are killed in the process. This is why Muslims are willing to blow themselves up, taking others with them. The 9/11 attack was the biggest ritual sacrifice to date by a handful of Muslim men. Over 3,000 people were killed during that attack, all for Allah. To the men who flew the planes, they believed that Allah would be so pleased that he would instantly grant them their new life with their new wives.

Islam is a Religion That Does Not Tolerate Criticism. We have all heard or read of individuals being killed because they did something horrendous, like oh, I don't know, drew a picture of Muhammad. The picture could be the most beautiful picture ever drawn, but it is against Islamic law to draw a picture or create a representation of Muhammad (like the one above). Any Jihadist worth his salt would view such an action as an affront to Muhammad AND Allah. The only proper course of action to take is to kill the person who drew the picture. It goes without saying that Allah's name should never be used in vain. This also could result in death to the perpetrator. It is interesting that you never hear anyone use Allah's name as a swear word, yet Jesus' Name is forever used as a curse word. In fact, it is not uncommon for Muslims to believe that Christians are weak, because we do not kill people who take God's Name in vain. The fact is that God will take care of it. He does not need His children to go around killing people for taking His Name in vain. Vengeance is His and He will repay.

It is this religion that incorporates war and politics that the American people are up against today. If Islam were simply a religion, that would be one thing. It is not. It is a religion that is based on war and politics to achieve what Islam demands. In other words, war and politics are used to bring the religion of Islam to the fore. War is the favored response to infidels, but politics will work just as well. This is what we are seeing with the desire of Muslims to build a mosque two blocks from Ground Zero. If I had my druthers, there would be no more mosques in the United States. The problem, though, is that the U.S. Constitution does not allow for picking on one religion to the exclusion of all others.

The Muslims know what they are doing in their attempts to build a mosque at Ground Zero. It is their way of saying "We WON! We have BEAT the infidels!" Whenever Islam has gone into an area and taken it over, the first thing they do is either convert the existing churches and synagogues to mosques or build brand new mosques. This is similar to planting a flag on the newly gained territory (or on the surface of the moon). It means victory. It means subjugation. It means empowering other Muslims to continue the fight to make Islam (and Sharia Law) THE law of the globe.

There are people fighting against this mosque at Ground Zero, and there are Muslims fighting against those people. The race card has already been played by those from the Muslim side. "Call someone a racist and they will back down" is the mentality. People are not backing down. To be opposed to a mosque near Ground Zero has nothing to do with racism and everything to do with wanting to keep the threat of Islam from continuing to grow.

Islam teaches no love for anyone. Muslims are not taught to love. They are taught to fight against others, overcoming them. Because Jesus taught love and because He died for humanity, He is seen as a weakling. Muhammad was the strong one, taking what he believed was rightfully his, unlike Jesus.

Jihad can be seen and accomplished either through politics or war. War is the preferred method, but politics will also do the job. On 9/11, Islam declared war on the United States. Over 3,000 people had their lives taken from them because of the intolerance of Islam. Many Muslims will tell us that it is the foreign policies of America that caused Muslim extremists to do what they did on 9/11. That is a lie. It would have come anyway one way or another because Islam is a religion that NEEDS to dominate everything. There is no tolerance.

Proponents of the 9/11 mosque want us to believe that this mosque will be for an interfaith dialogue. Wrong. It will only appear to be for an interfaith dialogue. Meanwhile, only Muslims will be allowed into the worship area, and it is there that they will be fed a steady diet of untruths, hatred, and a sense of superiority over everyone else.

The proponents of this mosque at Ground Zero are liars, and they can lie because they are allowed to lie when dealing with infidels. It is their normal, native language. Every time a Muslim mosque is built anywhere in America, it is Islam saying, "Here we have conquered." They will not stop all by themselves. They will only stop when they are forced to stop. It is up to all true Americans to fight the threat of Islam wherever it is found. To ignore the threat is to voluntarily come under the subjugation (or execution) of Islam.

51

Betwixt and Between: Obama's Agenda

(Blogged: 07/20/2010)

President Obama deserves respect for two reasons:

1. God placed him in office
2. He holds the highest office in the land

Apart from that, though, it becomes difficult to hold your tongue. On one hand, I would like President Obama voted out of office as quickly as possible. I know that many would be against that, likely because they simply do not "get it" or they prefer getting handouts from the government. On the other hand, I also realize that if what God reveals in Scripture is going to happen, it cannot happen without individuals like President Obama coming to the fore.

If you look at many Psalms, they present pictures of the huge thorn in the side that the state of Israel is going to create during the end times, or last days. This has been happening on a greater scale with much more frequency. Don't tell a Preterist this though, because they will simply accuse you of wanting these things to happen (you know, you get what you wish for). The truth of the matter, though, is that this is really the first time a U.S. president has come out so virulently against Israel and for the Palestinians. It's certainly possible that previous administrations felt and believed as Obama's administration does, but they were much more careful about how they presented their ideas.

IF the Bible is true, there will never be a lasting two-state solution. In fact, if the Bible is true, Jerusalem will not be split up, part of it siphoned off to the Palestinians (who are not any particular culture at all, but Yassar Arafat's coup de grace in the sense that while he literally created a Muslim Palestinian, he killed the idea of a Jewish Palestinian, even though there were plenty of Jewish Palestinians at the time) and with part of it (the part without the Temple Mount) going to Jews.

One previous policy adviser to the president (Peter Ferrara) was recently quoted as saying, "*He engages in rhetoric, which can be described as 'calculated deception,'" Ferrara observes. 'Or basically, he's playing us'.*"[80] Ferrara goes onto give an example. "*The former policy advisor recalls stump speeches like one Obama gave in Nevada: 'He goes out to Las Vegas and gives this speech, and he says, 'You know, when we were trying to pass the healthcare reform bill, everybody talked about all these scary results that were going to come out of the health bill. And now look; we passed it three, four months ago, and where are all these scary results they were talking about?'"*

---

[80] http://www.onenewsnow.com/Politics/Default.aspx?id=1093328

Ferrara points out that healthcare reform legislation will not go into effect until 2014, and since the effects of those changes will not be recognized for several years, he wonders, *"Just how stupid does [Obama] think we are'."*[81] Apparently, Obama either thinks we are idiots, or he couldn't care less if we see through his charade. Is Obama unaware of the fact that states are already turning their attorneys loose on his healthcare bill? The Federal government will be inundated with lawsuits from states who are barely surviving now financially. Again, either Obama does not care, or he is oblivious. I think it's the former, because with respect to the Tea Party, he laughed as if it was simply a miniature Schnauzer that barks ferociously but has no teeth. Does he not see that the Tea Party is made up of people who want real change and not to be taxed to death or forced to buy something that they cannot afford (i.e. Obama's healthcare package)?

Columnist Thomas Sowell recently stated: *"This year's target is the Tea Party. When leading Democrats, led by a smirking Nancy Pelosi, made their triumphant walk on Capitol Hill, celebrating their passage of a bill in defiance of public opinion, Tea Party members on the scene protested.*

"All this was captured on camera and the scene was played on television. What was not captured on any of the cameras and other recording devices on the scene was anybody using racist language, as has been charged by those playing the race card.

"When you realize how many media people were there, and how many ordinary citizens carry around recording devices of one sort or another, it is remarkable -- indeed, unbelievable -- that racist remarks were made and yet were not captured by anybody."[82]

So, the NAACP does what they do best and refers to the Tea Party as made up of racists. Two black senators were apparently subjected to

---

[81] http://www.onenewsnow.com/Politics/Default.aspx?id=1093328
[82] http://www.onenewsnow.com/Perspectives/Default.aspx?id=1094144

racial slurs and epithets by Tea Party members a while ago, yet there is little to no evidence to support their accusations. When you can't beat someone, you play the race card.

Sowell continued with comments related directly to the Tea Party and President Obama. *"Some critics of the Tea Party have seized upon banners carried at one of its rallies that compared Obama with Hitler and Stalin. Extreme? Yes. But there was nothing racist about it, since extreme comparisons have been made about politicians of every race, color, creed, nationality, ideology and sexual preference.*

"Some Obama supporters have long regarded any criticism of him as racism. But that they should have to resort to such a banner to bolster their case shows how desperate they are for any evidence.

"Among people who voted for Barack Obama in 2008, those who are likely to be most disappointed are those who thought that they were voting for a new post-racial era. There was absolutely nothing in Obama's past to lead to any such expectation, and much to suggest the exact opposite. But the man's rhetoric and demeanor during the election campaign enabled this and many other illusions to flourish."[83]

So we have President Obama, who is supposed to be respected by authentic Christians because God states clearly that He puts anyone who is in power there in the first place. We are supposed to pray for our leaders. Under Obama, that is extremely difficult to do, so I pray for him the only way I know how, in which God is glorified; "Father God, please accomplish your will in and through President Obama!" I fully believe that God will do what He needs to do to accomplish His goals. He is certainly not held captive by anyone, much less a president of the United States.

We are seeing all kinds of things happening in this country that are not pleasant. We see the rise of the New Black Panthers, who believe

---

[83] Ibid

intimidation of white people (or anyone who does not vote their way - for the person they want in office) is perfectly acceptable. At least one of these situations has ignored by the Justice Department and Eric Holder. This is the very same Justice Department (and the same Eric Holder) who decided that the new law in Arizona was unconstitutional before even reading the law. This is the same justice department who has opted to sue the state of Arizona because they believe the Arizona law to be racist (there is that word again). It does not seem to matter that thugs were intimidating people at voting locations (and in spite of this intimidation being ON VIDEO, the Federal Government has dropped the charges).

It does not matter that Arizona approved a law that gave them the ability to do what the Federal Government said they should do. None of that seems to matter. The Federal Government has decided it is time to sue Arizona and with amazing hypocrisy, the president of Mexico wants to join in the lawsuit. Of course, this is in spite of the fact that Mexico's immigration laws for illegal immigrants are tougher than America's. There, they do not refer to illegal aliens as "visiting immigrants." They are often brutalized in any number of ways, or deported (if they are lucky). Many of the illegals coming from Mexico often brutalize other illegal aliens also coming from Mexico or force them to be drug runners for the cartels. No one cares about that, though. The Federal Government seems not to care that states like Arizona cannot continue to foot the bill for the healthcare and education overload that illegal immigrants place on the system. Instead of doing what it should be doing to protect our borders, our Federal Government seems intent on pulling down the borders either by eliminating the fence and border patrol, granting blanket citizenship to those who are here illegally, or both.

It seems to be time for racists of color to come together and create a sense of ill will between the races, allowed and encouraged by our own Federal Government under the Obama administration. Unfortunately, people like this are starting to come out of the woodwork. Whether these individuals want to intimidate voters or wish to exterminate whites (as at least one black college professor has publicly stated), the reality is that this is a growing concern, and the Federal Government seems to be willing to do absolutely nothing about it. By doing nothing, they encourage it.

However, if we keep all things in perspective, it is still true that God is in charge. There is no doubt. This does not remove culpability from people. It simply means that they are allowed to do what they do under the banner of God's full sovereignty. Otherwise the world cannot arrive to the place of anarchy that is needed in order for the coming last world dictator to come to the throne. We cannot have peace one day and anarchy the next. The system must break down in stages, and President Obama is simply one in a long line of individuals from across the globe that are playing their part in the coming human holocaust. In that sense then, God's will is being accomplished, though President Obama and other leaders believe it to be their will.

It is really difficult to discern how bad it will get before the Antichrist makes his appearance and is revealed to the world. He will be revealed when he steps up onto the world's stage and enters into or brokers a covenant with Israel and other countries, guaranteeing her safety for seven years (the last "week" of Daniel 9:27). That is when the world will see this leader and go "Ooh, ahh!" That is when he will be seen, but it will not be for three and a half years that he will be seen for what he truly is, and until then, most will be taken by his disguise.

When President Obama was first elected, some thought, "Wow, this guy could be the Antichrist!" I seriously doubt it, because the Antichrist - I believe - will play his Anti-Semitism much closer to his chest. He will pretend to be the friend to the Jew. He will not talk about how much he can take away from Israel, but how much he can do for them, while placating the Islamic world at the same time. President Obama's intentions seem to be only (and pointedly) for Muslims. It is as if he is president of the United States in name only, but is doing all he can to further the cause of Islam. There will be no such distinction with the coming one-world ruler. That man will seem to be for the Jew and Israel. Obama is anything but, and is only held in check by conservatives in Congress (and the United States) who actually see what he is doing and want him to stop.

Though President Obama appears to not notice, he has changed his tune somewhat. However, he seems to be ready to change it again if what the Palestinian Authority is stating is true, that the United States supports the idea of carving up parts of Israel and Jerusalem. The P.A. has also been told by this administration not to worry about the results of the coming November election, as this will not in any way affect Obama's foreign policy.

As Christians, we must pray for our leaders, and so we should. We can do this by earnestly praying that God and only God's purposes will be accomplished in and through President Obama and the other leaders of this nation. That is a prayer God will honor, and in doing so the authentic Christian will be blessed. After all, whose will do you want in your life (if you are an authentic Christian)? If it's not God's then there is a huge problem.

52

Islam Rising

(Blogged: 07/27/2010)

I have decided to publish a number of blogs related to Islam. In fact, these will probably go into a book that is on the drawing board as well. People seem to be unaware of Islam's roots, intentions, and demands. Proponents of Islam do not want democracy. They want total control. They reject freedom, demanding allegiance to Allah. They want to go back to the stone age when women were nothing more than furniture - an object to be used and tossed when done.

Islam has no room for anyone who disagrees with it. While everywhere we read and hear that we are to be tolerant of other religions, Islam has no such desire. In fact, they take advantage of the tolerance of others, using it to their advantage. Orthodox Muslims believe that they are at war with the rest of the world. To them, it is a battle for survival. They do not plan on losing.

Now, if I am a Christian, why am I worried? I'm not worried in the sense of wondering what the outcome will be, nor am I worried about my salvation or where I will be upon my death. I am not worried at all. I am concerned about what is happening in the world. I am concerned that there are too many people doing nothing. I am concerned that Islam is forcing open one door after another because people of the world are allowing it.

What concerns me is that I cannot sit by and do nothing while people throughout the world come face to face with the totalitarian threat of Islam. Sharia Law is such that all verdicts are final and irrevocable. It goes back to the Code of Hammurabi; an eye for an eye, one less hand for a thief, losing your head if you commit adultery (for the woman). Execution if you are gay.

The world is going backwards, and the reality is that few realize it. When Ray from Prophezine.com brought up the fact that Six Flags celebrates Muslim Day, I was incensed enough to write to them. I received a response, which said in part, "*In response to your inquiry about days that appeal to other religious and cultural groups, we do host a number of events during our season. In 2010, these events included Praise in the Park on June 12 featuring a concert with gospel star Hezekiah Walker, a concert on June 19 starring Christian music artist Jeremy Camp, Festival Latino on June 20, and an upcoming Caribbean Day this Sunday. A Jewish heritage event is also being planned at the park and the date will be announced soon. These events are all open to the public. In addition, a number of local churches and synagogues host private events at Six Flags America throughout the season.*"

The woman who responded to me also assured me that Six Flags does not discriminate based on anything. My response to her was:

"Thank you for your response...

Unfortunately, while you may "host" certain events with Christian artists, are those days referred to as "Christian Day"? If not, then of course you are discriminating, whether you believe that to be the case or not.

If you really want to provide fun days for every guest, then it would seem that it might be far more inclusive to have NO day set apart for one particular group (including Christian), than to set specific days aside for specific groups. The truth of the matter though is that Six Flags is a business and the almighty dollar is what guides the decision-making process. If Muslim Day did not make money for the park, it would be eliminated, regardless of your claim of non-discrimination.

As I indicated previously, Islam is not merely a religion. It is a political AS WELL AS military movement.

All you folks are doing is segregating by drawing attention to one particular group over another. For a group to host a private event at a Six Flags park is one thing. For any group to have a day dedicated to them and them alone (though others are welcome to come) simply smacks of the same type of mindset that the Civil Rights movement of the 60s hoped to eliminate.

It is also interesting to note what many Muslim groups are saying about these events and how grateful they are to Allah for what they consider to be successful events. While these comments can be taken any number of ways because of their generality, some comments are far more pointed.

Thanks again for your time and your attempt to dispel my uneasiness."

The plain fact of the matter is that Six Flags DOES discriminate, as I pointed out. Beyond this, Islam is a religion built on discrimination, yet they are being pandered to and placated by people who have no clue. I cannot let that go by unchecked. I cannot sit here and do nothing, so I am writing. I am warning. I am bringing this to your attention so that you can tell and warn others. If we do not, the United States under the Islamic Obama Administration will become what the Netherlands has already become, Islamic nearly to its foundation. I do not want that, and I would be willing to bet that most people in the United States do not want that. However, most people do not believe it has a chance of happening. That is error. Not only does it have a chance of happening, but it IS happening. Are you going to do anything to stop it?

One of the things that Christians can do is pray. The other thing that Christians can do is preach the gospel of Jesus Christ. Another thing that Christians can do is NON-VIOLENTLY resist all attempts by Muslims to Islamatize your town, county, state or country. God's will is going to be accomplished. However, He expects His children to act responsibly and to resist evil wherever it is rising.

Allah is Satan. Allah, through Islam, is a religion of hatred and dhimmitude. Violent Muslims will not stop unless they are stopped. They will not give in because someone says "Please." They stand with Satan and his attempts to take over the world.

This is the day when all Christians are to be lights to the world, shining His light on the works of darkness. This is the day when authentic Christians are to stand as beacons in dark places. This is the day when true believers should never turn and run, but stand firm. Muslims need Jesus. They need the truth. Whether they listen or not is not your choice to make. It is God's. Authentic Christians must preach to all people the gospel of Jesus Christ. A day is coming when that will not happen.

I would ask that you to watch this video: http://shutking.blogspot.com/2009/12/watch-fitna-movie-muslim-plan-for-world.html

I will warn you that it is violent and some of the images will shock you. Please also note some of the language on that Web site will likely offend. However, the video offers a glimpse into the heart of the Muslim extremist. Please pass the link onto as many people as possible. Pray for God's strength to stand against this tremendous evil and preach His gospel in spite of the odds. His Word will not return to Him void.

Please check this blog in the days ahead for more information on Islam. In the meantime, buy a copy of the Qur'an and read it for yourself.

53

Julea Ward's Upper Education

(Blogged: 07/28/2010)

I just finished reading that a court upheld a university's decision to expel a graduate student due to her unwillingness to counsel homosexuals. The university believes that the expulsion is necessary because of the student's religious views.

"A federal judge today ruled in favor of Eastern Michigan University's recent decision to remove a Christian student from its graduate program in school counseling because she refused to provide counseling for homosexual clients on the basis of her religious beliefs.

"The student, Julea Ward, had filed a religious discrimination lawsuit against the school leading up to today's court ruling after she was told by the school that she would 'only be allowed to remain in the program if she went through a 'remediation' program so that she could 'see the error of her ways' and change her belief system about homosexuality', according to a Fox News report."[84]

While I'm sure Gay activists are out celebrating, they seem to be missing the point. What the university was effectively stating was that Ms. Ward needed to change her religious beliefs, or be expelled. When she refused to do so - which would have amounted to denying Christ in her view - the university felt it had no recourse but to expel her. Apparently, at least in this first round, a Federal court agreed with the university.

Now, stop and think for a moment. What Julea Ward said was that she was unable to counsel homosexuals due to her religious beliefs. She believes that the practice of homosexuality is wrong, according to Scripture. She is not wishing the death of homosexuals, nor is she out protesting the homosexual movement or lifestyle (as far as I know). Her decision was based solely on her belief that the Bible is the final authority. She was given the choice of entering a "remediation program," in which her views would be subjected to criticism and possible ridicule. In essence, the school gave her the choice of changing her beliefs about homosexuality, in spite of the fact that she simply chose not to counsel homosexuals, or expulsion.

Again, what Julea Ward was not doing was counseling homosexuals against their lifestyle, or attempting to persuade them to change their lifestyle. She was simply opting out of counseling them at all. Apparently though, Eastern Michigan University firmly believes that if someone graduates through their doctoral program, they are required to counsel to all people, regardless of anything. This is absurd

---

[84] http://www.bible-prophecy-today.com/

to say the least. The idea that a student should be forced to counsel someone whose lifestyle they disagree with is not only asinine, but demagoguery on the part of the university, and yet we have a Federal court agreeing that this should be done.

Consider this, though. When it comes to homosexuality and Islam, there is not only a complete lack of willingness to treat homosexuals as human beings, but they are routinely executed by hanging. When President Ahmadinejad was in New York and spoke before a university crowd, he bragged that Iran did not have homosexuals. Though jeered at, he obviously spoke the truth, because anyone who is found to be a homosexual is put to death.

I personally know of no authentic Christian who wishes homosexuals be put to death. Though I, along with other true believers, may state that homosexuality is wrong, this does not mean that my preference is that homosexuals should be executed! It is one thing to believe that homosexuality is wrong, and it is quite another to execute them for their "crime."

Julea Ward is a graduate student who has been expelled for daring to say that she would have a difficulty counseling homosexuals. I would think that a homosexual would prefer this type of truth, as opposed to hearing some Christian attempt to preach to them during a counseling session. Of course, I could be wrong. What boggles my mind is why the instructors at Eastern Michigan University are upset with Ward because she is unwilling to counsel homosexuals? If I were a counselor, I would feel uncomfortable counseling a woman who might come to me with certain difficulties in her life that are related to being a woman. How could I - as a man - respond or provide aid to a woman who truly needs help from another woman, someone who can offer insight? I have often thought it strange that many OBGyns are men. While they can certainly learn about a woman's anatomy, and read the books, and discuss aspects of what it means to be a woman, and what it means to experience menopause, etc., how on earth can a man truly understand what it means to be a woman? Short answer: they can't! Yet most women continue to go to male gynecologists. It does not make sense to me, but there it is. I could tell homosexuals that their lifestyle is wrong according to Scripture, but I could not relate to them and I could certainly not speak to them as if I am aware of how they think. For that, it takes someone who has actually come out of that lifestyle; and whether homosexuals like to admit it or not, many have and have become Christians as well. These are the people who have ministries with practicing homosexuals, though the homosexual community would very much like to silence these people as well.

Julea Ward has simply stated that she would willingly remove herself from a situation in which she found herself counseling a homosexual. She did not say she would wish the homosexual dead. She said she could not counsel a homosexual. For this, the university decided that Ward needed to be brainwashed to their way of thinking.

In the meantime, great travesties of justice are taking place throughout the world, with homosexuals being executed because of their lifestyle. I'd like to ask what the instructors of Eastern Michigan University are doing about that. Anything? I can't imagine that they are, but again, I could be wrong.

Islam metes out punishment through Sharia Law. It is a mob mentality that guides the people who deem themselves executioners. Found some homosexuals? No problem. They will find a tree or overhang, some rope, some necks, and place the perpetrators on the back of a flatbed. After someone gets done reading part of the Qur'an, the driver of the truck simply pulls away. They don't even have the decency to ensure that the individuals are killed instantly. As the flatbed pulls away, the condemned fall a foot or so, hardly enough distance to break a neck. There they float, struggling to breathe and slowly dying.

The real problem lies in the fact that people hate Christianity so much that they do not see that Islam is coming at breakneck pace! It has already turned The Netherlands into a virtual Islamic Republic and it is on the way to doing the same thing to Great Britain. What country is next? Certainly the United States is in their sights, and we are seeing this attitude at Ground Zero, with the demand for a mosque, as well as elsewhere in the United States. Oklahoma is moving ahead with plans to outlaw Sharia Law in their state before it becomes a problem. Others are taking notice.

So while people rail against "hate-mongering" Christians and Christianity, Islam with its stone age mentality is slowing encroaching on the world. Islam wants nothing less than to rule the world. They believe they will, and IF they do homosexuals will wish for the days when people simply SAID that they could not counsel a homosexual. Of course, it will be too late for that because with Sharia Law in place, the death penalty is a foregone conclusion.

I used to be for the death penalty in the United States. But frankly, if the state wants to pay for a lifelong incarceration for a convicted felon, that's fine. There is always a chance that the person is innocent, and it seems that DNA is proving it more and more. There is also the constant chance that someone on death row will turn his life over to Jesus Christ. If it could happen to the thief on the cross, then it's never too late as long as a person has breath. By the way, Rome did not necessarily put people to death for simply stealing. It was more likely that this particular thief was much more than a thief, though he had been found guilty of thieving.

The days are coming when this world will turn itself upside down. Already "right" is "wrong" and "wrong" is "right," as evidenced with the Federal court's recent decision with respect to Julea Ward as well as other areas, from the Federal courts to the White House. But in the days and years ahead, we can be assured that Muslims will not care about what the courts think. They have their own legal system and it is called Sharia Law. It supersedes any other rule of law. There are no appeals, and there is no long drawn out stay on death row. Conviction brings swift punishment. This is what is coming to the world because too many people are doing nothing to stop it.

I recall watching part of an interview with a group opposed to the mosque at Ground Zero on CNN not long ago. The news reporter was clear in her support FOR the Imam, also on the show that day. CNN made it appear as if the group opposed to the mosque really did not have their story or facts straight. The Imam got the last word and the news reporter was effusive in thanking the Imam for coming on the show that day. People either have no clue, or they are told not to have a clue. In either case, Islam is overtaking the world, country by country.

Some may argue that these are the extreme Muslims, or the jihadists, but not the average Muslim. I disagree, but let's say that is a correct assumption. Even so, since there is precious little protesting (if any) by the moderate and conservative Muslim, then the extremist or violent Muslim wins by default. These Muslims fear nothing, and they are unafraid to say that they WANT and plan to get world domination. This is what they are working toward. Check the news in Great Britain if you do not believe me!

We need to get into Islam in much more depth. I want to start defining terms and outlining the belief system that Islam is founded upon. I also want to discuss aspects of Muhammad - who he was, what he stood for, and how he lived. The reality is found in there somewhere and it is that information that is guiding way too many Muslims today. They are on a roll and they believe Allah is on their side. They are not afraid of violence and they use it frequently as a weapon of condemnation to those who stand against them.

Islam sees itself at war with the world. IF you are not a Muslim then you are the enemy, and it is as simple as that. We need to wake up to the fact that they see the world as their oyster, something to conquer for Allah. Even the Muslim Day at Six Flags is a method of "conquering" because they believe the success of it is due to Allah. As companies cater to Muslim beliefs (forbidding employees to wear shorts at Six Flags, for instance), Muslims are winning. People do not realize this, nor do companies, because it is the dollar that speaks loud and clear. It yells, "Give Islam what it wants!"

The more we cave in to the demands of Islam, the more we give up. Eastern Michigan University is fighting the wrong battle. While they may have been successful in their win (for now) over Julea Ward, I cannot help but wonder what would happen if the student had been Muslim? Would the courts have decided the same way for the Muslim as they decided for the Christian? I seriously doubt it.

There is an undeniable respect for Muslims today that they have not earned. Yet it is there and it is likely born out of fear of what violent Muslims will do if they do not get their way. Christians are hated, while the perpetrators of one of the most heinous religions ever established are treated with kid gloves. If the courts ruled against a Muslim student, there would be hell to pay. Protests would occur and demands for Sharia Law would be chanted, along with "Allah is Great!" Who wants that? Those protests could easily give way to violence and again, what city wants to have to send in the National Guard to quell a riotous crowd? Better to ALLOW the Muslim to have his/her way, while finding a way for the university to have something as well. Why? Because violent Muslims will kill if necessary to win their point, while Christians will not (and should not).

In a few years none of this will matter, because Satan's Trojan Horse - Islam - will have gained the victory from within, as they have done in The Netherlands and as they are now doing in Great Britain. While some of the more violent Muslims are willing to fly planes into tall buildings, many more are more willing to condense their hate-filled rhetoric into chants that create a strong sense of uneasiness with people. "Let's give them what they want, so they will go away!" has repeatedly become the response to the demands of Muslims. They will not go away. They plan on taking over. What are you going to do about it when they come into your neighborhood making demands that are given to no other group? Better come up with an answer now.

54

Arizona and the Courts

(Blogged: 07/29/2010)

Recently, the courts temporarily eliminated a number of key points from the new law in Arizona. Bleeding hearts, liberals, and some people of color are very happy. Law-abiding citizens are not. The former objects to the idea that a person has to prove that they are in this country legally. The latter believes that this is not an unreasonable demand.

There are many photos on the Internet, which tell a story. It is a story about how people completely misunderstand and misrepresent the law. In the photos are people holding up signs that say essentially that just because they are Mexicans or Hispanic, they are not here illegally. No one is saying that because someone is Mexican or Hispanic, they are here illegally. The race card plays well in the media and in discussions, but it is not what the new Arizona law stems from. What the law is saying is that people should have to prove their legal residency and/or citizenship IF they are pulled over for a traffic violation or have become suspect to a criminal offense. The people who actually believe that the law allows for and encourages police officers to pull someone over based on race also likely believe that Tawana Brawley was telling the truth...

(And by the way, whether this was Mexico's homeland or not is not the point. If we go back far enough, we learn that Spain invaded Mexico and overran the Aztecs, virtually taking their land from them. So if any Mexicans alive today are related to those Spaniards who overran Mexico, then it would stand to reason that they should give back what was taken from the Aztecs. How far back do we go to prove who is right and who is wrong? I guess we can start with Adam and Eve and move forward from there...)

I was not around when plantations and slaves existed, yet I am often seen as the perpetrator of racism against blacks, in spite of the fact that the blacks living today were not slaves on plantations either. I owe them two things (which I owe everyone): 1) respect as another human being, and 2) the sharing of the Gospel of Jesus Christ. That is all I owe anyone and that is all they owe me.

While certain groups erroneously believe that the law in Arizona would grant law enforcement officials the right to pick any Hispanic-looking person out and demand that they provide proof of residency and/or citizenship, it is simply not true. Then again, if that is what people believe, it seems that no amount of explanation will change their beliefs. It is like trying to speak intelligently and calmly to a Jihadist Muslim who has bombs strapped on his back and his hand on the trigger. He will not listen to reason because he has been brainwashed to believe that all non-Muslims deserve death. His reasoning facilities - if he ever had them - have been taken over by and replaced with emotional rhetoric and jargon. (When I say "if he ever had them," I do NOT mean that he may have been stupid all of his life. What I mean is that from an extremely young age, many Muslims are brainwashed to believe the tenets of Islam without question.)

In normal situations, a police officer has every right to demand proof of identification and address when he/she pulls a person over for any type of traffic violation. Moreover, if the person is suspected of being involved in a crime, then it goes without saying that law enforcement has every right to determine the legality of their presence in this country. However, is the world "normal" today? Not from where I sit.

Not long ago, I was rushing to get to a class I had to teach. I had left the house a bit late, and I knew I was going to be late to class if I did not speed it up. Unfortunately, my haste invited the attention of the Highway Patrol. I was promptly pulled over, told I was speeding, and asked to present my license and proof of insurance. Why? Because law enforcement would ASSUME that I am not who I said I was unless I could prove it. They would also assume that I did not have insurance unless I could prove it. Did they have a right to ask for and expect me to show proof of I.D. and insurance? Of course they did. In spite of this, there are too many people who drive on suspended licenses and/or without insurance. If they never do anything wrong, they are never pulled over. If they are never pulled over, it is never discovered that they are without proper I.D. and/or proof of insurance.

Police Officers do not generally sit on the side of the road and say to themselves, "*Aha! That guy looks like he has no insurance!*" They pull someone over IF they have broken some law. During the course of the brief investigation, if it is determined that their I.D. is not in order or if they do not have insurance, they are cited for breaking those laws as well. Is this wrong? Nope. Watch any reality-based cop show and you can see for yourself that officers are bound by the law. They pull people over based on the way they drive, or if they are speeding. There is a path that many drug-runners take from Florida that goes up through Georgia. The police are aware of this and look for cars that are breaking some law. They do not look for cars in which the occupants "look like" drug runners. What does a drug-runner look like, anyway?

Unfortunately, bleeding heart liberals and special interest groups believe that this law will play into the race card, allowing and even encouraging law enforcement to demand proof of residency and/or citizenship at whim. This is patently absurd and untrue. If law enforcement officials did this, that would be ALL they would have time to do.

The race card plays very well in the media and for the average person. However, it is not as if I can go anywhere in this country without having to prove who I am and why I am in this country.

I recently was invited behind the scenes at a major movie studio in Burbank. I had to prove to the guard that I was who I said I was before I was let in. This was in spite of the fact that the person I was with was very high up in the studio. In fact, he also had to show proof of his identification. If the guards had simply let him pass without showing I.D., they would likely have been fired.

Consider the fact that every time I fly anywhere, the airport security ASSUMES that I am NOT who I say I am. If I go to the skycap to check my luggage, they will ask me my name. I have to prove it is my name by showing them some form of state-issued identification. Once they are satisfied, I can move on, which means going through actual security.

At the official security entrance I must show my boarding pass and my license AGAIN, because these guards assume that I am not who I say I am, in spite of the fact that someone else had just checked my I.D. These security guards take my license and shine a special light on it that will immediately tell them if my I.D. is forged or if it is real. In other words, security does not believe who I am if I just tell them. They must see proof of it. It is their job to DOUBT who I am until I can PROVE who I am.

We have come to accept and expect this at airports. You cannot fly between states or countries without having to prove who you are. I also use a CPAP machine, which is a machine prescribed for people with sleep apnea. At one time I carried the machine as a carryon because I did not trust the luggage handlers to take care of it gently. However, every time I took it through security it HAD to be swabbed, I'm assuming for explosive materials. In other words, whether I looked as if I was a terrorist or not, it was ASSUMED that my CPAP machine WAS a bomb. They had to be certain that it was NOT a bomb before they would allow me to go on the plane with it.

As I go through security, I must remove my shoes and place all loose articles like keys, belt, wallet, cell phone etc., in a separate bin to go through their machine. I am also required to open my laptop and put it in its own bin for inspection.

Now I am not a terrorist. I have never had, nor ever will have, any intention of blowing a plane out of the sky. Yet to the security at the airport, I am a terrorist until I can prove that I am NOT. Hence, the reason for security. They are there to eliminate all chances of someone getting on board a plane with some incendiary device that will blow the plane up.

You hear people say, "Yes, I think going through security is a great idea, if it ensures that we are all safe as we fly." In other words, when it comes to flying, most people have no qualms about giving up their rights in exchange for feeling safe.

Consider the IRS. To them, I am GUILTY until I can prove my innocence. If the IRS says I have not paid all of my taxes, it is up to me to PROVE to them that I have done so and that they are wrong. If I cannot prove that they are wrong, even if they are, then I will be required to pay the taxes they say I did not pay. This is done through liens on my paycheck, or on my home, or whatever, until the debt is satisfied. These are only two situations in which I am ALWAYS considered guilty until I can prove my innocence.

In Arizona, liberals, special interest groups and some people of color balk at the idea that they have to prove they are here legally. They say it is discriminatory. If that is discriminatory, then I am being discriminated against every time I fly, or every time the IRS decides it will audit me.

On one hand, Hispanics argue that it will merely be Hispanics that will be targeted under Arizona's law. This could be; however, we need to remember that the illegal alien problem we experience in this country stems from the steady flow of individuals from Mexico, land of many Hispanics. We also need to remember that the law does not extend only to Hispanics. It extends to *everyone*. Law enforcement officials in Arizona would have the right to check the legality of anyone and everyone IF they are being pulled over for a driving infraction or detained in the suspected commission of a crime.

When I was pulled over for speeding, I provided my state-issued driver's license and proof that my car was covered by an insurance company. The police officer also ran my plates to determine whether or not I had any outstanding warrants, or if my car was properly registered or stolen. They were within the law to do those things.

In essence, by showing my state-issued driver's license I was proving that I am in this country legally. Anyone who has a problem with that should probably go live in another country altogether. I have no problem with proving my residency or citizenship because I am proud to be an American; though I will say, it is becoming more difficult to be proud of this country.

Now, what is so wrong about having to prove that I am here *legally*? What is wrong about having to prove that you are in ANY country legally? Nothing. Nothing at all. However, some people believe that every law that is passed is racist and therefore should be tossed out.

As much as I hate it, I must jump through all the hoops that airport security throws in my path. If they want to do so they can also pull me aside for an even greater inspection, including being patted down or having my carryon luggage more closely scrutinized. They have done so on a number of occasions, while everyone else goes through without having to be subjected to the additional harassment that I am being subjected to. Frankly, I think it's ridiculous when I see an elderly person who has a difficult time walking being subjected to this type of search, but maybe security knows something I don't.

Everywhere, someone from some culture is decrying the alleged racism in this country. We are hearing it more and more, and unfortunately, our first black (and Muslim) president has done little to nothing to quell the uneasiness between races. If anything, his complete silence and his stance *favoring* Islam have made things worse.

What is also interesting is the fact that many Muslims object to the laws in the United States because of their particular beliefs, yet no one invited them to come here. They are certainly welcome to be here if they are here *legally*, but they are also required to obey the laws of this land. Muslim women are supposed to be covered with Burhkas, and when applying for a state-issued driver's license they object to uncovering their faces. Our laws are for people who live and reside in the United States. They are not for people who live under the cultural norms for THEIR country and wish to bring those cultural norms to this country. They have willingly relocated to this country, in which case they SHOULD follow our laws whether it is convenient for them or not. If they cannot show their faces for a driver's license, then they should not be given a driver's license.

What if a Muslim woman is arrested for some infraction? While she is being booked and her mug shot snapped, would she be allowed to continue to wear her Burkha? You see where this is going?

If the world was a place in which trust was the overriding factor and there was no need to fear others or be suspicious of them, we would have few problems. However, any idiot should be able to see that this is not the case. Terrorism is rampant and is arriving in the United States. Frankly, I am surprised that it took so long for the attempted Times Square bombing to happen. I am surprised that we have not experienced what Israel experiences with suicide bombers, but there will likely come a day where these things will happen increasingly. In light of this, people should understand the need for increased security.

Without having to follow the laws, we have anarchy. This seems to be what many bleeding hearts want - anarchy. But then you have diehard Muslims who want Sharia Law and ONLY Sharia Law. While that may be fine for their country, it is NOT what this country was founded upon, nor should the U.S. become a country that follows Sharia Law.

There is a tremendous amount of Mexican gang and drug-related crime in Arizona. The drug cartels are moving into that area from Mexico in droves, and they are illegally moving their drugs across private ranch lands to do it. I'm sorry that these are Mexican individuals, who obviously look Hispanic because they are Mexicans from Mexico, so that it stands to reason that the bulk of law-breakers that come into Arizona are Mexicans. As such, the inconvenience of having to prove that you are in this country legally comes into play, and for the most part it will fall to Hispanics to prove that they are indeed here legally. I am sorry that the preponderance of crime in Arizona is related to the drug cartels from Mexico. While that is not the fault of all Hispanics, at least some are involved in the drug culture as runners. Again, though, does this mean that law enforcement officials will stop every Mexican or Hispanic person because of the way they look? Even if they wanted to, it would be impossible.

It is no different than me having to prove that I am who I say I am every time I fly, or every time I deal with the IRS.

People need to wake up and realize that the bleeding heart liberal politicians need to go. We need to secure our borders and we need to do it yesterday. We need to make it safer for the people who are in this country legally, and if that means that some are inconvenienced, then so be it. Gov. Jan Brewer of Arizona is doing what she believes is within the bounds of law to enforce the Federal law that is on the books already. For her sake and the safety of all Arizonans, I hope she is successful in her fight through the courts.

I do not like being herded around like a cow at an airport, yet the same people who complain about the law in Arizona think nothing of the discriminatory actions by every airport security team. It is that way because of terrorists and the criminal element.

If Arizona did not have a problem with crime coming in from Mexico, this would be a non-issue. Because Arizona is right next to Mexico, illegal immigrants (NOT "visiting" immigrants as President Obama calls them) come into Arizona in wave after wave, bypassing and thumbing their nose at our legal system. They come to better their lives in many cases, because Mexico hardly takes care of their poor and underprivileged. It is much better for Mexican citizens to sneak into the United States rather than remain a burden for the Mexican government. Though many illegal immigrants come here to earn an honest day's wages, too many come here to make themselves rich from drug trafficking.

If Arizona's borders were secure (along with other states that exist right next to Mexico), this would not be necessary. However, it seems that President Obama prefers to spend our taxpayer dollars elsewhere rather than to continue to build the fence that was begun under the Bush Administration, a fence that would go a long way in keeping people out who come into this country illegally.

If someone comes into this country illegally, they are not "visitors," but criminals. They have already broken laws. They then drive cars without licenses and/or insurance. They break a ton of existing laws because they are under the radar. Yet they fill up the lobbies of healthcare centers in many states. Their children sit in seats in schools meant for children who are here legally.

In a world where terrorism is at an all-time high and growing, we cannot hold onto our own cultural norms, believing that we are somehow above the law or suspicion. It is not only self-centered, but imprudent. We cannot have safety without impinging on certain rights.

Look at Islam. It wants no freedom, only Sharia Law. It treats all non-Muslims as infidels, worthy of death. When Muslims who believe only in Sharia Law come to this country, demanding special treatment because of their religion, they are placing themselves above the law. They should not be given special treatment any more than I would be if I moved to a country in which Sharia Law already exists. It would probably not be long before I would be executed for sharing my faith with Muslims.

All around us, society moves via statistics. Young men are discriminated against by insurance companies because of their age, and it has been proven that a majority of young men have a lead foot and make foolish decisions while driving. Do ALL young men make those mistakes? Nope, but it does not matter because they fall into a category that ALLOWS insurance companies to ding them simply because they are part of that category. While someone may say "Yeah, but the insurance companies are not segregating by race!" that may be true; however, they are segregating by gender, which is essentially the same type of discrimination.

In a perfect world that will one day be here when Jesus Christ returns and metes out perfect justice regardless of race or gender, these types of discriminatory efforts will not be in place. Until then, it appears that race and/or gender will always play a part in how laws are determined. If you have not gotten used to it, then you need to start.

55

Islam: What Is It and Who Started It?

(Blogged: 07/30/2010)

The best place to start in defining Islam is to determine how it began and who began it. Islam itself really begins with Muhammad, Islam's main prophet who lived in the A.D. 600s. It is clear from history that Muhammad's life is filled with anger, violence, and some say even pedophilia, because of his alleged penchant for very young girls.

Definition of Islam: "*A monotheistic religion characterized by the acceptance of the doctrine of submission to God and to Muhammad as the chief and last prophet of God.*"[85] That definition is as good as any.

---

[85] http://www.answers.com/topic/islam

Ultimately, Muhammad is the starting point for Islam. As noted, it is a monotheistic religion, meaning they believe in one god. Because Christians believe in a triune God - or one God in three Persons - Christians are seen as being polytheists to Muslims. This is not true. Christians are not polytheists at all, but monotheists. We cannot help the fact that the Bible reveals one God in three separate Persons. Because people cannot wrap their brains around that also does not mean it is not true.

Basic Tenets of Islam

- Monotheism - in Islam, only Allah exists as god
- Allah Encompasses Everything
- Allah is Near to Man
- Allah Created Everything
- Allah has Power over Everything
- Allah Sees and Knows Everything
- Allah is Sovereign
- The Torah and the New Testament are Corrupt
- The Qur'an is a Guide to the Muslim
- Belief in Angels
- This Life is Temporary
- Man is Tested throughout His Life Here
- Death is Not Annihilation
- There is Life After this Life
- A Judgment Follows this Life
- Paradise and Hell exist
- We are to Please God

A good portion of what Muslims believe is found within the Qur'an. The Qur'an is essentially a short book of things that Muhammad is believed to have said and taught. Along with the Qur'an, there are many Hadith (or sayings). Between the Qur'an and Hadith, Islam is explained to its adherents.

Sharia Law is the sacred law of Islam. It is non-negotiable and there are no appeals. Unfortunately, there are differences of opinion with respect to the tenets of Sharia Law by those within Islam. Sharia Law covers a range of areas and topics for daily living in the Muslim world, such as:

- Purification
- Prayer
- The Funeral Prayer
- The Poor Tax
- Fasting
- The Pilgrimage
- Trade
- Inheritance
- Marriage
  - Polygamy
  - Divorce
- Justice
  - Legal and court proceedings
  - Penalties
- Diet
- Liquor and Gambling
- Customs and behaviour
  - Rituals
  - Dress codes

Within Islam, there are three major divisions:

1. Sunni
2. Salafi
3. Shi'a

So depending upon which group a Muslim is associated with, this will determine how they view not only Sharia Law, but all aspects of Islam, including Jihad.

Jihad in its most basic sense means "struggle." All Muslim men will go through this as they struggle to follow the way of Allah. For many Muslims, it means an inner struggle, an emotional struggle overcoming the barriers that keep the Muslim from progressing.

For the extremist Muslim, jihad is taken to mean a physical or outward struggle with those of the world who are not part of Islam. These Muslims view themselves as being at war with anyone outside of Islam. These enemies - or infidels (unbelievers) - are believed to be keeping the final Mahdi, or Savior, from coming to earth. The Jihadist, or extreme Muslim, waits impatiently for this Mahdi to appear, and they believe that by physically fighting the world they can eradicate those who stand against Islam.

Obviously, in this sense even the more conservative Muslims are often seen as being against Islam, as far as the extreme Muslims are concerned. This has created friction, war and even combat with one group of Muslims going after another group of Muslims.

While many people may believe and assert that the extreme Muslim (also known as Jihadist, or violent Muslim) is in the minority, the reality is that these Muslims have been making and are continuing to make themselves known worldwide. In fact, it does not matter if they are the minority or majority because their murderous actions speak for themselves, and they remain a continual threat to the entire world.

Many of these Muslims firmly believe that by killing infidels (along with themselves, as in the case of flying planes into the WTC or by blowing themselves up in a crowded market area) they will immediately be ushered into Allah's presence. They will then be rewarded with 70 virgins.

Islam is a religion that was born - unfortunately - on violence and evil. It stands juxtaposed against Christianity. When Islam says to kill the infidels, Christ says to love those who use you and persecute you.

Because Jesus taught us to love one another, to love our enemies and strive to do good to those who hurt and/or persecute us, he is seen as weak to the Muslim mind in general. Consequently, Christ's followers are also seen as weak.

Extreme Muslims are willing to kill to defend Allah and Muhammad. No one is allowed to draw a picture of Muhammad, even if the picture is thought to be complimentary of him. To draw a picture of Muhammad is to invite your own death.

Further, extreme Muslims believe that anyone who curses or ridicules Allah or Muhammad must also be put to death. Because Christians do not kill people who take the Name of Jesus as a swear word, we are seen as being weak-willed.

The difference, of course, is that God is perfectly capable of defending Himself. He also tells us that vengeance is His alone. He will repay all the evil in this universe. No imperfect creature can put themselves in the place of perfect judge, as He is the Perfect Judge. All have sinned.

Allah is seen as a god who delights when his followers kill infidels. In fact, much of the Qur'an and the Hadith preach hatred, anger, violence, and vengeance. I recently saw a few videos in which very young children (ages 3 to 5) had been brainwashed into thinking and believing that Jewish individuals are "apes and pigs." They said this with all sincerity.

Extreme Muslims teach their children not only to hate the Jew, but to hate anyone who is not Muslim. They are taught that to die for Allah brings great reward. Strapping yourself with bombs and blowing yourself up along with others reaps tremendous benefits. This is what children are being taught.

Sharia Law takes us back to the days of Hammurabi's Code - an eye for an eye, and tooth for a tooth. Democracy - while it is certainly not perfect - has laws based on compassion.

I just read today, in an email from Ray at Prophezine.com, that a judge in New Jersey upheld a Muslim man's right to rape his wife if she refused to have sexual contact with him. According to Islam, it is the wife's duty to have sex whenever the husband wishes. If he does not get her to have sex willingly, she must give it unwillingly, and the angels will curse the wife until morning. A New Jersey judge agreed with this, essentially stating that Sharia Law trumps (as Ray said), America's democratic laws.

What people are failing to see is that while Muslims certainly may have the right to practice their religion in this United States, they do not have the right to break the laws of this land in so doing. All 50 states have laws against husbands raping their wives. Apparently, though, if you are Muslim and your religion teaches that women can never say "no" to a husband's desire for sex, then you are exempt.

In future blogs, we will go into greater detail regarding Islam and how it is working itself out in this country. We will most likely start with an article on the Five Pillars of Islam. Stay tuned.

56

President Obama Chooses Islam

(Blogged: 08/11/2010)

Funny, but the more you learn about our world, the less you want to know. Most of us are undoubtedly aware of the "plot" to build a mega-mosque at Ground Zero, and it is scheduled to open on the anniversary of 9/11 in 2011.

Many of us are also aware that the main man behind the goal to build this mega-mosque, dubbed Cordoba House, which is said to be a worship center for all faiths, is Feisal Abdul Rauf. Of course, this shows how many Muslims view people in the world and in the United States. The day infidels (non-Muslims) will be allowed to worship alongside Muslims is the day that the Antichrist is in power.

What many of us may not know is that this same man - Imam Rauf - is being paid by the United States' State Department. Isn't that something? He is going on a trip to the Middle East where he will...do...something. Let's let a spokesperson for the State Department explain it:

"He is a distinguished Muslim cleric," said State Department Spokesman P.J. Crowley. "We do have a program whereby, through our Educational and Cultural Affairs Bureau here at the State Department, we send people from Muslim communities here in this country around the world to help people overseas understand our society and the role of religion within our society."[86]

Regarding Rauf, and in the words of actress Jody Carlson (credited as "Girl in Studebaker") from the movie *American Graffiti*, "Ain't he neat?" He's "neat" because he has dutifully pulled the wool over the eyes of Americans and has gotten a real leg up from the man in the Oval Office. I can think of no one better to send "overseas [to help them] understand our society and the role of religion within our society." Actually, I can think of a ton of people.

Do you understand what is happening here? The U.S. State Department is sending a hardcore Muslim - who refuses to say that Hamas is a terrorist organization, AND lays at least some of the blame for 9/11 at the feet of America - overseas to teach people about American society and the role of religion in that society! I am missing something, something huge. I just don't get it. The man hates America in spite of his rhetoric, yet he is employed by America to essentially be an ambassador to other countries to explain to them how we live and what makes our society so great.

Okay, raise your hand if you think there is something fishy going on here.

---

[86] http://liveshots.blogs.foxnews.com/2010/08/09/us-state-dept-sends-mosque-imam-to-mideast/#ixzz0wKECFQSO

Yes, I see those hands, folks! In my previous blog, I quoted a gentleman who said it like it is regarding "King" Obama - that he treats himself and his family as if he were actually the Monarch of the United States. While Michelle is gallivanting off to Spain, spending oh...about one million dollars of taxpayer money, people in America are having a very difficult time finding a job. My 19 year-old son looked for what seemed like ages. It was only after a neighbor actually pulled some strings that he was able to secure employment! I know many people who aren't even looked at or noticed by anyone, in spite of the fact that they have filled out too many applications to number.

So what is going on? Well, it should be obvious, and it is obvious to all except the diehard "I love Obama!" fans, that piece by piece, Lord Obama is destroying this country as fast as he can. What does he hope to gain? A number of things, and while this upcoming list is not complete, it covers the basics:

- o friendship with Islamic countries (for HIMSELF, not America)
- o destruction of the capitalistic system this country was literally built on
- o a solid move toward Socialism (you know, government health care, buying the corporations so that they are government owned and run, caring less about the strength of America's borders - things like that)
- o the sale of America down the river to become part of the one-world order
- o a solid place in the coming one-world order where he will be part of the leadership
- o race riots

Ultimately, almost everything that His Majesty Obama does is designed to bring this country down. The only time he backs off even slightly is when the pressure is so much that he can no longer avoid it, so at that point he plays along because that is what his narcissism forces him to do and it is in his best interests. This is what these folks do who are so enamored with themselves that they see nothing else in the world except them and their needs and desires.

I'm convinced that Obama cares nothing for the American people at all. Why should he? He was likely born in Kenya, spent much of his growing up years outside of this country getting the best education possible (and who paid for it, we have no clue, just like where his real birth certificate is hiding), and took up with people from ACORN and others who are known for their hatred of the United States. He spent quite a number of years listening to an ordained man rail against America based on Black Dominion Theology (if you don't know what that is, PLEASE buy a book on it!) who spewed racist rants from the pulpit too often.

This man - Barack H. Obama - is out for himself and those he wants to do favors for; but remember, he wants to do those favors so that he will receive benefits in return. Because of that, I feel quite certain that he put the pressure on the State Department to create a "program" whereby they could pay for Imam Rauf to travel abroad and do God knows what. Moreover, during this entire process of the debate concerning the mega-mosque debacle, the Mayor of NYC - Bloomberg - has been nothing but quiet. Not even a peep, in spite of the fact that his own electorate has demanded answers from the man. Top that off with the fact that the alleged committee to determine which buildings might be designated historical landmarks all agree (9 to 0) that the building that Rauf wants to turn into a mega-mosque should NOT be given landmark status, thus clearing the way for it be torn down and remade into a worship center for all faiths...choke...cough.

Ultimately, by doing all that he has done our illustrious president has chosen Islam over Christianity, and therefore chosen Islamic countries over this country. He seems to be brushing right past the U.S.

Constitution, doing whatever he wants to do to ensure that his will is what is put into practice.

It all seems quite dour...IF we look at it solely from a human perspective. As I have said previously, while President Obama or any other leader has plans for this country, they will only be able to do what God decrees, though they will firmly believe that it is their will that is going into practice.

As I was writing more of my commentary on Revelation - End of the Ages - I came to the part in Revelation chapter 16 where the text seems to say something that is contradictory. We know that God never contradicts Himself, so what could it possibly mean?

Revelation 16:14 - "For they are the spirits of devils, working miracles, which go forth unto the kings of the earth and of the whole world, to gather them to the battle of that great day of God Almighty."

Revelation 16:16 - "And he gathered them together into a place called in the Hebrew tongue Armageddon."

Note in verse 14, we read that the (three) spirits of the devils go throughout the world working their magic before the kings of the earth. They do this for one purpose: to gather them to battle against God at Armageddon! It is clear that the responsibility lies with these three devils.

However, if we look at verse 16, the "he" in that verse references God (from the context of the surrounding verses) and therefore God Himself is the One who claims to be responsible for gathering the kings of the earth against Himself. How can that be? Which is correct? They are both correct. God has purposes and He decrees what occurs. Because men are fallen, and because evil spirits are fallen, all God needs to do is find someone that already has it in their heart to do what God needs done. He then chooses that person (or persons) and accomplishes His will through them. Is He going against their so-called "free will"? Absolutely not, since they have already determined in their heart what they want to do and are planning to do. He uses them and their desires to accomplish what He needs done.

The person God uses in this way bears the responsibility for the wickedness of their heart and their desire to overthrow God. On the other hand, the authentic believer who desires in his heart to please God is also used by God for His purposes. That Christian then enjoys the reward of pleasing God because that Christian wants - in his heart - to do the things that please God. God looks around and finds that person who desires to be a missionary in Africa, let's say. God illuminates that individual's heart further and opens doors so that they learn that His will is, in fact, for them to become missionaries to Africa.

Now in both scenarios, each individual - the person (or demon) with the evil thoughts and desires and the authentic Christian with the righteous desires and thoughts – is doing what he/she wants to do. God merely uses them for His purposes. In both situations, the individuals wind up bringing glory to God because what is accomplished is exactly what God wants to be accomplished. One of the individuals actually pleases God though, and that is the authentic Christian.

What we have is a president who does whatever he wants to do, and he seems not to care at all about what people think of him. He reminds me of someone who always has that laugh ready to go, the laugh that says nothing can threaten him. I enjoy the show "The Mentalist" on TV. It's a fairly decent show. What impresses me is the way actor Simon Baker portrays Patrick Jane on the show. His character comes from a background in which he was a fake psychic. After the murder of his wife and daughter, he quits being a fake psychic and uses his powers of observation to help the CBI (California Bureau of Investigation) solve crimes. The show supposedly takes place in Sacramento, and when my wife and I went down to Burbank at the invitation of some folks who got us on one of the stages, it was very interesting to see how they tried to replicate parts of Sacramento in the show.

At any rate, Patrick Jane always seems nonplussed. Someone says something to him that would offend the average person, and he simply shrugs it off with that knowing smile, the smile that says, "I know what you are trying to hide, but you're not hiding it from me." It works and it appears authentic. This is exactly how Obama comes across to me, as someone who has a real hidden motive or agenda and hides it with a knowing smile, or a facade that says, "I'll play along...for now."

When President Obama first became president, people began talking about the possibility of him being the Antichrist. A number of people came out to fend that charge off, including myself. It just did not seem to fit him. He did not seem intelligent enough. He didn't seem as though he had enough experience in leadership and global policy to be that kind of a leader.

Lately, I've been contemplating Obama quite a bit. If he is in fact not the Antichrist, then he is an obvious precursor to that man of sin. I watch how Obama literally "plays" PM Netanyahu and Israel, doing what he wants, giving a little here and taking more there. It appears to be a game to Obama. I could actually envision this man - President Obama - coming to Israel and its leaders and offering them a deal that would give them peace and a Temple in exchange for this or that to benefit the Palestinians. Now, think of it. If Israel's leaders were offered a covenant of peace, which included the chance to erect their Temple, why would they not jump at it?

According to Scripture (Daniel 9:24-27), Antichrist brings a peace accord to the table which allows Israel to rebuild her Temple and begin the practice of sacrificing animals once again. But why does the Antichrist do this? He is not doing it because he is feeling magnanimous. He is doing it because he is looking ahead to that point in future time when he will enter the Holy of Holies, sit down and dese-crate the Temple by declaring himself god. By merely entering the Holy of Holies he will have desecrated it, but he goes further, just as Antiochus Epiphanes did in 168 B.C.

To me, it makes sense that the Antichrist could possibly arise from the United States leadership. After all, the United States has been one of the strongest supporters of Israel for years. It is not so strange, then, to have someone who would come to the fore from America and who can bridge the gap between Islam and Jew, creating a peace accord that will supposedly last for seven years.

In President Obama, we have a Muslim man who would overthrow this country in a moment if he could. He needs to appear to be play-ing within the rules, even though he has stepped outside of them on numerous occasions. He is a Muslim who has the ear of a least some within the Islamic community, and as leader of this nation, he also has access to Israel's government. Muslims will trust a Muslim, and in this case, because of his political position, Jewish leaders of Israel would trust him as well.

I cannot think of any situation in which Islamic countries would trust a non-Muslim. While they might enter into a covenant with non-Muslims, according to the writings of Islam that covenant is non-binding, so they could break it any time they felt the need. However, by putting Antichrist into the mix as a Muslim, who has the ear of Jews, Muslims, and professing Christians, he would be able to accom-plish things that no other individual would be able to accomplish.

Is President Obama the Antichrist? I still have no idea. What I know is that he is Muslim, prefers to cater to Islamic countries, can pretend to enjoy Netanyahu's company, and projects an aura of narcissism like no other. Does that make him the Antichrist? No, but it does not eliminate the possibility either.

57

President Obama Has Spoken

(Blogged: 08/14/2010)

I s it a surprise? Are we actually sitting here, reading about Obama's expressed support for the Ground Zero mosque and wondering how that could happen? Nope.

From the get-go, Obama has been pro-Muslim, pro-Islam, anti-Christian, and anti-American. He has proven it repeatedly. This latest stance of his is merely another of the same kind of demagoguery.

What amazes me is that many of the people who voted for him (I was not among them) are surprised by his actions. They shouldn't be.

During his election run, all he said was "Change is coming!" and "Yes, we can." Oh, he also stated without equivocation that he would NOT raise any taxes.

Change is Here

The phrase "change is coming" can mean anything. People heard it and said, "YES!" Unfortunately, Obama never explained what he meant, and as soon as he realized that no one expected him to explain it, he kept his mouth shut, allowing people to believe what they wanted to believe.

Since being elected to the highest office in the land, we have seen what he meant by "change is coming," and it is not good. So far, we have seen that his definition of "change is coming" means:

- open borders between America and Mexico
- siding with terrorists (ACORN, etc.)
- believing himself to be god (essentially doing whatever he wants to do, consistently ignoring the voices of Americans)
- disregarding the laws of this land (never showing a valid birth certificate, etc.)
- being pro-Islamic and pro-Muslim
- being anti-Christian
- eliminating the National Day of Prayer so he could pray with 50,000 Muslims - he did not want the National Day of Prayer to offend anyone. Instead, he himself decided to offend by siding ONLY with Muslims.
- ignoring the individuals from the New Black Panther party who were essentially causing problems at voting precincts. They stood in front of the entrance with one of the individuals wielding a big nightstick.
- directing the Justice Department to sue Arizona for attempting to enforce the Federal Laws on illegal immigration

- sending his wife (and 40 guests) on a vacation to Spain at tax-payer expense
- consistently giving away large sums of money to outside interests and foreign countries, while Americans go without jobs
- pushing a national health care package that forces people to PURCHASE health care, unless you're a Muslim. Muslims are exempt from having to purchase health care insurance, so it will be GIVEN to them at taxpayer expense
- doing all he can to turn this great nation into a Socialist country
- constantly taking every opportunity to throw Israel under the bus
- treating Netanyahu as if he were a wayward child

Now, on top of all the things mentioned above (not an exhaustive list), he comes out in full support of the Ground Zero mosque - the Cordoba House - in spite of the fact that the majority of New Yorkers and much of America believes that building a mosque at or near Ground Zero is not only a slap in the face to America, but a huge affront to all who died in the 9/11 attack.

He Really Does Not Care...About Your Opinion

Obama seems either unwilling or unable to care about the ramifications of his decisions. This is how a fully narcissistic individual thinks. It has been stated on numerous occasions by me and others that he is acting as if he is the KING of America, not its president. For some reason, he believes that if he says something that should be enough.

In the case of the Cordoba House, he believes that Muslims have a right to build their mosques in America and practice their religion just as other religions do. The mosque is going to be built on private property, so what is the problem?

Let's Repeat

The problem is that Islam is not merely a religion. It is a political and military movement as well. I know of no other religion that incorporates these three branches into one. Islam has no ability to reason with other religions. Therefore the adherents of Islam have no ability to reason with others. To them, it is Sharia Law or nothing.

To the radical Islamic, all infidels (non-Muslims) must die. The alleged purpose of the Cordoba House, touted as a place of interfaith, where people from all faiths will be able to worship, is absolute nonsense. It will not happen. Non-Muslims are not allowed into the inner sanctum where actual worship in Islam takes place. Too many of these mosques have also been fronts for terrorist activity because it offers them safety from the world's prying eyes. No one who is not Muslim can go behind that curtain.

Now, Obama is in full support of the Ground Zero mosque. It would not surprise me to hear Mayor Bloomberg finally come out in favor of the mosque as well. He has been strangely quiet throughout this entire process, in spite of the demands of the people of New York. He obviously has his marching orders, and it would not surprise me to find out that they came from the White House; play along or be tossed from the political scene.

President Obama seems to have no conscience. He does what he wants, says what he wants, and completely ignores the foundational basis of this country. He seems to believe that he was given a blank check when he became president, a check that is his to use as he sees fit.

The truth of the matter is that this particular president is pulling this country apart. He has done nothing to quell the uneasiness between races though he is in the perfect position to do so. Instead, he has consistently come out on the side of Black America, ignoring the fact that many white citizens of this country voted for him (not sure what they were thinking, unless they themselves have socialist leanings).

Destroying America Brick by Brick

Obama is not only NOT good for this country, but left to himself, he will destroy it. Oh sure, that sounds like an over-exaggerated claim, but if his track record is any indication, then we can expect more of the same from him: doing what he wants, in spite of the voice of the people.

Does it surprise anyone, for instance, that he is so cavalier about the illegal alien problem in America? He has yet to prove that he himself has the right to be president of the United States. If he was actually born in Kenya, Africa for instance, then he clearly has no legal right to be president because he was not born here naturally. If he is essentially a usurper, then how could he actually come out against any illegal alien who simply walks into this country without proper papers or passport?

Moreover, why should we expect him to do anything less than side with the Mexican president in wanting to overturn the new law in Arizona? We have already talked about Mexico's infamous anti-immigration laws that treat illegals coming into Mexico from South America as much less than human beings.

Pro-Muslim to the Core

Why should we expect anything but a pro-Muslim stance when he spent 20 or so years attending a church where the pastor routinely slammed America, and spewed his racist ideology (based on Black Dominion Theology) from the pulpit, week after week?

When Obama was running for president, ALL of this was neatly swept under the rug by the media, and they continue that tactic. They were dutiful in their desire to discuss nothing that would make

Obama look less than perfect. That type of rancor is reserved for Republicans and Conservatives.

Where are the Woodwards and Bernsteins of Watergate fame? Where are the reporters who are willing to dig, even if it means walking right into danger? Where are the individuals who are willing to buck the system in order to bring out the truth?

People like Glenn Beck and others are panned and ignored as raving lunatics. The rest of the media smiles benignly at any suggestion that President Obama himself is a racist, has no legal standing to be the president of the United States, and is pro-Muslim and anti-Christian. They sadly, knowingly shake their heads in dismay that anyone would accuse Obama of not being eligible to be president, or that he is pro-Islam, to the detriment of this country.

The truth seems to be far more sinister than originally thought. Obama has only one thing on his mind, to the exclusion of everything else: he wants his agenda, and only his agenda, pushed through.

Currently, it is said that he is trying to find some way to grant blanket amnesty to all (or most) illegal aliens, and he is hoping to find a way to do this by bypassing Congress. That is illegal, but that does not matter to Obama, because if he was not born in this country, then everything he is doing and attempting to do as president is illegal!

I realize God is in control and I also realize that we are to pray for our leaders. Last night, for the first time since Obama was elected, I began to pray that Obama would start to feel so much pressure from the American people that he would resign.

Obama and the Antichrist
I cannot help but wonder if God has allowed Obama's election to startle Americans into realizing what it will be like under the rule of the Antichrist. We have talked briefly about this before. The Antichrist will be like no other. He will be narcissistic to a fault, fully unable

and unwilling to see another viewpoint. He will push his own agenda from day one, though it will seem as though he has the interests of others at heart. It will be for show, until he can become more overt about doing what he wants to do, and to heck with anyone who thinks differently.

Since it is clear that the news media is fully unwilling to take a hard look at Obama, then it is up to authentic Christians to get on their knees and look to the one who makes kings and dethrones them. Unless God has a problem with it, I am going to pray that He will bring about Obama's resignation long before the next election in 2012.

IF God sees fit to remove this man from office, we will hear the charge of racism repeatedly - that's a given. Even the media will jump on the bandwagon because it is such a hot button issue (and a ratings bonanza).

I have no idea what God has in store for this or any other country in the coming days and even months. It may be that God will keep Obama right where he is, allowing him to continue his work of dismantling this country piece by piece. If God chooses to do that, then so be it.

Pray for the Resignation
In the meantime, I am going to pray that He will remove President Obama from office through resignation...nevertheless, not my will, but His be done. Will you join me?

58

God is Sovereign

(Blogged: 08/01/2010)

It is very easy to become wrapped up with all of the events that are occurring throughout the world. It is easy to focus on what President Obama is doing, or is not doing. We can become distracted by the constant threats of war in the Middle East, or the economy, or our own jobs, or a million other things besides.

This is at least one reason why some people do not study Eschatology (End Times, or Last Days prophecy), because they believe it is more of a reason to be sidetracked than anything else. It definitely could become that, if we are not careful.

What is worse than becoming sidetracked with prophetic discourse, though, is failing to remember that in all things, through all things, and in spite of the way things look, God is absolutely in control.

A dear woman in my church just called me to share this very thought. She did so because her son called her and shared it with her. Years ago, this son was on the wrong side of God and his life was a total mess. Now - as she said - she and her son speak the same language. They both know God is fully sovereign, and 100% in control.

It is not wrong to focus on the events of the world. It is certainly not wrong to study about the various cults and religious groups who are opposed to Christianity. Some believe it is never okay to study about cults per se, because what a Christian should be doing is simply studying God's Word. I agree that the answers are in God's Word. I also believe that by knowing how those from cults think, we are much more able to provide those answers from God's Word.

I marvel at how far from God people are today. I recall that President Obama canceled the National Day of Prayer because he did not want to offend anyone (presumably those who are not Christian). However, he had no problem worshiping with over 50,000 that day in Muslim prayer. He apparently saw this as neither offensive or contrary to the biblical principles that this country was built upon.

President Obama is merely representative of many who believe that God does not exist (as the Judeo-Christian God), or that if God exists at all, then this God may very well be different things to different people. Because this thinking has become prevalent, many are completely unable to see how far from center this country has gone. They fail to recognize the godlessness in many of our leaders today.

If we stop and look around this world of ours, simply focusing on the world itself, we might be very tempted to declare that God is not here. We may erroneously believe that God is not involved in what happens on this earth, and things are left up to chance.

However, if we look at this world, and then look up, we will soon conclude that God has never abdicated His throne. If He is on His throne, then He has not given up, or set aside His sovereignty either.

As we continue our study in Islam and other things that connect with the End Times leading to the Tribulation, we must never forget that God is sovereign. He and He alone directs the affairs of men. There is no one who can stand in His presence, unless He gives them leave to do so. God is overthrown by no one, including the enemy of our souls.

I would encourage you to read Psalm 2, for it is there that we gain a tremendous picture of God and how He views the efforts of puny man. We are no kind of threat to God. He literally laughs at the efforts of foolish men to cast off the "chains" of His sovereignty. He warns us repeatedly that we should "kiss the Son, lest He be angry with us." In order to do that, we need to humble ourselves. Too many are unable to do so because they think too highly of themselves.

In a world that is in constant turmoil, it is easy to begin focusing on the situation. When this happens, our eyes are taken away from the Lord of all. The situation makes us feel angry or frustrated and, if allowed, even hopeless. Yet there is nothing hopeless about this time in humanity's history. In fact, though things are gearing up for the greatest conflict that has ever existed (or will ever exist), God is STILL in control. Nothing will happen that does not have the stamp of His approval.

God is sovereign. He knows all and He controls all. For the Christian, there is nothing more comforting. It reminds us of who we are and what our salvation means. It should also remind us that the time is short and there are many who still need to hear the Gospel of Jesus Christ, in order that they might be brought into the Kingdom as well.

I hope this blog has been an encouragement to you. As I stop to consider God's eternal rule, based on His sovereignty, I stop and I marvel. God is good. He is sovereign, and He will prevail. Amen? Amen.

Yo, Deb!

More Books by Fred DeRuvo

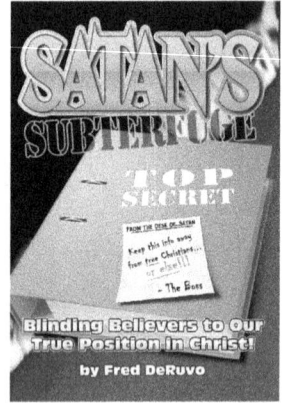

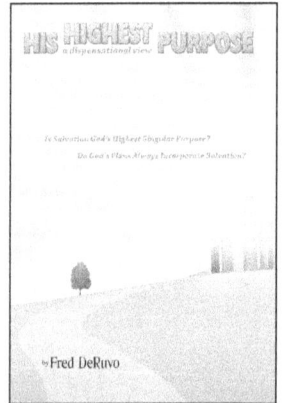

www.studygrowknow.com or wherever quality books are sold!